Global IT Management

A Practical Approach

Robert Barton

Copyright © 2003 John Wiley & Sons Ltd, The Atrium, Southern Gate, Chichester, West Sussex PO19 8SQ, England

Telephone (+44) 1243 779777

Email (for orders and customer service enquiries): cs-books@wiley.co.uk
Visit our Home Page on www.wileyeurope.com or www.wiley.com

Other Wiley Editorial Offices

John Wiley & Sons Inc., 111 River Street, Hoboken, NJ 07030, USA

Jossey-Bass, 989 Market Street, San Francisco, CA 94103-1741, USA

Wiley-VCH Verlag GmbH, Boschstr. 12, D-69469 Weinheim, Germany

John Wiley & Sons Australia Ltd, 33 Park Road, Milton, Queensland 4064, Australia

John Wiley & Sons (Asia) Pte Ltd, 2 Clementi Loop #02-01, Jin Xing Distripark, Singapore 129809

John Wiley & Sons Canada Ltd, 22 Worcester Road, Etobicoke, Ontario, Canada M9W 1L1

Wiley also publishes its books in a variety of electronic formats. Some content that appears in print may not be available in electronic books.

Library of Congress Cataloging-in-Publication Data

Barton, Robert (Robert A.)
Global IT management : a practical approach / Robert Barton.
p. cm.
Includes bibliographical references and index.
ISBN 0-470-85433-2
1. Information technology—Management. 2. International business enterprises—Communication systems—Management. 3. Management informations systems. 4. Computer architecture. 5. Strategic planning. I. Title.

HD30.2.B367 2003
004′.068—dc21

2003057192

British Library Cataloguing in Publication Data

A catalogue record for this book is available from the British Library

ISBN 0-470-85433-2

Typeset in 10/12pt Garamond by Laserwords Private Limited, Chennai, India
Printed and bound in Great Britain by Antony Rowe Ltd, Chippenham, Wiltshire
This book is printed on acid-free paper responsibly manufactured from sustainable forestry in which at least two trees are planted for each one used for paper production.

Contents

Foreword

IT departments have many challenges, but the one that comes to mind is the handicap of having the word *technology* in the department name and no mention of the term *business value*. I would not call it a legacy, because managing technology is still an important part of what IT needs to do, but in exploiting IT over the years, technology was often developed simply for the sake of technology and without genuine consideration of business value. Certainly, misguided expectations of what can be achieved with technology alone were a root cause of some of the disappointments concerning IT today.

So beyond simply delivering technology, what is it we need to do in IT? As a CIO, I see two major focus areas. The first is to appreciate that a more professional approach needs to be taken to running IT systems. Of course, business processes frequently depend on them and they account for most of the IT budget, but nevertheless, the correlation between business value and IT operational costs often remains unclear. We need demonstrable service reliability and performance, in line with business requirements. The second focus area concerns new IT investments. Business environments and available technology continue to evolve fast, but capturing the right opportunities and making the right investments takes an IT organization that understands business value and a business organization that is aware of what can be achieved with technology. Having such an organization does not happen by chance, you have to work towards it.

I like to think of this evolution in IT along the lines of an IT function as a firm delivering information products to the surrounding business. IT needs to manage the quality and value of core products, but it also needs to be tuned in to the business and be able to innovate and deliver new, added value products. This idea of a firm-within-a-firm brings me to the topic of this book. Global IT management is like the art of running IT as a global business, developing the right balance of local and global products, and capitalizing on any global opportunities for improving performance. It goes without saying that the human element in global IT management will always play a crucial role. But it helps a great deal to have as a foundation a solid and practical approach to working together around the world. The themes presented in this book reflect the realities of global IT business today and the lessons learnt from failures in the past. You need to be determined to align your global IT organization with genuine business requirements and you need straightforward processes that make that alignment tangible. The key to success will then be achieving the best combination of operational integrity, cost leadership and continued delivery of new value to the business.

Peter Sany, CIO of Novartis
one of the world's leading pharmaceutical companies

Table of Exhibits

Table of Figures

Table of Tables

Acknowledgements

For their substantial advice and feedback concerning the core book material, I would like to extend my warmest thanks to: Eric Graber, Eva Hörner, Simone Rehm and Olivier Rolland.

For their time and effort in assisting me with the industry examples, I'd like to thank the following IT executives: Piet Kock (Philips), Olivier Gouin (Nestlé), Ludo Vandervelden (Toyota), Peter Sany and Rene Ziegler (Novartis), Thomas Escher and Martin Leuthold (UBS).

For their ongoing professional support in the whole publication process, I would like to thank the following at John Wiley: Sarah Booth, Lorna Skinner, Darren Reed and Renée Last.

And lastly, for her patience and tolerance, I'd like to thank my wife, Ulrike.

1 Why globalize IT management?

The high level justification of any IT function is ultimately that a company needs an organization dedicated to ensuring that information technology is exploited as effectively and efficiently as possible. Such an organization is in a position to take a professional approach to provision of information services to the business, including applications, infrastructure and support. The real question here is why it is advantageous to manage IT on a *global* basis when it would appear, at least to the average business user, that the majority of service is delivered locally. The answer is to be found in a range of straightforward business and IT reasons, some or all of which will apply to any particular company.

In considering first of all the business reasons, it is worth thinking back briefly to what has been achieved to date by the information processing capabilities that IT provides:

- IT presents a plethora of utilities such as spreadsheets and e-mail that cut mundane administration costs and generally improve the office environment and personal productivity.
- Client server systems such as SAP provide sufficient process transparency and control to allow devolution of decision making to local managers, cutting out several layers of middle management and enabling better synchronization, streamlining and integration of business processes.
- The flattening of traditional hierarchies is further supported by real-time management information systems and applications for communicating priorities, negotiating budgets and managing incentives. Together they open up the possibility for new approaches to organizing businesses, for example along the lines of the matrix structure introduced by G. Lindahl to ABB.

Notice how there was no intrinsically global aspect to the above achievements, in fact quite the opposite: with no binding dependence on central mainframes and control, IT has enabled widespread local autonomy in businesses. The situation starts to look distinctly different when the latest requirements placed on IT are considered that result from current business developments in an increasingly competitive marketplace:

- Businesses see tighter integration with customers, suppliers and partners as a way to alter the marketplace to their advantage and to realize the same benefits of traditional process synchronization, streamlining and integration, albeit applied to processes that extend beyond company boundaries. The Web technology utilized has by default global reach and, furthermore, the security implications of opening up internal systems to third parties are global.

- Businesses want to exploit improvement in international transportation and relaxation of trade regulations to regionalize or globalize selected business processes, either in the interests of internal efficiency or better meeting demands of global customers or partners. Fulfilling the accompanying global information requirements requires a global approach by IT (although it should be noted that the very autonomy which client server systems allowed affiliates to develop in the first place now presents an obstacle to implementing global processes).
- Bundling of particular information services with traditional products and services is seen as an opportunity to achieve competitive advantage. Examples range from remote maintenance of equipment to computerized tuning systems in cars. There is an innovative side to this that usually occurs within affiliates, but it needs to be complemented by the development of executive level understanding of the options opened up by IT, and that requires high level, global dialogue between executives and IT counterparts.

This is by no means an exhaustive list of the business drivers for managing IT on a global basis, although it does highlight how a number of current business developments can explicitly require global IT management. The nature and intentions of a firm will dictate which ones apply. Even without direct business drivers in a firm, there is an additional series of well-founded IT reasons for implementing global IT management:

- Consolidated IT efficiency can be improved by acting on local weaknesses and strengths identified in benchmarking across local IT units. Actions can still be local or alternatively take a global approach, possibly by pooling certain activities such as vendor negotiations for commodities or consolidating excessively fragmented service provision.
- The cycle of technology obsolescence occurs on a global scale, so high level planning of new technology assimilation and architecture in general can be carried out globally for the company, allowing affiliates to dedicate efforts to immediate operational priorities.
- Managing the steady accumulation of systems on a global level can be the best approach to controlling the overall complexity of systems and making sure that this neither exposes today's operations to unnecessary risks nor is so inflexible as to exclude future business options. As an indication of such complexity, one well-known oil company discovered that for the migration of its installed base of PCs to Windows® XP, a total of 25 000 applications and packages needed to be adapted to the new environment and tested.

The approach presented in this book does not, however, assume that any particular set of the above reasons is taken as the justification for global IT management. The point of departure may simply be a business executive who intuitively supports the idea of global IT management and has engaged someone to build it up, or a fully fledged global IT organization may already be in place. What is important is the intention to be *systematic* about ensuring, on the one hand, that IT can respond on a global scale to impending business requirements and, on the other hand, that viable opportunities for managing IT more efficiently and with less risk are identified and exploited. Being systematic about this task does not mean micro-managing everything that happens in affiliate IT departments, but it does mean that at least overall IT architecture, strategy, standards and control need to be actively managed. These are exactly the processes that will reveal where the benefits lie in global IT for a particular firm and take concrete steps to realize these benefits, or at least spawn initiatives to do so.

This book proposes straightforward work streams for managing global IT architecture, strategy, standards and control. Most of them have a practical exploratory component, aiming to look closely at business and IT aspects in each domain before targeting and implementing specific changes. This combines the value of quickly producing tangible results with the more subtle mid-term benefit of raising IT and business understanding of the options IT offers on a global level. This ensures that the gap between expectations and reality (so often responsible for disappointment in IT) can be managed, and that the skills are there to select and implement global opportunities when these arise.

Exhibit 1 – introduction to featured firms

To provide context to the approach presented in this book and give the opportunity to compare and contrast approaches in different industries, several major global firms kindly agreed to be featured in the text. Each chapter contains an exhibit that briefly visits the firms to see how they approach a particular aspect of global IT management. The following paragraphs introduce the firms to be featured.

Philips

Royal Philips Electronics is one of the world's biggest electronics companies, with 170 000 employees active in more than 60 countries. The firm has five divisions serving the businesses of lighting, consumer electronics, domestic appliances, semiconductors and medical systems. In several of the domains covered, such as lighting and diagnostic imaging, Philips is the worldwide leader.

Nestlé

Nestlé is the world leader in food and nutrition, operating in more than 80 countries with more than 250 000 employees, of whom about 3500 are in IT. Management of the business is primarily by region and country, but some product groups such as water or pharmaceutical products are managed globally.

Novartis

Novartis is one of the world's largest pharmaceutical companies, operating in over 140 countries with 77 000 employees, of whom about 2400 are in IT plus 1000 ongoing contractors. The company has two divisions dedicated respectively to pharmaceuticals and consumer health. The former is further subdivided into business units covering therapeutic domains such as oncology or transplantation, while consumer health comprises business units such as baby foods or over-the-counter medication.

Toyota

Toyota is the world's third largest automotive company with manufacturing facilities in 27 countries and 247 000 employees of whom roughly 5000 are in IT. Most income is generated by the global automotive and financing divisions which are organized by region, although Toyota also has a growing portfolio of other ventures such as telecommunications in Japan. This text focuses on the global automotive division.

UBS

UBS is a major global financial services group with nearly 70 000 employees worldwide, of whom about 12 000 are in IT. The group as it stands today was formed in 1998 in a merger between Union Bank of Switzerland and Swiss Bank Corporation. It is organized in four primary business groups which are dedicated to domestic retail banking and global services in wealth management, asset management and investment banking.

2 Organization

Introduction

The foundation of successfully managing IT on a global basis is to have an appropriate IT organization in place. Depending on the scale of global ambition, that organization may not need to differ much from the status quo. Perhaps the reporting lines simply require adjusting to allow more transparency across locations in objectives. The IT organization can then move on to managing selected aspects of IT globally. In practice, the ideal compromise for a business between local and global IT management may not initially be clear, and a more iterative approach may have to be taken, attempting one or two global processes before any significant organizational realignment. This gives an organization the opportunity of realizing some tactical benefits, for example by pooling negotiations for software licences, while assembling a better appreciation of IT operations and culture across locations. But as head office enthusiasm for global processes grows or recedes, recurrent checks need to be made that the underlying IT organization matches intentions. Reporting lines and investment controls must be strong enough to resolve the predictable conflicts of interest which can otherwise repeatedly stall global initiatives.

This chapter sets the initial scene by introducing the main factors to consider and options available in constructing a global IT organization:

- The range of core services that most IT organizations need to provide.
- The forces between business and IT that influence evolution of the IT organization.
- The basic constellations that global IT organizations commonly take.

The chapter then moves on to present practical guidance for forming those basic elements in a global IT organization that almost every global firm can benefit from. These focus on achieving global IT management of architecture, strategy, standards and control:

- Profiles for key management positions and supporting institutions.
- Clear distribution of responsibilities between global and local elements in the organization.

Subsequent chapters concentrate in turn on each of the global IT processes: here the same people and positions can be seen again, but in the direct context of the sequence of activities that need to be carried out to manage IT architecture, strategy, standards and control globally.

Core IT services

The detailed structure of global IT organizations is as varied as the range of businesses carried out by companies, and yet with the exception perhaps of companies where IT forms an integral part of the end product, the essence of IT service requirements remains very similar. Requirements all revolve around management of applications, infrastructure and information, and the basic organizational building blocks for carrying out these tasks are fairly standard. The variety observed in IT organizations delivering this service appears to be primarily a product of the rapid growth over time of IT, all the while exposed to pushing and pulling from various parts of the business and IT itself. The challenge is to recognize whether the inherited status quo will support or stand in the way of business progress. The process to systematically manage the fit between business intentions and the overall structure of IT in terms of organization, applications and infrastructure, is presented in the next chapter; here the focus is kept on IT organization by examining more closely the core IT services and the forces influencing development.

Viewed from a business perspective, the whole idea is that the business should be supported in exploiting information technology to its advantage. Achieving that ideal means IT delivering the following three core services that are normally required irrespective of the size or geographic spread of a company:

- *Run applications*: Business applications such as enterprise resource planning, customer relationship management or supply chain management systems need to be reliably operated and maintained, and business users supported in using these applications.
- *Run infrastructure*: The whole IT infrastructure, on which business applications run and which ultimately provides users with a modern office environment, needs to be operated and maintained. The infrastructure itself covers PCs, data centres, networks and basic office tools such as e-mail and wordprocessing. Users likewise need to be supported in using the infrastructure.
- *Integrate new solutions*: Information needs that remain unmet with deployed applications need to be resolved. This activity can range from development of simple end-user applications or decision support queries to assistance in selection and deployment of entirely new systems.

Open to debate is just how far services should go beyond simply operating computers into the realm of actively supporting the business extract benefit from IT. But two issues are clear. Business processes are increasingly dependent on complex IT systems and the amount of information accumulated by systems is large. This opens up threats and opportunities for a firm and it is an implicit expectation that IT manage both. In this respect IT really needs to provide one further service which is overall planning to ensure, for example, that systems are reliable, information is secure, and that complexity is managed to keep business options open. The more potential impact information technology has on a firm, the more important this planning service becomes.

While the above services summarize the business demand for IT, the IT organizations supplying these services tend to be broken down slightly differently into departments or functions reflecting the respective expertise and skills involved in service delivery:

- *Technical services*: responsible for running business applications, covering database administration, systems administration, and version or production control. They also provide key consulting input to applications development.
- *Operations*: responsible for data centre facilities management, monitoring of production servers, testing, information security, response to failures, disaster recovery, capacity planning and availability planning.
- *Networks*: responsible for the physical installation and maintenance of equipment and the mid-term development of the overall network architecture.
- *Client services*: responsible for activities concerning users' PCs, covering user training, procurement and customization of clients. The latter generally include remote or desk-side support allowing new installations, physical relocations, additions of hardware such as extra memory, and changes in configuration.
- *Help desk*: provides the initial contact point between users and the IT organization for handling events from simple user queries and requests for specific services to registering incidents and problems. The help desk in turn interfaces tightly with the other units to instigate necessary action.
- *Development*: dedicated to responding to business information requirements which remain unmet with existing systems. These activities can be in-house developments or integration of packaged systems developed by third parties.

Although this basic departmental breakdown can be expected to remain fairly steady, a shift in the underlying skills is likely to occur. Originally, the skills pooled in each department were orientated towards those required physically to implement the service. But certain services are now commonly farmed out to third-party service providers and the required IT skill in that domain is actually good management of another vendor or service provider. Furthermore, IT operations are no longer so insular: supply chain management, for example, may extend directly into suppliers and customers. Setting up this type of integration requires new skills in working with IT departments in partner companies. Overall, an IT organization will need to deliver the services above, but its success in doing so is influenced to an increasing extent by its skill in working effectively with other companies.

Forces shaping IT organizations

The source of the variety in IT organizations providing the relatively standard set of services shown in Figure 2.1 is twofold. On a rather mundane level and in common with any other business organization, there is always a background tendency for certain managers to conduct empire building, drawing clusters of resources under their own control. Viewed in a positive light, this can be seen as simply handing management to the most capable person at the time, but mid-term it can distort the hierarchy by bending it around an individual who may later leave the firm. On a level more specific to IT, there is an intrinsic tension between IT and served business functions that arises from the fact that IT serves several functions and locations, each with their own distinct priorities. In their demand for service, the business functions tend to pull IT resources into their own organizations for a number of reasons:

- Project delays and accumulated backlogs are believed to stem at least in part from inflexible central IT operations and a disconnect with immediate local or functional business requirements. IT staff dedicated to the specific user population are perceived as closer to business realities and more responsive to new demands.
- In pooling operations to serve several units, IT normally retains collective control over priorities such as information security or investment levels and the allocation of limited resources between respective business units. The latter commonly prefer setting up their own operations to "competing" with each other for pooled IT resources.
- Business functions or affiliates may have a tradition of autonomy and simply be accustomed to purchasing, developing and running their own systems. This desire to control their own destiny is reinforced by the growing range of IT products and services available at apparently competitive rates on the local market.

Overall, this pull in the direction of served functions and locations fosters proximity to specific local or functional business requirements, but leads ultimately to dispersion or fragmentation of the IT organization and systems. By contrast, IT exerts a force in the opposite direction, tending to consolidate the IT organization in supplying service. The following are the main drivers:

- Larger IT organizations are better able to recruit and develop quality staff by offering both exposure to pooled expertise and clear career development

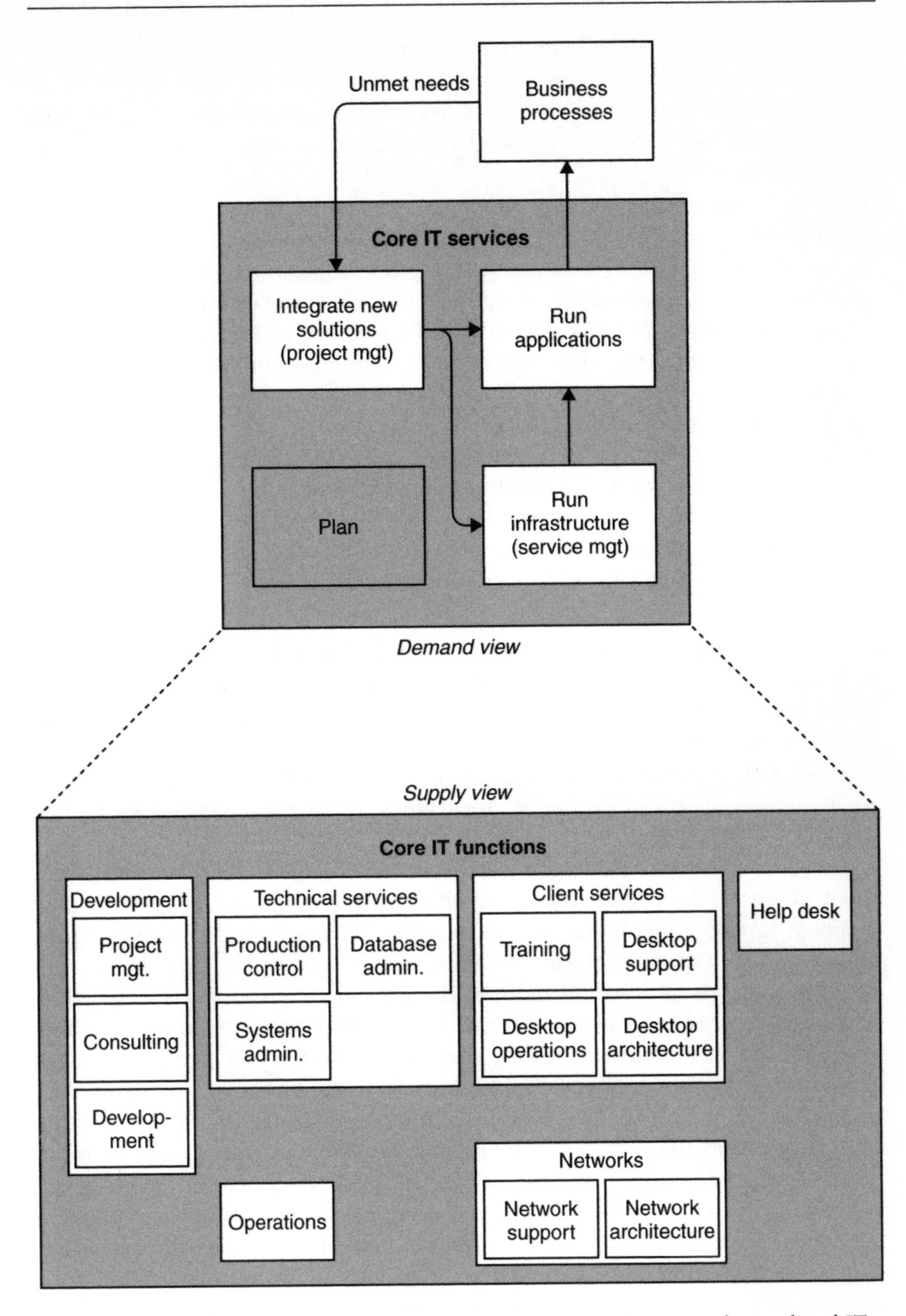

Figure 2.1—Core IT services and functions viewed from business demand and IT supply perspectives

paths. They also allow economies of scale, for example by using the same systems administrators on computers serving several business functions. The size of the organization allows explicit implementation and tight control of low profile, but essential processes for information security and disaster recovery.
- There is significant interdependency between the processes for supplying IT service. For example, in problem management, help desk calls need to be passed on smoothly to any of the application, network or client service units. Positioning services in the same organization assists both coordination in running services and assembly of teams for integrating new solutions. This also alleviates the common problem of a lack of appreciation of the operational environment in assessing project costs and designing new solutions.
- The evolving structure and complexity of systems across served functions can be managed to avoid mid-term development of information "silos". In the latter, steady state information needs in a particular function are met, but any integration of business activities with other units is hindered by incompatibility in information or systems.

There is one further force that acts at a slight tangent to the natural tension between business and IT organizations. That force is essentially the desire to transfer supply of IT services out of a company into the hands of a third-party service provider. In most cases, this force emanates from executive business management and is normally founded on the belief that the added value of implementing a service in-house does not warrant the time and effort that needs to be invested.

These basic forces can be observed shaping IT organizations in most firms today (Figure 2.2). Even within a small firm at a single location, individual business functions may tend to take on some IT tasks for themselves. Firms with several locations requiring IT services experience the same forces, but the physical separation of locations and the extra distinction between central and local IT organizations simply adds a degree of freedom to the resulting organization. The same is true of global firms, but the fact that the physical separation extends across national boundaries accentuates two particular factors. One factor is that, in principle, as the coverage of an IT organization extends globally, the greater are the potential economies of scale in pooling IT services, especially given the wide range of favourable locations from which pooled services can be run. India, for example, has now become a major centre for global help desk operations. But conversely, business information requirements and service expectations can vary so widely from country to country that such economies cannot genuinely be realized.

The other factor is that domestic IT operations are naturally favoured by their intrinsic proximity to served business units and international differences in language, time zone, culture, tax and legal environments. The impact of culture is certainly difficult to judge, but should not be underestimated. One component

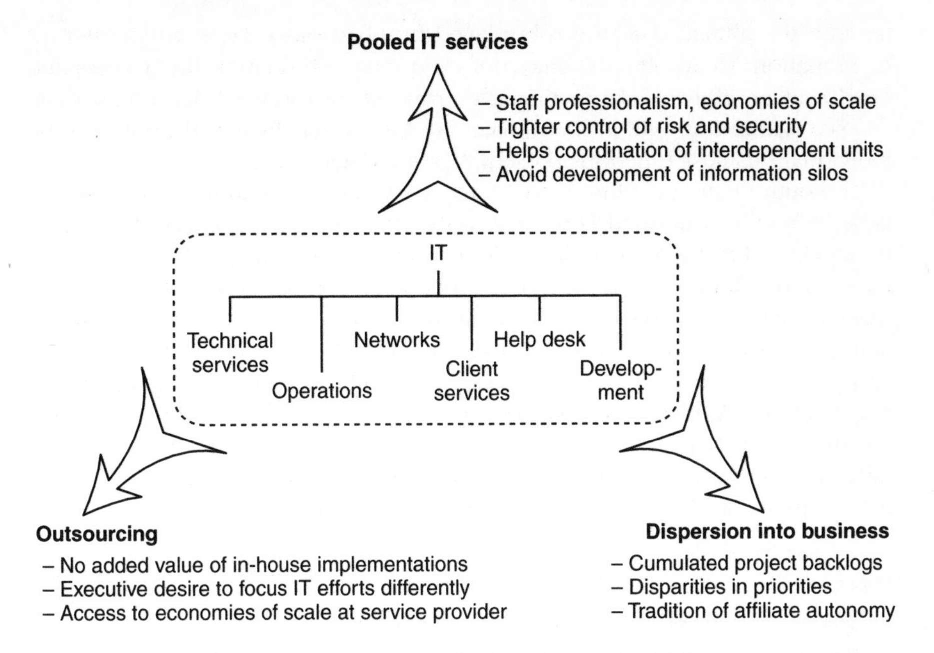

Figure 2.2—Forces shaping IT organizations

of culture that merits particular attention is the allegiance that evolves gradually from working with colleagues. Simply for reasons of the historical growth of an average affiliate, perhaps with its own IT systems, that allegiance between business and IT is normally local. Only in cases where an affiliate has been served from day one by head office IT is the allegiance likely to be different.

In summary, the forces shaping IT organizations can be viewed as the natural tension between local and global optimization. On the one hand is the attraction of local business proximity and short-term responsiveness in favour of IT resources concentrated locally or even dispersed into business functions. On the other hand is the draw of a pooled IT organization aiming at a more efficient, commoditized service with long-term global viability.

Basic organizational variants

There are two extremes of IT organization that can in principle result from the forces between IT demand and supply in global firms: either totally decentralized or centralized. In the former extreme, each affiliate has its own distinct IT organization which delivers all IT services to the respective affiliate. Typical examples are multinational firms with a financial holding or "black box" style corporate approach to managing local commercial operations. The IT services themselves may or may not duplicate those provided in other affiliates, but either way the responsibility and authority for IT implementation lie with the affiliate and the role played by head office IT, if any, is that of coordination. Head office IT may not even have information on IT costs and headcount in affiliates. In particularly pronounced forms of decentralization, the IT organization within an affiliate can be further dispersed right into the individual business functions present at a site (Figure 2.3).

By contrast, at the other end of the scale in the centralized extreme, a large, centrally controlled core organization provides harmonized IT services to satellite affiliates which themselves only carry out those IT tasks which have to be done on site. Typical firms with central IT organizations are financial institutions where IT forms a key foundation of the core business, although industrial firms which have expanded from a strong home market such as the USA often have powerful head offices and also run central IT organizations. Affiliates are obliged to use the services provided by head office which essentially exerts a monopoly on IT services within the company. The range of responsibilities of local IT staff is strictly limited, and the bulk of the responsibility and authority lies with the central IT organization (Figure 2.4).

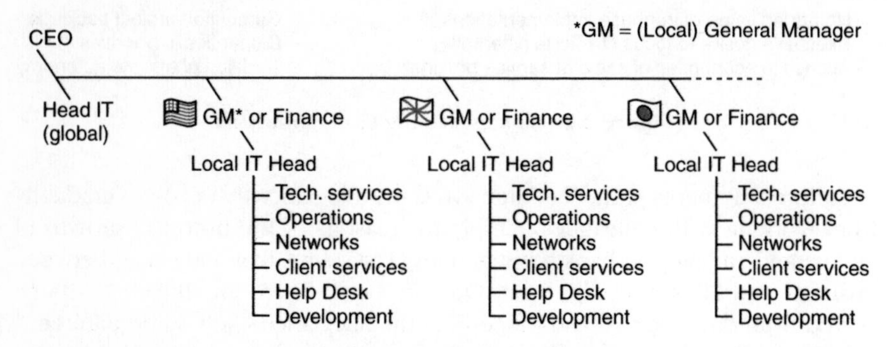

Figure 2.3—Decentralized IT organization. (Scope of services offered in each location may still vary)

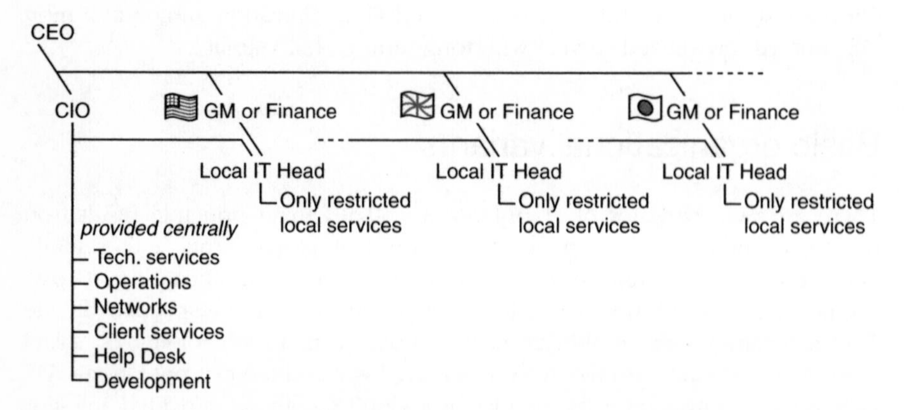

Figure 2.4—Centralized IT organization

Most IT organizations fall somewhere between the two extremes of centralization or decentralization, with one of the most common constellations being global management of wide area networks, regional data centres, and local help desks and support. In some cases, the current organization can be the result of a series of past compromises made during mergers or acquisitions; in other cases the structure may be directly driven by the CEO's vision of perhaps cutting costs or risks, supporting business strategy, or just leaving affiliates to run their own business. In a cost transparency driven approach, an otherwise decentralized IT organization may, for example, add direct reporting lines from local IT heads to a central CIO, but without explicitly offering any services centrally other than consolidated reporting and control of IT costs. One subtle flavour of compromise is the globalized IT organization, which follows in the footsteps of global manufacturers and pools implementation of specific services wherever in the world that service can be provided at least cost. Note that the location may depend on the service in question, and certainly does not need to be head office.

The degree of freedom behind the variants above is the ability in a multinational firm to distribute or consolidate the IT organization geographically. However, the IT organization can also be distributed across business functions in any particular location. Where the served business functions or units are large and their requirements sufficiently specific, dedication of at least part of the IT organization to them may be warranted. The special case to recognize is where each respective business function or unit is run globally, in other words IT is required to provide service to a matrix business organization. For example, IT may need to support several distinct business divisions, or certain line functions such as supply chain management have been globalized within a business. The common response to this challenge is for the IT organization to adopt a matrix structure that faithfully reflects the matrix structure of the business served, although where a matrix organization may be justified for a business as a whole, the IT organization is an order of magnitude smaller and runs the risk of becoming excessively fragmented in smaller locations. Note how a matrix IT organization is fundamentally a sophisticated interface to the businesses served and a flexible response to potentially conflicting priorities between geography and function. However, the matrix itself precludes neither centralization nor decentralization, which will still be determined by the choice in overall distribution of IT resources within the matrix (Figure 2.5).

Two sides to a coin

In IT, as in any complex business, the organizational structure is key. On one side of the coin, it forms the underlying control structure for directing and coordinating the diverse efforts of employees. But on the other side of the coin, the rigidity of that same structure intrinsically sets limits on what can be achieved by an organization. These limits become apparent whenever initiatives run counter to the prevailing structure, for example by straddling distinct

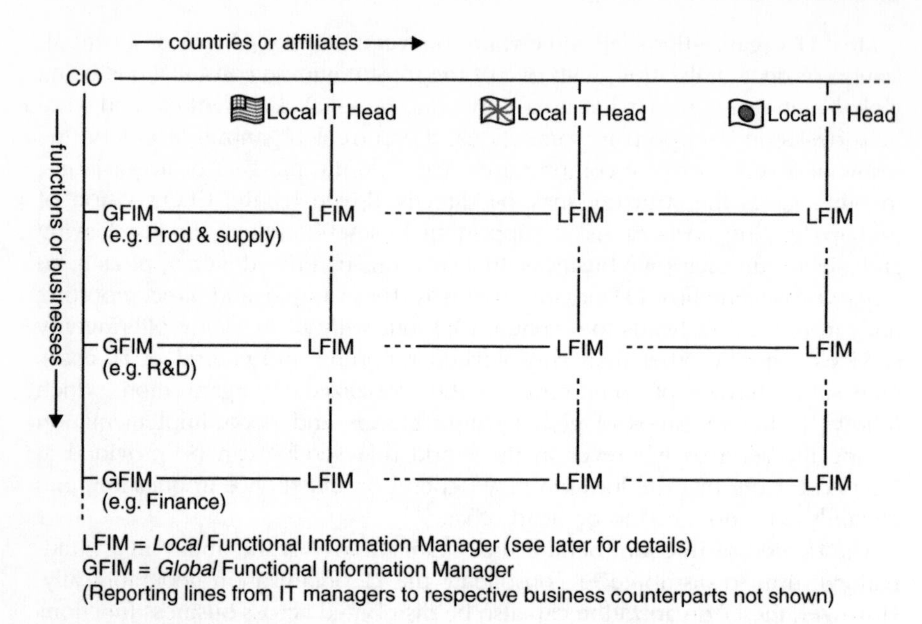

Figure 2.5—Matrix IT organization reflecting business structure

branches of the IT and business hierarchy: decentralized IT organizations do not respond well to global business information requirements, and the converse is true of centralized IT organizations. The recurrent determining factor in these issues is who has the authority to set policies and direct investment of personnel and money, and on what basis his or her priorities are set. This is not "politics", but people simply doing what the hierarchy indicates they should do—and escalating issues several stages to resolve divergent priorities is not something that can be done on a regular basis.

Appreciating the practical limits of the current IT organization is very important and can avoid a great deal of fruitless, misdirected effort. The issue is the following. The motivation behind global IT management is to ensure that information technology is exploited as effectively and efficiently as possible in the company as a whole, but this can spawn initiatives that overstretch the organization and exceed its limits. Such initiatives are common and yet usually fail. Most of us are familiar with well intentioned strategic initiatives which never went beyond the planning stage because the levels or distribution of resources available simply did not match intentions and the authority to change them lay elsewhere. Equally, even after consensus in the global IT community on the suitability of a global IT standard, certain local implementations are blocked solely because of local investment priorities.

Two levels of ambition crystallize out of this for global IT management. The first is to try and achieve as much as possible for the business within the bounds of what is feasible with the current IT organization. Even pooling licence negotiations globally for a *de facto* standard such as Microsoft Office®

can bring value. The second level of ambition is directly to address whether the limitations imposed by the current IT organization and controls are appropriate for the degree of global effectiveness and efficiency the business requires, and to implement any necessary changes.

Exhibit 2 – global IT organization in featured firms

Philips

The corporate CIO is responsible for IT as a whole at Philips and reports directly to the Vice-Chairman of the Board (CEO). Reporting in turn to the CIO are two distinct domains. One consists of the respective division CIOs responsible for the provision of division specific services such as enterprise resource planning and other business applications. The other domain is dedicated to providing the underlying corporate infrastructure common to all divisions. The bulk of corporate effort focuses on IT infrastructure, building up and maintaining a set of globalized shared services, often on the basis of services already shared across divisions within a country. This fits well with a business culture of harmonizing common business processes and rationalizing implementation. For example, Accounts Payable is handled worldwide for Philips by four regional service centres. The main IT services managed globally are wide area networks, desktop and local infrastructure, e-mail and groupware, internet technology, security, and IT purchasing and contracting. Each service has its own core team at head office, complemented by a global service management team managing local deployment of services by country or region. Looking more to the future, the next major step is seen as the consolidation of data centres.

Nestlé

Until recently, the IT organization at Nestlé was highly decentralized, with each location or market generally running its own independent IT operations. This faithfully reflected the way in which the business itself was managed. The only global IT activities that took place were capital expenditure reviews, setting of certain guidelines, negotiation of non-binding global contracts and the development of global systems such as those used in manufacturing. The situation has now changed radically as part of a major business initiative called "GLOBE" to implement best practices for key business processes throughout Nestlé, cutting cleanly across traditional organizational boundaries. Globalization of IT forms such an important part of the GLOBE project that the corporate CIO reports to the business leader of the GLOBE project, who in turn reports to the CEO. Likewise, the scope of accompanying global IT activities has been greatly extended to include implementation of global IT standards in applications and infrastructure and complete reorganization of IT operations to three regional centres. At the time of writing the organization is in a transition phase, but the intention is to reduce local IT activities to the minimum necessary.

Novartis

When Novartis was created from a merger in 1996, the IT organization was entirely divisional, with most IT operations having a domestic focus. Progressive globalization of R&D and supply chain functions in pharmaceuticals was supported by introduction of a matrix IT organization led by a CIO reporting directly to the divisional CEO. This formal structure proved successful in responding to diverse functional and domestic business requirements, while informal efforts in global IT community building also led to smooth implementation of common standards in networks and basic IT infrastructure within the division. Novartis undertook several divisional restructurings to reach its current form, but the success of the IT model within pharmaceuticals was recognized and the lead for IT as a whole in Novartis was passed to the pharmaceuticals division, with the pharmaceuticals CIO promoted to also fulfil the position of corporate CIO. Global services covering all divisions are now maturing and include e-mail and groupware, support for mobile users, networks, security, and server and desktop infrastructure.

Toyota

Following the manner in which the business itself is run, the IT organization at Toyota is highly regional. Within each region, two CIOs run historically independent IT organizations supporting the distinct manufacturing and sales divisions for the region. In most regions, both report to the respective regional Chief Operating Officer (COO) without formal reporting for regional CIOs extending further up towards corporate IT. On a global level, single standards for groupware and common applications such as order entry have been established and previously regional telecommunications operations are being globalized, but the real emphasis of global IT is on coordinated planning and architectural alignment across regions. Here the main integrating element is annual Global IT Committee summits, chaired by a corporate executive vice-president. The committee is composed of all regional COOs and CIOs together with both corporate IT and corporate business planning representatives. The latter share joint responsibility for managing the process and report progress each quarter directly to the Board. The global IT summits are followed by annual regional summits held six months later that are likewise chaired by corporate business executives, but otherwise composed of regional IT and business executives.

UBS

IT resources are allocated to UBS' four primary business groups in separate IT units, each serving a respective business group along the main user principle. Cooperation across IT units is, however, of great importance both in meeting requirements and improving efficiency. For example, IT units cooperate to support business functions such as credit and market risk management that are led centrally for the entire bank. Depending on the location, one or more IT units provide the necessary service to the user population concerned. The bank also makes common use across all IT units of technological infrastructure to reduce complexity, strengthen security and exploit volume synergies wherever possible. Throughout, the key integrating element is the IT Committee which reports to the bank's Group Executive Board and is composed of the heads of the respective business group IT units and additional key IT professionals. The committee has the mandate to set policies, standards and directives, to coordinate resolution of common issues, and to exploit synergies for UBS as a whole. Sub-committees with representation from impacted IT units are used to implement initiatives driven by the IT Committee, the main examples to date being common electronic workplaces, networks, enterprise systems, server platforms and market data services.

A practical approach

When considering how best to run IT in a global firm, the major consolation is that best practices exist for almost all of the IT activities shown in Figure 2.1. Three key public domain best practice frameworks are known under the acronyms COBIT®, ITIL® and PRINCE2®, and the large consulting firms often have proprietary frameworks of their own. The Appendix introduces the frameworks and shows how the approach presented here fits in, but one recurrent weakness of the overall best practice landscape is that the global perspective is neglected. There are no best practice structures for a global IT organization, nor is there a best practice set of particular IT activities that should be managed globally. Perhaps this reflects the reality that each set-up simply has its own features and limits, but especially in the face of natural resistance by perhaps well-run local IT operations, there is a driving need to concentrate initially on those processes that are more effective when run globally *and* that provide tangible value to local operations.

The approach proposed here is to focus global efforts on coordinating and leading specific elements of local planning processes. Global processes are established for managing IT architecture, strategy, standards and performance control (Figure 2.6). The provision of the core services of new solutions integration, running applications and infrastructure is left intact, at least in the interim. The emphasis is on integrating global considerations and opportunities into the detailed local planning that occurs wherever resources are concentrated, not on migrating local planning activities to head office. One small head office group leads the processes, collaborating mainly with local planners and two important committees dedicated respectively to governance of strategic and operational issues.

There are a number of advantages to this approach. From the outset, the processes are designed so that the value generated by managing each domain globally is maximized without causing major overhead for affiliates or head office. Each process also features active collaboration between head office IT, local IT and business counterparts. Beyond the exchange of

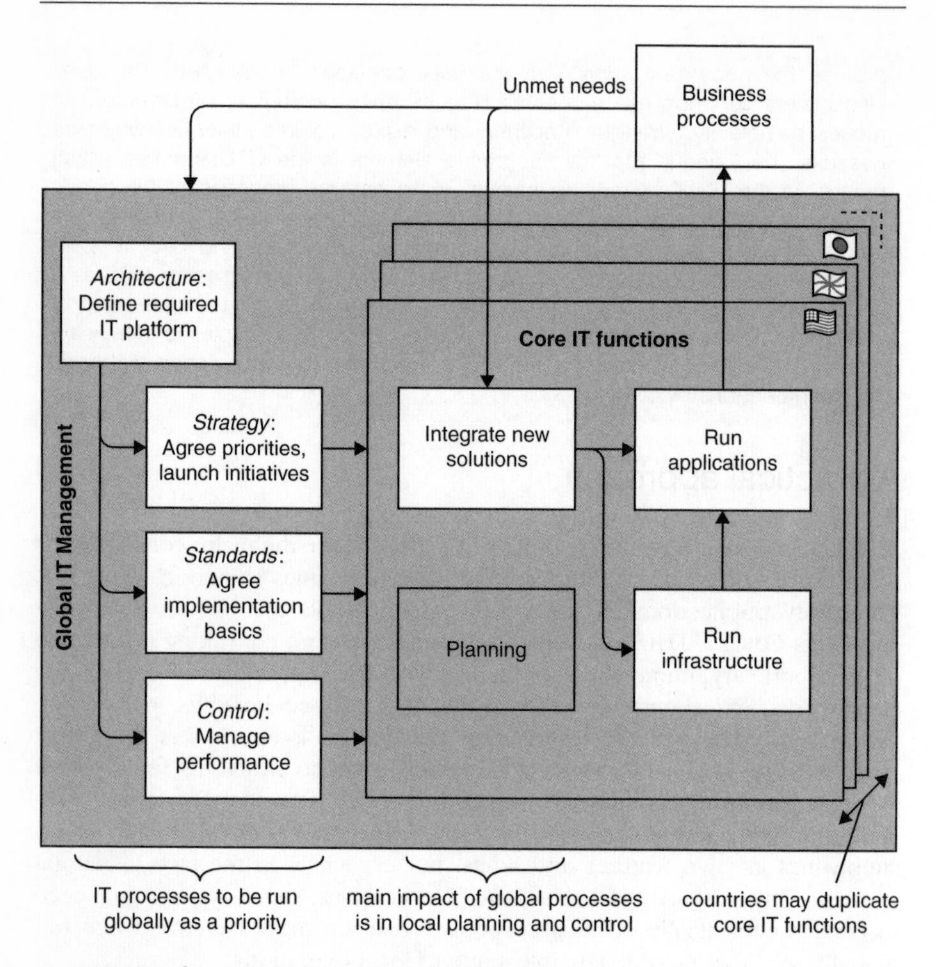

Figure 2.6—Global leadership and coordination of key planning elements as first priority

information on local and global priorities, this collaboration fosters development of new global allegiances that can become key enablers for future initiatives. Lastly, in as far as this is possible, the committees are used to access available resources, but where this proves insufficient, the information collected by the global processes provides an effective foundation for justifying structural changes. In this way, while the prime aim is to achieve what is feasible within the current organization, the foundation is also laid for changing this if it proves to be a barrier to meeting global business requirements.

The sections following in this chapter present an overview of the requisite organization. Many of these elements will then be revisited in detail later in the direct context of the individual global processes presented in each subsequent chapter.

Key players and institutions

Chief Information Officer

The key position in global IT management is that of chief information officer or "CIO". This term for someone who heads a firm's IT organization is relatively new, but it does convey the business flavour of the role.[1] A CIO is expected to be a serious executive counterpart who contributes actively to the direction and success of a company. This business side promotion of IT leadership is reflected in the increasing proportion of CIOs reporting directly to the CEO and participating in executive committees. The remainder usually report to the CFO for historical reasons, as IT originally entered most firms in the form of transaction systems used by the finance department. What needs to be targeted for the success of the role is a viable and productive combination of the following factors:

- Leadership quality of the individual.
- Level of the CIO position within the hierarchy.
- Range of CIO objectives and responsibilities.
- Extent of CIO resources and authority.

The main driver is the range of objectives and responsibilities, because this is what a firm is aiming to achieve in developing global management of IT. The overall objectives are invariably forms of expected improvement in cost, value or risk. The spectrum of responsibilities goes from consolidated reporting on IT activities, through management of central services provided to affiliates, to establishing specific IT components as an integral part of business strategy. Depending on how far IT has been globalized to date, a large proportion of responsibilities may focus on managing existing operations. But the following less operational, more planning orientated responsibilities recur and are fairly standard:

- *Architecture*: ensure the overall pattern of accumulating IT systems and resources matches mid-term business needs on a global scale.
- *Strategy*: agree IT priorities in line with current business priorities and implement required initiatives.
- *Standards*: manage global complexity and exploit opportunities for cost savings by establishing selected standards.
- *Control*: manage basic IT performance in terms of cost, value and risk across affiliates (Figure 2.7).

[1] Heads of large domestic IT operations sometimes also carry the title of (local) CIO. To avoid confusion, this book assumes one (global) CIO, with the others referred to as Local IT Heads.

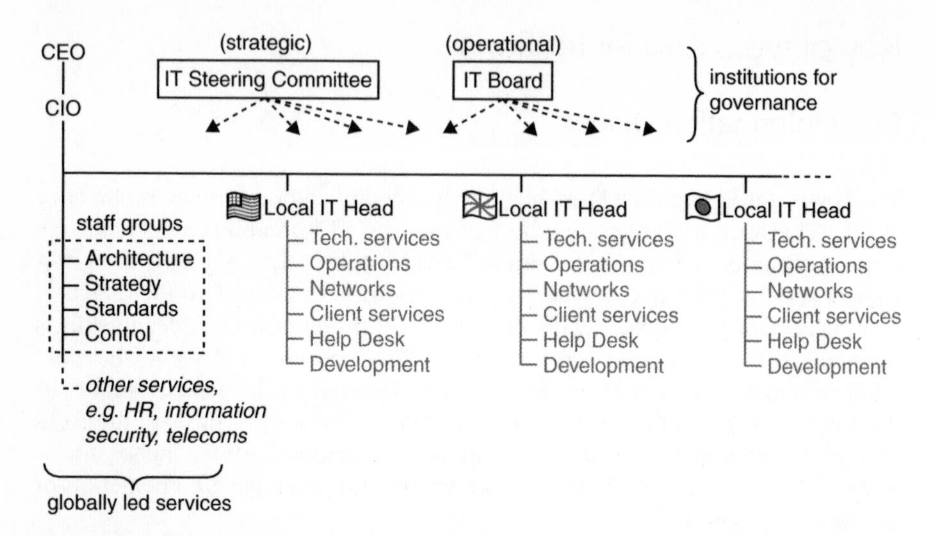

Figure 2.7—Overall organizational chart for managing core global services

Together, this core set of generic responsibilities can both deliver value rapidly and ensure the mid-term health of the IT organization as a whole. To this may be added more specific responsibilities such as global human resources management or information security. But recalling the target of finding a viable combination of leadership, positioning, responsibilities and authority, the extent of responsibility for an activity needs to be balanced with sufficient resources and authority to make something happen. By design, the processes presented in this book are economical with resources, but achieving a sensible level of authority for a CIO is intrinsically delicate, simply because more authority for a CIO means less authority for local managers. To reach an accepted compromise, there are three complementary types of formal authority that can be put at a CIO's disposal:

- Power can be granted, sometimes in conjunction with committees, to set mandatory policies in particular domains and approve or refuse local exceptions.
- Affiliates may be obliged to present IT budgets and investment requests above threshold values to the CIO, and the CIO can veto their approval by local management.
- Local IT heads can formally report directly to the CIO.

While passing IT budgets and investments through the CIO ostensibly enables global cost transparency and control, the most far-reaching form of authority is the reporting structure. Certainly, while local finance may still retain primary control of local IT investments, solid reporting lines from local IT heads in major locations to the CIO are a major aid to influencing behaviour and ultimately forming a global team willing to address global improvements. Without this authority to at least partially determine local IT heads' objectives, incentives and rewards, the assignment of the title "CIO" appears superficial and somewhat deceiving. In most cases, local IT heads will need to report both to the CIO and the local general manager or head of finance—in formally sharing control, the local manager sets operative and business specific targets, and the CIO sets objectives which are relevant on a global scale. For example, the CIO may require participation of an affiliate in benchmarking IT performance across affiliates. The key error to avoid is overuse of direct reporting lines to control too much, constraining the ability of local IT heads to manage their operations well. An initial step can be to focus on assuring cooperation in those IT processes being launched globally, namely architecture, strategy, standards and performance control.

Despite the choice in types of formal authority, imbalances between responsibility and authority are still relatively common, particularly in decentralized firms, but they can be partially compensated by sufficient sponsorship from the executive to whom the CIO reports, i.e. the CEO or CFO. In the absence of both authority and active sponsorship, achievements by the CIO are likely to be restricted to tactical efforts from which every involved affiliate benefits.

Local IT heads and functional information managers

The overall IT hierarchy forms an essential part of delivering an IT service, but more important than the concept of a single ideal organization is to know whether the *de facto* organization in place today is able to deliver the specific type of service the business requires. The architecture process in the next chapter presents a systematic approach to judging whether this is the case, including at the same time other important perspectives such as the applications and infrastructure landscape. The two key features of the organization that enter this equation are:

- The nature of the organizational interface to the business.
- The distribution of resources and authority within the organization.

In straightforward cases such as the decentralized organization shown in Figure 2.3, these can be one and the same thing. The local IT head forms the formal reporting interface to the business, and resources are organized by IT function directly below, each serving supported business functions to the best of their ability. In centralized organizations, clearly the resources are pooled under head office control, but local IT heads may form the interface to local businesses for the entire service or just provision of local infrastructure.

More complex constellations are produced where the organizational interface to the business explicitly incorporates positions dedicated to individual line functions, normally reporting both to the business function they serve and IT. Such positions are termed here "functional information managers" (FIM).

An FIM is intended to form the main point of managerial contact between a particular line function and IT. The key aspect to note is how far resources and authority fall under an FIM. IT resources may remain pooled across served business functions, in which case the FIM is basically an account manager for a line function that can effectively liaise with IT and represent the line function's priorities in IT resource allocation. Alternatively, the FIM has accumulated its own resources, such as application developers, partly to run its own operations, ultimately just leaving generic infrastructure services to the core IT department.

The FIM construct reaches its zenith in the matrix IT organization shown in Figure 2.5, which features both local and global FIMs as the interface between IT and line functions on a local and global level. In a firm which has chosen this approach, the same flavours of resource distribution are feasible as above, albeit with the extra dimension of shifting resources globally within a particular functional IT department. The additional feature on which to focus is whether the multiple reporting lines (three for a local FIM!) are configured well enough that the interface to the business is transparent and actually achieves a working balance between local and global priorities (Figure 2.8).

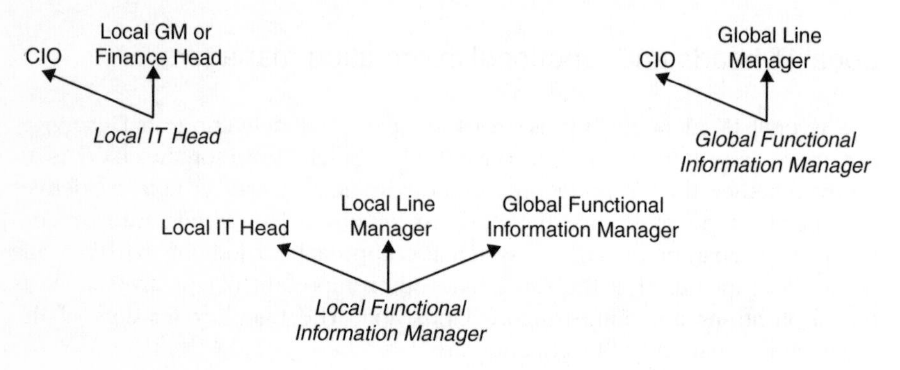

Figure 2.8—Multiple reporting lines in matrix IT organizations

Steering Committees to support governance

Several characteristics of global IT management encourage the use of committees. For example, the geographic dispersion of an organization can make it hard for head office alone to be well enough informed about diverse requirements to be able to reach balanced decisions without involving others. Physically bringing together key members of IT and business management on a regular basis also helps seal contacts and build useful allegiances. Lastly, the power of a CIO to decide single-handedly on global matters is often weaker than would appear in the organizational chart: committees reassure the community of adequate discussion and consensus on issues, while reinforcing the status of resulting decisions with an official stamp of approval.

The use of two committees is recommended to support global IT management and both feature prominently in the processes for managing architecture, strategy, standards and control. The first is the "IT Steering Committee", whose mandate is to set global IT strategy, launch and resource strategic initiatives, and finally to review overall progress. It meets twice a year and is composed of a globally representative mix of key business executives and their IT counterparts, each chosen not so much for their nominal positioning in the hierarchy, but rather because they make the decisions that are of relevance to IT. The primary product of the IT Steering Committee is a succinct statement of global IT strategy which is subsequently cascaded down into the organization by the strategy process. A full profile of both committee and process is given in Chapter 4.

The second committee is the "IT Board" which focuses on more operative IT issues, meets more regularly, e.g. four times a year, and is composed solely of key IT managers. To avoid proliferation of committees and aid coordination of meetings, the IT Board can be made up from those IT managers in the IT Steering Committee, adding extra members only if necessary (Figure 2.9). The board mandate is as follows:

- Serve as an instrument for executing IT strategy, i.e. turning decisions taken by the IT Steering Committee into reality.
- Form the main institution for discussion and official approval of IT policies such as choice of certain standards and controls.
- Act as a forum for regular communication between IT counterparts from comparable organizations in other affiliates, identifying and exploiting global opportunities.

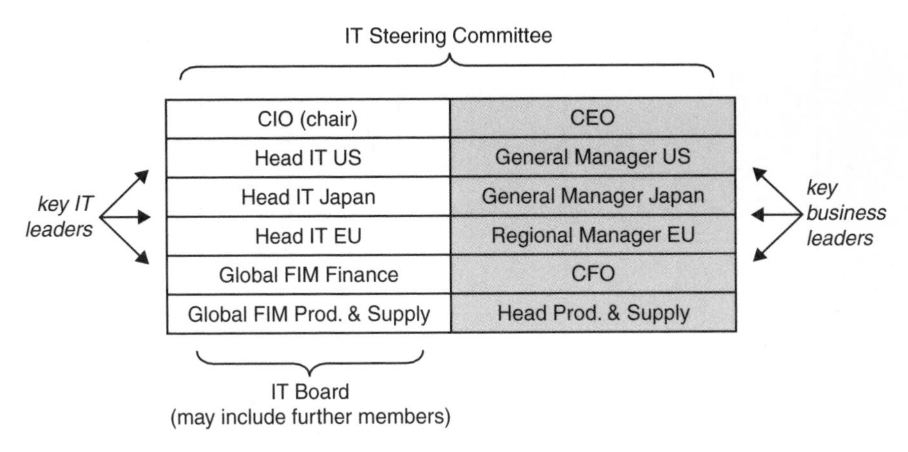

Figure 2.9—Example composition of IT Steering Committee and IT Board

Both committees are aimed at discussion, consensus and decision making, rather than physical planning. The groundwork preceding and following

Table 2.1—Division of responsibilities between members of proposed global IT organization

Work stream		CIO	IT Steering Committee	IT Board	Local IT organizations	Global IT management staff group
Architecture	Map current situation				Provide information on business processes, applications, infrastructure	Coordinate information collection, collate results
	Adapt to requirements			Approve recommendations	Prepare recommendations	Prepare recommendations Feed approved recommendations into strategy, standards, and control work streams
Strategy	Agree strategy	Champion agreed strategy	Set top level strategy			Prepare decision material and execute follow-up
	Align organization	Champion agreed strategy			Integrate overall priorities explicitly with local priorities	Moderate cascade of priorities into organization
	Implementation	Champion agreed strategy	Resource and initiate strategic initiatives	Operative responsibility for implementation	Execute local components of strategic initiatives	Report back on progress to IT Steering Committee

Standards	Define new standards			Approve new standards (may need to escalate to IT Steering Committee)	Contribute local expertise and definition of requirements	Prepare business case, negotiate with vendors (in collaboration with purchasing department)
	Maintain standards			Approval for controversial standard updates only	Respective standard owners track and report required updates	Ongoing publication of current standards and latest changes
	Handle exceptions	Approve request for exception			Assemble and present business case for exception	Moderate process
Control	Develop scorecards			Mandate approval and later approval of denition	Local planners and controllers assist in metric definitions	Develop mandate and alternative scorecard proposals
	Deploy scorecards	Align motivation with scorecards			Report agreed information	Initiate collection and analysis of information
	Operate scorecards			Act on findings		Market IT performance and progress

meetings is accomplished as an integral part of the global IT processes run by the global IT management staff introduced below, in collaboration with local planning departments. For both committees, the same reality check applies as for the CIO, namely that the extent of the mandate should only go as far as the authority and resources to which the members of the committee have access. Otherwise, committee meetings take place with extensive discussion and final agreement, but nothing happens as a result.

Global IT management staff

In most global firms, while the CIO has ownership for global IT architecture, strategy, standards and control, he or she will need the support of a staff group to define, lead and moderate the respective work streams. Ideally, each process needs its own dedicated staff member. But irrespective of its size, the aim of the group is on the one hand to manage the work streams so that tangible value is extracted on an ongoing basis, and on the other to chart the most effective direction for IT to take in the company. As an accompanying activity, the group can run more general internal communications and build up a sense of global IT community through organization of global IT newsletters, intranet Web sites, exchange visits or conferences. The staff positions are discussed in more detail in each respective chapter in this volume, but Table 2.1 shows a summary of their activities and the interdependence with other parts of the organization.

Moving towards action

This chapter has reviewed the capabilities and limitations exhibited by different constellations of IT hierarchy, responsibility and authority. Together, these set initial boundaries on what can be achieved by managing IT on a global basis without making direct changes to the organizational structure. With or without changes to the organization, two other important factors play a role in how much is achieved by global IT. First, a great deal depends on the quality of the employees within the organization and the skills they possess. Secondly, much depends on the choice of global activities on which these people are asked to focus their attention. The architecture, strategy, standards and control work streams are presented as those global activities that are easiest to set up and most likely to produce positive results without generating excessive overhead. Each of the following chapters is dedicated to a respective work stream and has the same basic form, with the first half of a chapter focusing on some of the material background and the second half presenting concrete work templates for moving towards action as shown in Figure 2.10.

Timing

An important feature of the presented work templates is that each work stream can be run largely independently of the others. They are, of course,

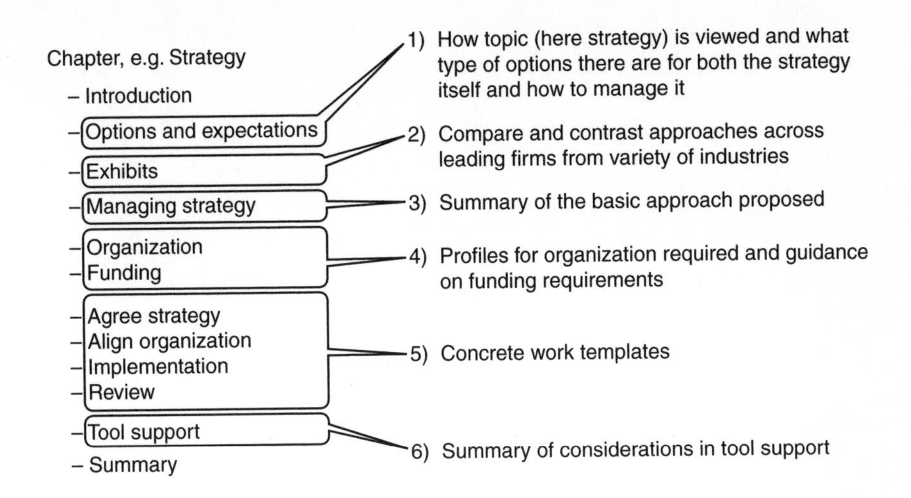

Figure 2.10—Chapters on architecture, strategy, standards and control have same overall structure

interlinked explicitly wherever the product of one process provides useful input to another, such as when certain standards are selected as a result of architectural considerations. However, each work stream generates value in its own right and does not strictly require the others to exist (although best results are achieved when all processes are run). This opens up the flexibility to selectively initiate certain processes and leave others for later. The advantage for a CIO is that those processes which deliver the most urgently required results can be launched first. The following points summarize the typical timing of results and can help a CIO know what can be promised within a certain time scale:

- Architecture delivers an accurate picture of the current situation within weeks/months, but genuine changes to the underlying architecture take years.
- Strategy can demonstrate tangible alignment of IT priorities to business priorities within weeks/months; the time scale for achieving results will depend on the nature of initiatives launched.
- Standards can show, for example, cost reductions through pooled vendor negotiations within weeks; by contrast, actually achieving harmonization of the deployed technology can take years.
- Control definitions, for example for scorecards, can be agreed within weeks/months and insights from information collection can be identified as soon as data is collected, although the concrete link to incentive and reward systems will take longer to realize.

3 Architecture

Introduction

The previous chapter on IT organization had the luxury of being about people, a topic everyone can immediately understand and appreciate. This chapter has the intrinsic handicap that even before considering how to manage IT architecture, views differ widely on what IT architecture actually is. Certainly it is the subject of many seminars, and definitions for IT architecture range from an IT blueprint to an all-encompassing planning process. Some insights can be drawn from the parallels with architecture in traditional bricks-and-mortar construction. For any particular building, the architect produces the overall design according to its intended use and draws up plans for building it. It is especially this idea of overall design that captures the essence of what IT architecture is. Imagine IT architecture as the overall design of a building. This is not an exhaustive inventory of applications or solutions, but rather the underlying structures that enable such solutions to exist or be developed. In most firms this will be the triad of core service infrastructure, backbone applications such as ERP systems, and last, but not least, the structure of the IT organization itself. Together, they form the IT architecture: a flexible foundation or platform for delivering information services to the business (Figure 3.1).

The IT architecture triad of core infrastructure, applications and organization appears quite neat. In reality, the historical growth of IT operations with changing technology makes the picture more complex. In most companies, the IT architecture is like the overall design of a building built up from successive extensions over the years, during which available materials have evolved from wood to bricks to concrete. This IT architecture may or may not stand in the way of meeting business requirements, but while business and IT attention is naturally concentrated on the day-to-day challenges and problems of delivering information services, it is important that the underlying IT architecture is explicitly managed as many recurrent operational problems have their roots in inappropriate IT architecture. The value of an architecture process is in being systematic about identifying genuine structural weaknesses or opportunities in the way IT is run and doing something about them. For an impression of how well architecture is managed in a firm, try considering the following questions:

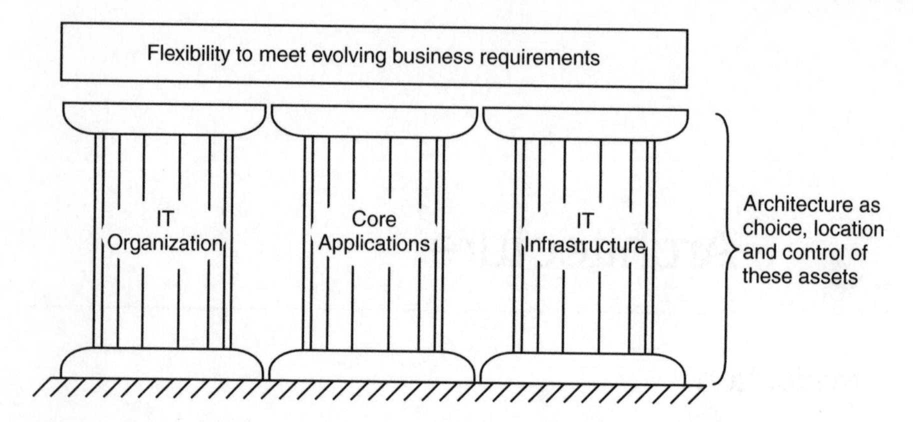

Figure 3.1—Conceptual view of IT architecture

- Is it clear how well the current IT architecture serves as a platform for meeting overall business requirements?
- Are IT efforts dominated by fire-fighting problems which have their source in the poor underlying structure of the IT operation?
- Do planners in functions and affiliates view IT architecture documentation as relevant and actually use it?
- Is it clear what aspects of the IT architecture need to be improved and how that improvement should take place?
- Do strategic initiatives or standards float in isolation or do they fit into the overall business support landscape?
- What has been achieved by IT architecture to date?

Many of the main consulting companies provide good services for IT architecture planning, but on the one hand the approaches can be quite comprehensive, tightly integrating many other processes, and on the other, the level of detail can be too fine to be effective at a global level. This chapter proposes a straightforward approach to managing global IT architecture which has just enough detail to be of value to affiliates and still integrates smoothly into the strategy, standards and control work streams (Figure 3.2). The latter are described in later chapters, but essentially form the part of the process where the findings of the architecture process are acted on and turned into reality. The key steps in the approach are as follows:

- Map at a high level the interplay of core IT infrastructure, applications and organization with supported business processes by affiliate or function.
- Identify what degree of global alignment or regional consolidation will make a platform that better meets evolving business needs.
- Feed key input on required architectural changes into the strategy, standards and control processes.

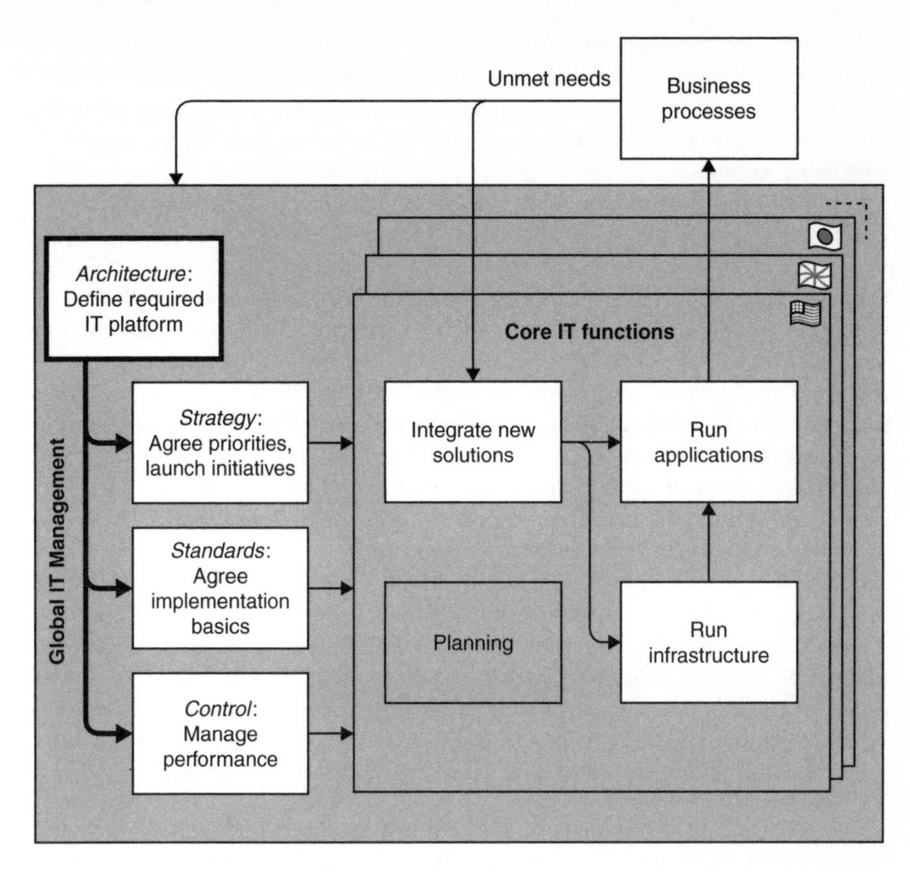

Figure 3.2—Positioning of global IT architecture

Options and expectations

At the highest level, IT architecture can be viewed as a firm's choice of IT assets such as core applications, infrastructure and organization, together with their location and control. Originally, the range of feasible architectures was tightly constrained by the availability of computing power, and most constellations revolved around centrally managed mainframes. But successive advances in networks, clients, servers and Web technologies have brought in so many degrees of freedom, that just about any hybrid of centralized or distributed services is feasible. In a way, modern architectures now revolve around networks, and the constraint is not so much availability of computing power, rather availability of skilled personnel. But while many architectures are now feasible, they do not all have the same value to a firm. In most branches business change is accelerating and this places a premium on flexible architectures that can act as an effective platform for waves of new IT solutions. And seeing a step further ahead, the IT architecture can in many businesses be taken beyond simple information services to become a real business asset and competitive weapon, an example being the introduction to travel agents of the Sabre online reservation system by American Airlines.

Seen at a more mundane level, global IT management is often faced with deep-seated problems. Globally consolidated IT costs may be far higher than expected, the responsiveness of IT to the need for new solutions may be characterized by year-long project delays, and meeting information demands of globalizing functions such as supply chain management may appear almost impossible. In short, there is a disconnect of some form between fundamental business requirements and IT service delivery. In many cases, inappropriate IT architecture is the underlying cause of the disconnect. Perhaps responsiveness to global information requirements is ultimately hindered by a global patchwork of local systems, inherited from historical affiliate autonomy or a series of mergers and acquisitions. Or conversely, exaggerated control of global standards may be stifling local innovation.

The issue is to identify what needs to be changed in the IT architecture and make that change happen. Both steps are usually non-trivial. While most changes at a global level distil down to implementing various degrees of alignment and consolidation across locations (Figure 3.3), there is a wide range of distinct domains to which these principles can be applied, each of which potentially holds the key to a target architecture that matches a firm's business information requirements. Here are some of the options:

- *Organization*: IT organization and control can be centralized or decentralized, and orientated towards geography or function (matrix organizations are essentially a hybrid of the two). Certain parts can be outsourced.
- *Infrastructure*: While users basically need a PC or similar device with access to company networks, the choice and physical location of servers and mainframes remains transparent and can be adjusted to suit business needs, for example through co-location at the same site.
- *Applications*: Head office control over affiliates' choice and tailoring of applications and technologies such as ERP systems can be tightened to meet global requirements or loosened to allow adaptation to exploit local business conditions.
- *Services*: Certain commodity services that do not require physical on-site presence, such as help desks and data centres, can be run locally, regionally or globally.
- *Information*: The extent to which information is more generally managed as an asset in its own right can vary from simple standardization of database access across affiliates to global data definitions governing, for example, a common chart of accounts.

The process to identify at a global level which changes to IT architecture make sense and are feasible must negotiate two hurdles. First, general

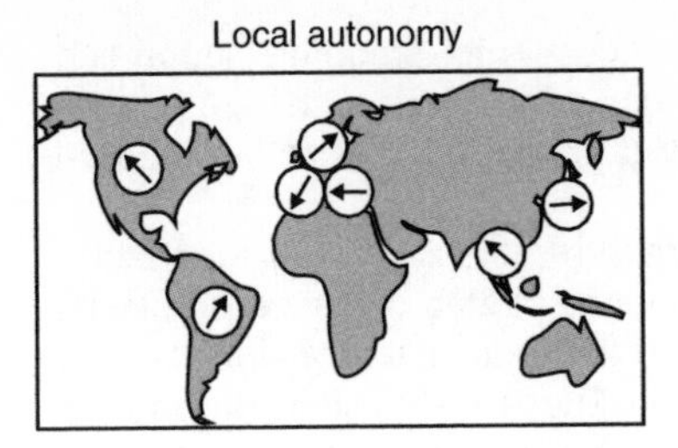

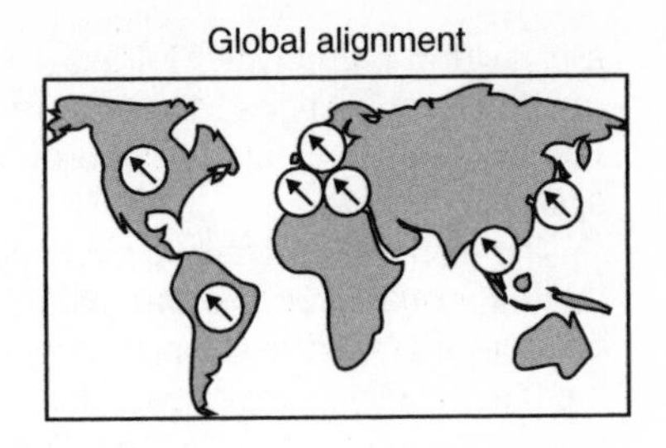

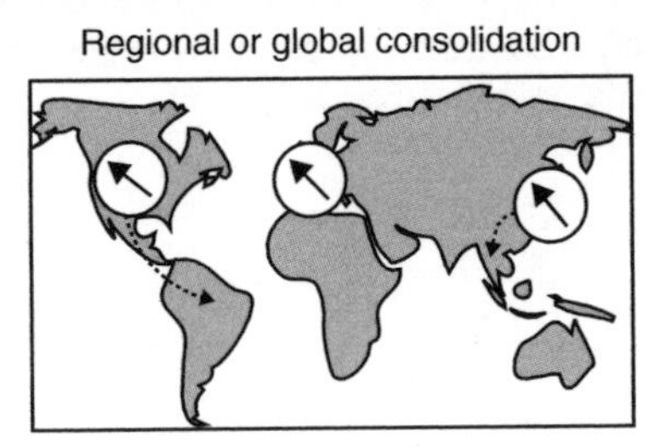

Figure 3.3—Alignment and consolidation as main degrees of freedom in global IT

management often focuses on the symptoms of a poor IT operation and the link to necessary change in the underlying architecture is not always easy to grasp. Secondly, local resistance to a global IT architecture process can be great, either because it is regarded as an intrusion in well functioning local planning, or because similar efforts in the past have proven to be intensive paper exercises yielding no concrete results.

After identifying necessary improvements to global IT architecture, the subsequent step of making change happen also has challenges, as global IT architecture is fundamentally political. Genuine changes in organization, infrastructure and applications directly impact not only IT personnel, but more significantly, business users and processes. Tackling these issues effectively forms the essence of global IT management, and the basic instruments at firms' disposal to do so are strategy, standards and control.

Exhibit 3 – global IT architecture in featured firms

Philips

A common underlying IT architecture or infrastructure is recognized as an important corporate asset for several reasons. Supply chain management is being globalized in response to the demand for standard products such as Philips digital displays which PC vendors subsequently incorporate into their products. Production remains decentralized, for example locating production as close as possible to customer production facilities, but overall, the supply chain is managed globally and that requires a harmonized infrastructure. In other cases, a clear and harmonized infrastructure is a prerequisite for smoothly supporting recurrent acquisitions, divestments, and co-engineering efforts with third parties. For example, four major acquisitions recently doubled the size of the medical systems division.

The approach taken to managing IT architecture at Philips is to feed architectural considerations and insights into the overall strategic planning process. Corporate IT and division IT departments each have dedicated architects who meet regularly to agree on architectural blueprints. These are then formally brought in as agenda items to CIO meetings. One example of current architectural priorities is the launch of an enterprise interconnectivity programme to develop uniform procedures for integrating enterprise applications.

Nestlé

The IT architecture at Nestlé is being drastically changed as part of the GLOBE project from decentralized to global. The current architecture is treated across the board as essentially legacy and is to be replaced by a new architecture that focuses on meeting the requirements of a common business process architecture, one of which is to support "off-the-shelf" best practice models for use by businesses according to prevailing market conditions. The new architecture builds on the SAP applications platform and has the following organizational components:

- Streamlined local IT organizations that focus on training users and assisting the transition to new systems, but without carrying out any developments of their own.
- Three regional operational centres where systems are implemented and supported, and any necessary adaptations are developed, for example to meet local regulations.
- One central competence centre where the kernel application template is maintained and the integration of regional adaptations into updates is controlled.
- One central operational centre running any global systems and providing operational support to head office and the central competence centre above.

Novartis

The IT architecture at Novartis is primarily divisional, and while the choice of core applications has been harmonized within each division there is a certain fragmentation which matches the nature of business information requirements. Novartis affiliates have traditionally operated with significant autonomy and have chosen to have their own IT operations. Furthermore, the pharmaceuticals industry exhibits extensive vertical integration, i.e. every function is present from research right through to marketing and sales, each exhibiting different levels of geographic spread and orientation. Information requirements are therefore very diverse, and particularly for globally orientated functions such as research it made business sense for individual functions to have some IT operations of their own.

Nevertheless, common processes are now being established to document and manage IT architecture throughout Novartis. This work has proven useful as a tool for supporting communication between IT and business counterparts, and it provides the foundation for identifying new areas where collaboration across IT units can be fruitful. As such it provides valuable input to high level discussions on IT strategy, mainly in communicating the complexity of the status quo and clearly positioning major initiatives in the IT landscape.

Toyota

IT architecture is one of the main areas where regional IT organizations cooperate globally. To date, the operations themselves have been held separate, even between the regional manufacturing and sales divisions, but there is significant effort to align choice of technologies and applications wherever the supported business processes are similar across locations, for example in human resources, finance and administration. Because of wide differences in dealer and market structure, marketing and sales systems remain regional. In manufacturing, the handling of IT architecture is orientated more towards the car being manufactured: development of a new car may be accompanied by construction of a new factory, processes and IT systems, all specially designed for that car. Once stabilized, the "mother" factory model is then used as the initial template for building further factories abroad.

The main work on global architecture is led by the Global IT Architecture Committee, chaired by corporate IT and composed of dedicated architects from each region. The committee meets quarterly and forms the main forum for dialogue on global issues and opportunities in IT architecture. Throughout, the approach is pragmatic and consensus orientated, with agreements, for example on standards, reported back to regional CIOs without any further escalation.

UBS

The IT architecture at UBS reflects the fact that each of the four "divisional" IT units serves the distinct needs of its respective business group. Each chooses the platforms, suppliers and products that best meet information requirements for their business group. Agreed company standards must nevertheless be adhered to, and IT units providing service for corporate business functions such as market and credit risk management need to meet central information requirements. Key throughout is a business-driven approach to architecture.

A number of initiatives such as centralization of previously regional mainframe operations have markedly improved efficiency. Today, one of the main architectural challenges lies in the ability of the IT units to respond to rapidly evolving and changing business requirements. Core operative platforms based on a design which stems from the 1970s will no longer be adequate for future business and market requirements given the evolution from a bank counter dominated business to one which requires 7 × 24 hour online service. A new core platform is now being set up to progressively replace the legacy systems in place today.

Managing architecture

Most local IT organizations beyond a certain size already manage their IT architecture, although the interpretation placed on it can vary in flavour from a short statement on overall IT structure accompanying annual planning to architecture as a comprehensive process from which all plans are derived. One could ask the question: "Isn't that enough, why manage architecture on a global basis?" But given the local scope of activity and perhaps in the interests of self-preservation, local planning processes will rarely report favourably on opportunities for global alignment or regional consolidation, and yet this may be just what is necessary to meet business requirements. IT architecture needs to be managed globally, and the more pertinent question is how. Integrated architecture processes that work well locally suffer when applied at a global level. Exhaustive data collection can obscure those few fundamental changes that need to be made to the global architecture. More seriously, whereas in local operations intentions are matched with *in situ* local resources for execution, this is often not the case at a global level and execution of global changes needs to be planned differently.

This book proposes a lean approach to managing global IT architecture, run by a small, dedicated central group collaborating with local IT planners or architects. The initial focus is on establishing a high-level picture of the status quo in each major IT organization. Information collection is kept basic enough to be manageable at a global level, while being sufficiently detailed to give a locally relevant picture of the current IT landscape. This picture can be used, for example, to give context to local project and budget approvals. The second phase is to analyze the consolidated architecture for weaknesses and to identify necessary changes on a global level. This does not necessarily imply alignment or consolidation; it may transpire that for the business in question, control appears too centralized and should be devolved. For the ultimate execution phase, instead of translating findings directly into detailed plans, recommendations are fed into the global strategy, standards and control processes. This places priorities concerning the core IT architecture into a more general business context that will include other priorities, and into the hands of processes that are more orientated towards execution.

Throughout, care is taken to control the scope and duration of IT architecture activity, concentrating at each stage on tangible interim deliverables that are of genuine value to both head office and local organizations. The following sections present the organization and processes for establishing and analysing the status quo. Later chapters on strategy, standards and control describe how findings are implemented.

Organization

Addressing underlying structural issues in an IT operation and shaping a firm's IT architecture to fit mid-term business needs is a fundamental part of good

IT leadership and a key responsibility for most CIOs. In this respect, one of the roles a CIO plays is that of chief IT architect. In larger scale companies, more operative issues can require so much immediate attention that systematic management of IT architecture needs to be delegated (Figure 3.4). In such instances, a small central group or individual reporting directly to the CIO can take on the task of ongoing management of IT architecture. Their mandate is to build up an understanding of the weaknesses and strengths of the current IT architecture and pass on recommendations for changes to the strategy, standards and control groups for execution. Activities are distributed in roughly equal proportions among the following:

- *Lead process*: visit sites and work with local IT heads or functional planners to maintain an overall picture of the current architecture. Lead the analysis of what changes are required. The aim is to pool and rationalize work on high level IT architecture.
- *Communications*: work with global IT strategy, standards and control groups to fit architectural recommendations into the context of overall priorities and available resources. Work with the CIO and IT Board to instigate and support execution of launched initiatives.

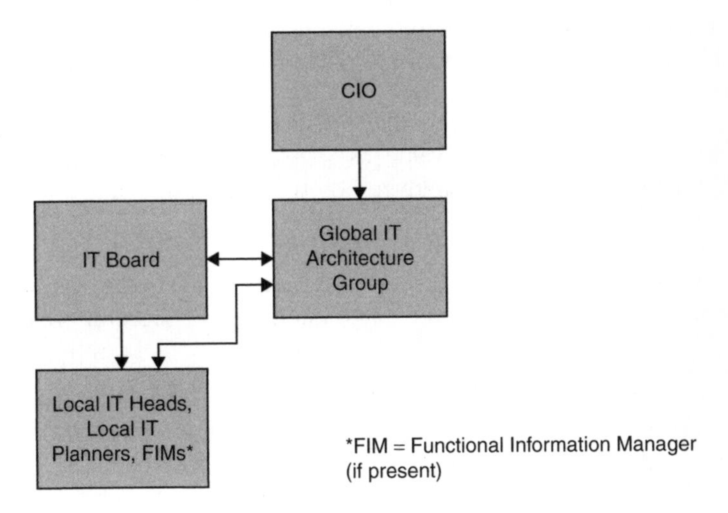

Figure 3.4—Organization for managing global IT architecture

The skills required for such a global role combine the conceptual and analytical skills of a traditional IT architect with practical communication ability. The latter is especially important in two domains. On the one hand, some affiliates may have experienced IT architecture as wasted effort in the past or they may feel directly threatened by the implications of cross-locational architecture. On the other hand, findings need to be crystallized out sufficiently clearly for everyone to be able to grasp the key messages and context. Both require a down-to-earth, pragmatic approach to dealing with people.

Funding

The funding requirements for global IT architecture should be minimal and limited to the cost of the Global IT Architecture Group and associated travel and consultancy costs. All these costs should be carried centrally.

Map current IT architecture

One of the complicating factors in capturing a firm's current IT architecture is the multitude of perspectives that can justifiably be construed as an integral part of the underlying IT structure. But attempting an approach that is too comprehensive will slow down proceedings and often conceal genuine insights, so an early decision needs to be made on exactly what the scope of mapping for the current IT landscape should be. The following guidelines to that decision can avoid many problems later in the process:

- Scale and timing of information collection should be such that contributing affiliates can easily devote the effort required on their part and receive useful interim results in time for annual planning. In most firms, receptivity will be minimal for architectural insights produced two weeks after budget finalizations.
- The picture of the current architecture should be of sufficient local relevance to be of ongoing value as a point of reference for succinctly describing to either IT employees or the business community how IT supports the business.
- The depth of information should be such that the picture of current IT architecture can reasonably be kept current through simple annual updates without repetition of the whole initial information collection cycle.

Define Scope (Step 1): The compromise recommended here is to map IT architecture using four figures, each constrained to a single page and depicting respectively the supported business processes, IT applications, IT infrastructure and IT organization. A distinct set of figures is drawn up for each affiliate or major function unless differences across organizations are negligible, in which case one set can be valid for all. The figures are necessarily a simplification, but they identify the essentials in each domain and help convey basic interdependencies. Important in a global context is that the format should be harmonized across affiliates and distinguish between local and global activities. The figures are as follows:

- *Business processes*: depicts at a high level the sequence of key business activities supported by IT. Wherever possible, the extension of activities into other affiliates, functions, suppliers or customers should be highlighted.

- *IT applications*: depicts the core business applications such as ERP systems and the main interfaces between them and applications in other domains.
- *IT infrastructure*: summarizes the choice of technologies and vendors from client PC, through middleware, Web environment, local and remote servers to networks.
- *IT organization*: summarizes the structure of the IT organization, including the distribution across new solutions integration, applications (help desk, competence centres, etc.), infrastructure (data centre, information security, etc.) and any outsourcing.

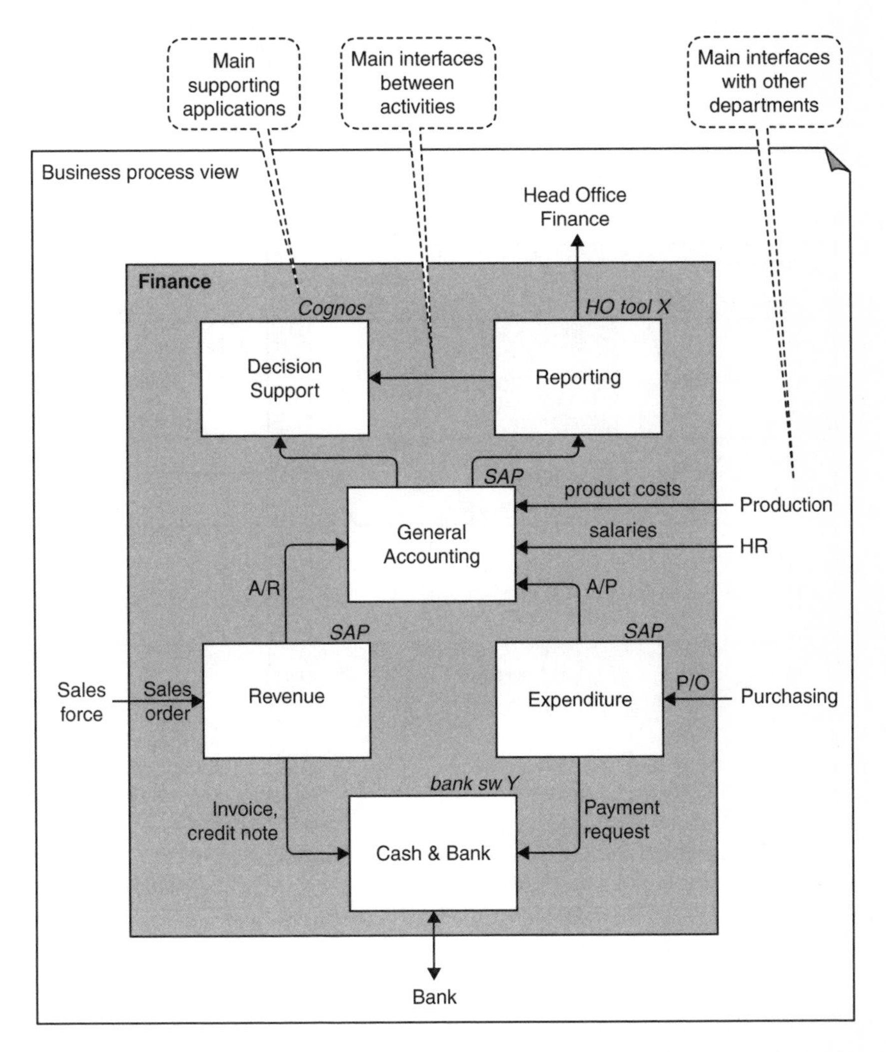

Figure 3.5—Sample target interim deliverable summarizing local finance business processes (elements can be colour coded to reflect business priorities for IT support)

Starting in this way with supported business activities gives business orientation to the representation of IT architecture, and careful labelling in figures helps trace basic infrastructure requirements directly back through applications to business activities. Should more detail be required, the logical addition to the picture is a further perspective focusing explicitly on the flow of information such as customer data between business activities. In most situations, the basic four perspectives above will be adequate on a global level for appraising the IT architecture across affiliates or functions. Figures 3.5 to 3.8 show the format for presenting the architecture for any particular unit.

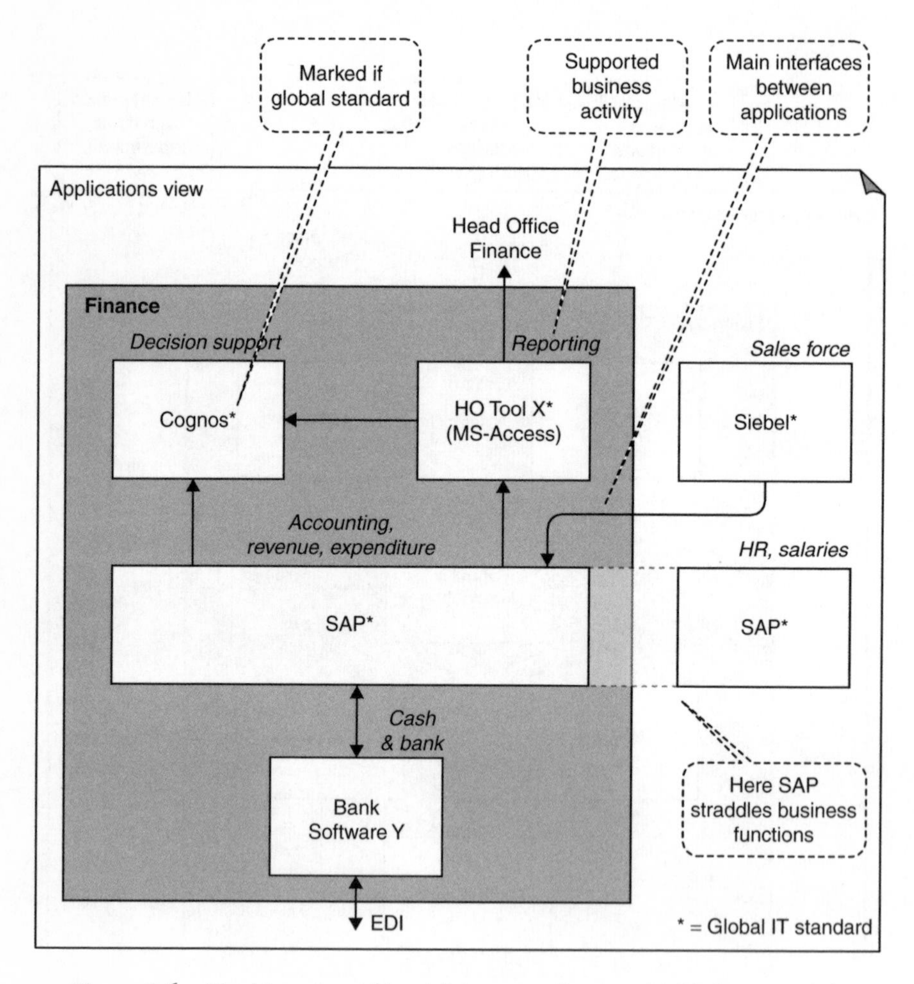

Figure 3.6—Matching view of local finance applications highlights essentials

Collect Local Information (Step 2): With the format for documenting IT architecture defined, the way to proceed to collect the information depends on the scale of the IT organization in affiliates and functions. In principle

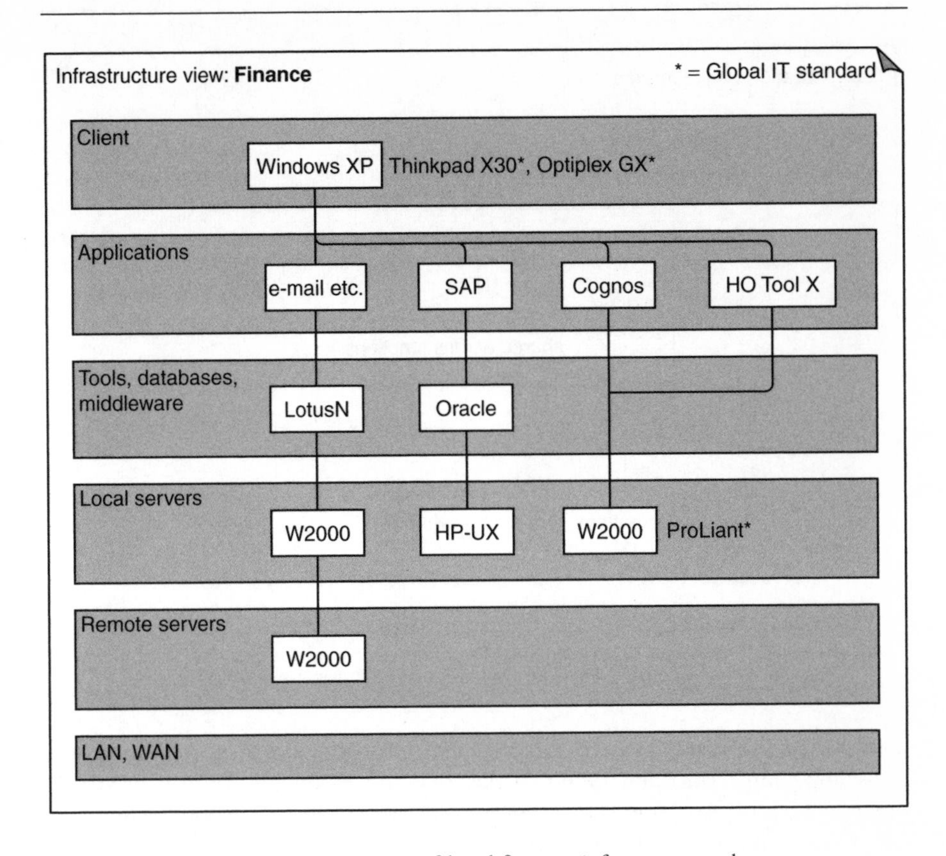

Figure 3.7—Matching view of local finance infrastructure charts core technologies used

this could be achieved through a simple questionnaire. In practice, and especially if there are a number of distinct functional IT organizations at a particular site, a physical visit to the site in question by the Global IT Architecture Group is more likely to reach a clear result and achieve local commitment to the initiative and later annual updates. Beyond the personal contact, there are further advantages of a visit. Experience and templates from other affiliates can be reused more effectively and the process moderated to keep the approach harmonized. The visit agenda can be set to complete the architecture during the visit, keeping a tangible limit on the effort required from affiliates. The information collected can already serve as an excellent point of departure for discussions between senior business and IT management.

Describe Global IT Architecture (Step 3): The information collected above is only a number of high-level views of individual local IT architectures. One last set of figures needs to be produced that summarizes architecture on a global

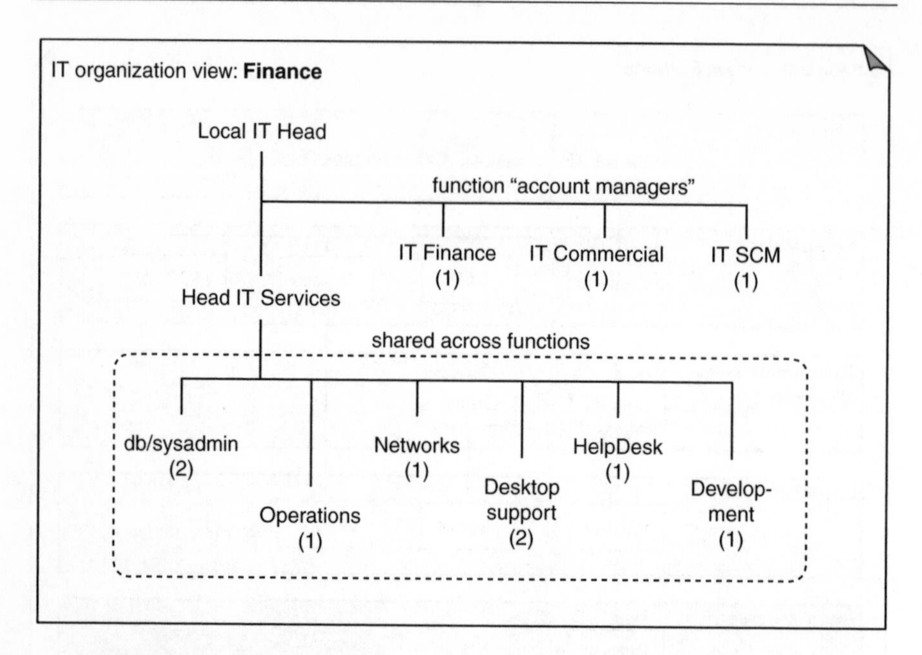

Figure 3.8—Matching view of local IT organization for serving finance

level for each perspective. In this instance the format can be left open, the most important constraint being to describe the essentials for any particular perspective on one page. For example, in the applications perspective, the summary could be a table of the different business applications in use and the locations where they are respectively operated. In the business perspective, there could be a view of the overall business hierarchy and statements on globalization of certain functions.

Publish Architecture (Step 4): Throughout, although not a necessity, the use of online systems for publishing IT architecture can facilitate the information collection process and add value to the result. For example, where explanations of the intricacies of IT architecture can be difficult and may remind affiliates of unproductive initiatives in the past, a simple online view of work completed to date in other affiliates quickly demonstrates what needs to be achieved and the immediate usefulness of the result in any event as a communication instrument. Likewise, during information collection, immediate publication of interim results, say on the company intranet, normally draws much more of the original author's attention to the accuracy of information than if it is believed that the architecture will simply end up in a filing cabinet. Finally, although the IT architectures remain high-level, significant amounts of information can be accumulated and online systems are needed to maintain easy, transparent access to information (Figure 3.9).

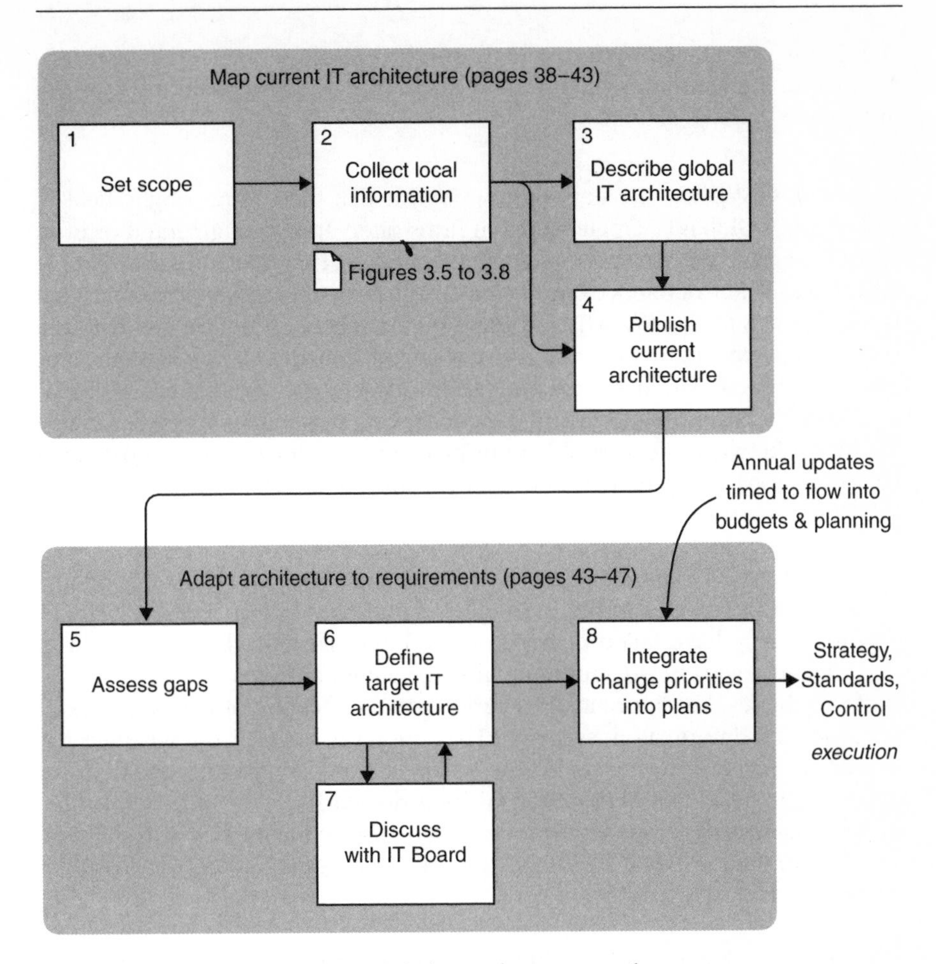

Figure 3.9—Global IT architecture work stream

Adapt architecture to requirements

Being aware of the current IT architecture is useful in its own right, but the greatest value comes from using the material to assess how well ongoing overall business requirements can be met, recognizing which structural changes, if any, are necessary on a global level. While the scale of this research need not be great, the impact of findings can be, so it is worth being systematic about the evaluation, although there is no magic recipe that guarantees pinpointing the correct findings. In general, best results are produced by a combination of management intuition and a more dry appraisal of collected information broken down into three stages. Stage one focuses on clarifying what the business requirements are that cannot be met with the current architecture. Such deficits are termed "gaps", i.e. gaps between what is required and the service that can be offered. Stage two moves on to establish what type of changes to the IT architecture are required to fill these gaps. The last stage focuses on integration of changes into plans. The overall procedure is shown in Figure 3.9 and is as follows.

Assess Gaps (Step 5): The key starting point is that there is no single ideal IT architecture. Global IT architectures in firms often appear fragmented or even chaotic, and yet this need not be unhealthy. Such IT architectures may simply reflect significant differences in business requirements across locations. What is important is to identify what business requirements cannot be met with the status quo architecture. There are two primary domains in which such gaps can be revealed. The first domain assesses how well the architecture copes with today's basic operational and performance requirements, by reviewing the match between the assembled business process views and corresponding IT applications, infrastructure and organizations, answering, for example, the following questions:

- Can sensitive IT failures be traced back to underlying weaknesses in global architecture? For example, rollout of a business driven international IT project may have failed or been delayed because of lack of alignment in IT technologies or organizations in place within affiliates.
- Does the level of information security match the extent of business dependence on information systems? This question focuses on whether the current architecture meets business expectations concerning operation of critical systems and defence against outside attack.
- Do business expectations on service and cost tie in roughly with the type of IT operation being run? Does the business genuinely expect excellent or just cheap IT service?

The second domain for revealing gaps focuses on the evolution of requirements, and in particular how well the architecture can respond to business change. Many architectures that manage current needs adequately prove to be particularly inflexible when needs change. This inflexibility may be built in to any aspect of the architecture, from technology to applications, infrastructure or organization, but the aim at this point is to assess what type of business change or innovation is expected, but cannot be supported effectively by IT. Key questions are, for example:

- If business is expected to increase significantly, how scalable is the IT infrastructure to respond to increased volumes or changes in configuration? For example, a new business strategy of acquisitions and spin-offs may require an IT architecture which can smoothly integrate or separate systems.
- If business innovation is to occur primarily on a global level, for example through globalization of supply chain management or the need to provide a single service to international customers, can the existing architecture respond adequately to global information needs?

- Conversely, if business innovation is to occur locally, for example through focusing on the specificities of local markets, can the architecture be responsive to wide-ranging local demands?

The aim at this stage is not to document the potentially manifold superficial weaknesses that any complex IT operation can have, but to focus on pinpointing fundamental business requirements that cannot be met with the current IT architecture.

Define Target IT Architecture (Step 6): This stage takes the gaps established above as the point of departure for identifying necessary changes to the IT architecture. On a global level, the levers available to close gaps are varying degrees of harmonization and consolidation applied to different aspects of IT. Some of the basic options in terms of organization, applications, infrastructure, service and information were presented earlier. Each of these should be reviewed, but while attention often tends to be drawn towards technology, the place to start is in reviewing whether changes are required to the IT organization and associated controls. Many of the issues were presented in the previous chapter on organization. It is crucial that the hierarchy of reporting and accountability matches the pattern of business information requirements. Therefore, if a business function is globalizing, the IT hierarchy will need to follow, in many cases from a status quo inherited from locally implemented client–server solutions. Additional changes to technology and service elements can then be identified to build a platform that closes the gaps in required service and flexibility.

With this method, proposed changes to the global IT architecture can be traced back to explicit business information requirements that cannot otherwise be met. Additional changes can be justified by the more generic need simply to cut costs and risks in meeting those information requirements. These changes capitalize on the options in delivering service that are opened up in global firms. To investigate these opportunities, the key assessments that need to be made are:

- Are there commodity services that could benefit from global alignment or coordination without deterioration of the local service provided? For example, vendor negotiations or system developments could be pooled if local choices in a certain type of system are harmonized.
- Are there entire services that do not need to be run locally and could benefit from economies of scale or choice of location if consolidated? For example, local data centres can be consolidated regionally or globally.

Overall, in capturing a target global IT architecture, it should always be considered that there are limits to the number of changes that an organization can absorb, and that whereas identifying necessary changes is relatively straightforward, achieving those changes in a global environment is an order of magnitude harder. The target architecture needs to be an objective that can reasonably be achieved and to which the IT and business community can relate.

Discuss with IT Board (Step 7): The findings revealed by the architecture process and the proposed target architecture need formal review by the IT Board. Where justified, plans can be discussed at the IT Steering Committee.

Integrate Change Priorities into Plans (Step 8): The previous step delivers a simple document specifying and justifying a few required changes to global IT architecture. Two points now arise. One is that while redressing faults in the underlying IT platform for delivering service is important, it is not the only priority. Business priorities may be focused entirely on an upcoming product launch and demand absolutely no disturbance of the status quo, irrespective of the motivation. Architecture projects therefore require context. The other point is that while changes to architecture are major undertakings, if the lean approach to global IT management is taken, then at least initially, few global resources will be available for dedication to execution. Both issues can be managed effectively by passing on required IT architecture changes formally as key input to the global IT strategy, standards and control processes. This gives both context and integration in processes that secure business and IT backing for initiatives. Later chapters are dedicated to treating each of these work streams. Here is a brief preview that highlights the interplay with architecture:

- *Strategy*: The global IT strategy process secures executive business and IT agreement on IT priorities, launches and resources associated initiatives, and cascades priorities and plans down into the organization. The main variants of agreed global IT strategy are direct support for a specific business improvement, incremental improvement in existing service, globalization of IT and outsourcing. Architectural priorities form a major input to the latter two variants.
- *Standards*: Global IT standards are managed with three distinct processes for definition of new standards, maintenance of existing ones and exception handling. Some standards may be opportunistic, but many form key integral components of the core IT infrastructure and their main justification is on architectural grounds, for example, the choice of a standard e-mail system.
- *Control*: The global IT control process manages the cost and, to an increasing extent, the value of IT activities. Partially allocated cost centres are used for cost accounting, improved business case definitions are used for individual project investment decisions, and lastly overall performance is managed through balanced scorecards. Architectural input serves in two ways. To begin with, reporting and budgeting controls need to complement organizational hierarchy and intentions. Furthermore, the architecture highlights which components other than organization form a key part of the architecture and likewise need monitoring.

The handover of required architectural changes effectively signals the end of the analysis phase and allows limits to be set for the scale and scope of the architecture process. Each year, the Global IT Architecture Group should return to the process, working with local planning colleagues to keep the picture of the status quo updated, and reviewing required architectural changes with respect to any evolution in the business and IT environment.

Tool support

There are many tools and multifunctional suites available on the market that can help record, represent and organize process and architectural information, for example, Microsoft Visio®, Casewise® and IDS-Scheer ARIS®. Given that in this instance the IT architecture for any particular affiliate or function is to be summarized in four pages, the sophistication required is minimal. Also, in a global context the range of people involved in information collection is wide. So probably the only tools everyone is familiar with are paper and pencil. Should the Global IT Architecture Group utilize a tool to rework input, this offers a little service to affiliates, while establishing the group as a certain gateway.

The genuine system functionality required is the transparent and appealing publication of the current architecture, normally on the company intranet, in such a way that users find the architecture for their own organization and can easily navigate across to others. An example has been prepared on the sample web site on `www.gitm.biz/architecture`. Note how the architecture for any particular site is placed directly next to the strategy, standards and control pages for the same unit.

The decision on whether to extend publication to include explicit details on the intended changes to the architecture is more sensitive, and is essentially a policy decision. In any event, intentions should only really be published once preliminary projects have been launched and all the stakeholders have been informed appropriately.

Summary

This chapter presented the key issues in global IT architecture and a business requirements orientated approach to systematically managing it:

- Map at a high level the interplay of core IT infrastructure, applications and organization with supported business processes by affiliate or function.
- Identify what degree of global alignment or regional consolidation will make a platform that better meets evolving business needs.
- Feed key input on required architectural changes into the strategy, standards and control processes for planning and execution.

While the return on global changes to the IT architecture can be high, changes are complex and often carry risk. Not surprisingly, proposals are exposed to significant management scrutiny. The steps above provide an effective framework for positioning and justifying projects that change the underlying way IT is run globally.

4 Strategy

Introduction

Strategy is not new: the word stems from the ancient Greek "strategia" meaning the art of war. Today, the idea of strategy has spread beyond its original military context to include business, and "strategy" is now commonly credited as the reason for the shining success or outright failure of well-known firms. For example, people say that IBM's success lies in its winning strategy of evolving from a manufacturer of computers to a deliverer of services. In contrast, the news may report that a losing strategy of expansionism lay at the foundation of Swissair's demise. Throughout, strategy is understood as those fundamental ideas that have been driven through to change a company for better or for worse (Figure 4.1).

Viewed from an insider perspective, the pressure to be competitive presents companies with a challenge. On the one hand, there are many potential possibilities for improving a business, but on the other hand a company's resources are limited and there is a real danger that spreading resources too thinly leads to no improvement at all. Strategy is about identifying the right options and focusing effort on those alone. In an IT context, the situation is not dissimilar. The demands on IT within a large firm can be complex, even conflicting, and the IT resources to meet these requirements are necessarily limited. But there is a further aggravating factor: the technology environment is evolving very rapidly. Together these form strong arguments for identifying priorities and formulating a clear strategy for IT.

Seen globally, the essential aim of IT strategy is to establish relevant priorities and turn these into reality. On the ground, reaching this ideal can be complicated by both differences across functions and between head office and affiliates. To see how close your organization is to fulfilling this ideal, try answering the following questions:

- Is the fundamental IT strategy documented succinctly and up to date?
- Do business counterparts know and support the IT strategy?
- Is alignment between IT departments in head office and affiliates tangible?
- Does everyone in the IT community understand the IT strategy?
- Do planners in affiliates and functions feel the strategy is relevant and actually use it?

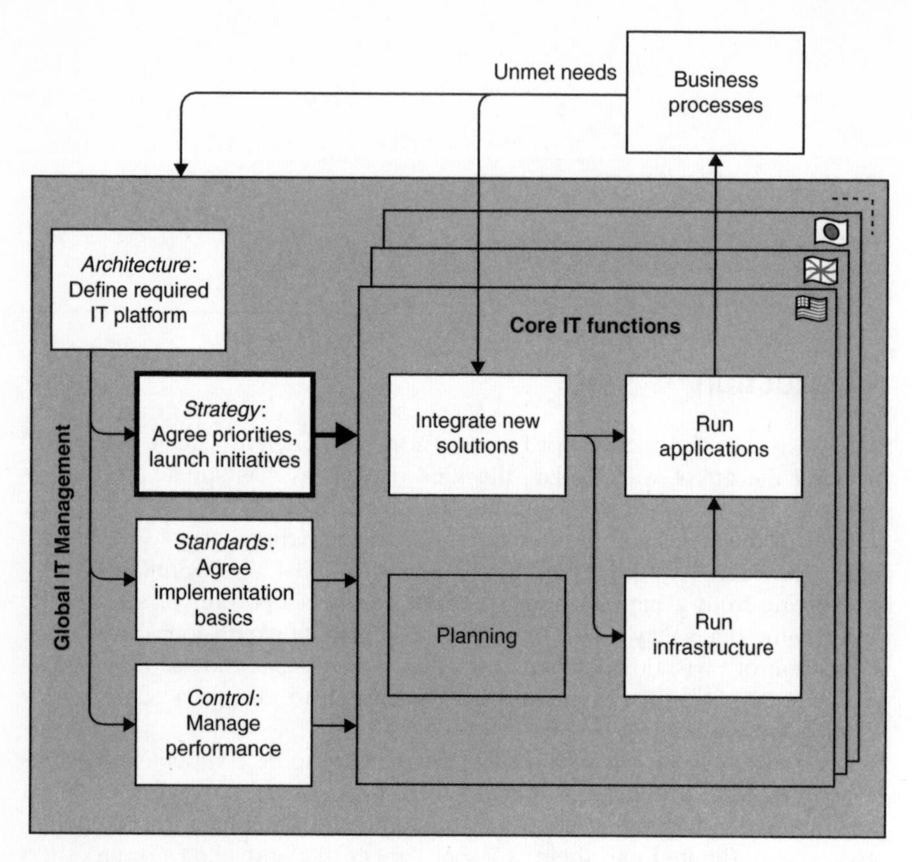

Figure 4.1—Overall positioning of global IT strategy

- What has the IT strategy achieved to date?
- What is being done to implement the current strategy?

Many organizations rightly invest time and effort in systematically establishing IT strategies and yet despite perhaps following a detailed and resource intensive methodology, cannot honestly give positive responses to all of the questions above. The idea of this chapter is not to find fault with these methodologies, but to cast light on those elements which need special attention in a global context. The main messages are to look beyond potentially exhaustive analysis and focus on the process of agreement on strategy and effective subsequent implementation in a global organization:

- Top-down IT and business agreement on IT strategy.
- Straightforward articulation of strategy and cascade of priorities into local and functional planning.
- Avoidance of well-known pitfalls in execution.

Options and expectations

The main demand for IT strategy within a firm springs from the three distinct populations of business managers, IT planners and the community of IT employees in general. Each population has its own reasons for needing an IT strategy:

- *Business managers*: Two factors concerning IT alert business managers. First, the levels of investment in IT are rising and range from about 1–5% of sales for industrial firms up to 15–20% for banks. Secondly, the dependence of business operations on IT systems availability is extending to include more and more core business processes. Without wanting to learn all the details, business managers have a vested interest in knowing and agreeing with underlying IT priorities, to make sure that enough value is reaped from IT investments while risks are kept to a minimum.
- *IT planners*: Local and functional IT planners naturally aim to anticipate and meet all the information needs of the communities they serve. Here too, operational resources are limited and specific priorities in resource allocation need to be set—and if there is to be alignment with any global business and IT priorities, IT planners need a clear statement of these overarching priorities and a practical mechanism for physically achieving and demonstrating alignment.
- *IT community in general*: As in other business functions, IT planning is regularly dominated by the annual budget cycle. Within the IT community, an exclusive focus on budgets can easily lead to a feeling of aimlessness and the accusation that there is simply no IT management vision beyond the current year. Relevant longer-term priorities and a sense of purpose beyond cost control need to be set and communicated if a negative atmosphere of aimlessness is to be avoided.

However, experience to date shows that the above needs are rarely met. Even at a local level, IT strategy commonly fails because of lack of top management acceptance, lack of resources to fully implement the strategy and the whole process being too slow. On a global level, the same problems occur but, in addition, global IT strategies often prove locally irrelevant or at a completely inappropriate level of detail. There are many cases of large IT strategy reports produced at great expense at head office that never go beyond the stage of paperwork.

So while the demand for IT strategy is there, actually establishing and implementing it is not without its challenges. Later sections will present the model for agreeing and implementing IT strategy. The following paragraphs, however, introduce the complexity of the material itself and some of the main options that firms have when identifying the strategy that best suits their business.

When thinking initially about IT strategy, it is worth taking as a starting point a view of those core activities which IT organizations carry out, i.e. the integration of new solutions, running business applications and running the supporting infrastructure. There will usually be substantial room for improvement in any of these activities. Perhaps new solutions take too long to develop, or applications are obsolete, or there are repeated network outages. Such weaknesses are fairly obvious and relatively straightforward to improve. But more insidious and harder to recognize are weaknesses in the interfaces between these core activities, and to the supported business community itself. For example, new projects might be handled and completed very professionally, but subsequent operation of new applications fails because little account has been taken of the operative environment in designing the solution. Or perhaps the dialogue between business and IT counterparts is poor and a great opportunity is missed simply because neither side adequately appreciated the possibilities.

Local IT departments are often well aware of these factors and have been planning and improving their operations on this basis for years; even if they have no explicit strategy, there will be an undercurrent of priorities which run through their plans. However, in large organizations there are two additional factors which enter the equation: information as an asset, and geography. In the case of information, where management see and to a certain extent appreciate IT personnel and systems as valuable assets resulting from IT investments, they often overlook the more general potential of accumulated information as an asset in its own right. For example, customer information is accumulated by field forces for their own purposes, but might that same information not also be of value to the marketing department? The geographic factor is more apparent: instead of a single, local IT operation, a firm may have IT operations in every site. On the one hand, this complexity can make a unifying strategy all the more important if alignment across sites makes sense, and on the other the possibility of shifting service provision between locations barely conceals a Pandora's box of issues.

In this landscape, there are many different tactical steps that can potentially be taken to progress IT. Viewed globally at a strategic level, however, there are only a few real options for a global IT strategy. These options distil down to the four generic strategies of business enablement, incremental improvement, globalization and outsourcing as depicted in Figure 4.2. The following paragraphs consider each of these themes a little closer. Notice how the situation is not dissimilar in business strategy: of all the nuances in approach, a business will ultimately succeed in differentiating itself from competitors by (1) being very innovative like 3M PostIts, or (2) being very intimate with customer requirements like SAS airlines, or (3) having excellent low-cost operations like Dell.[1]

[1] M.E. Porter, *Competitive Advantage*, Free Press, 1985, 1998.

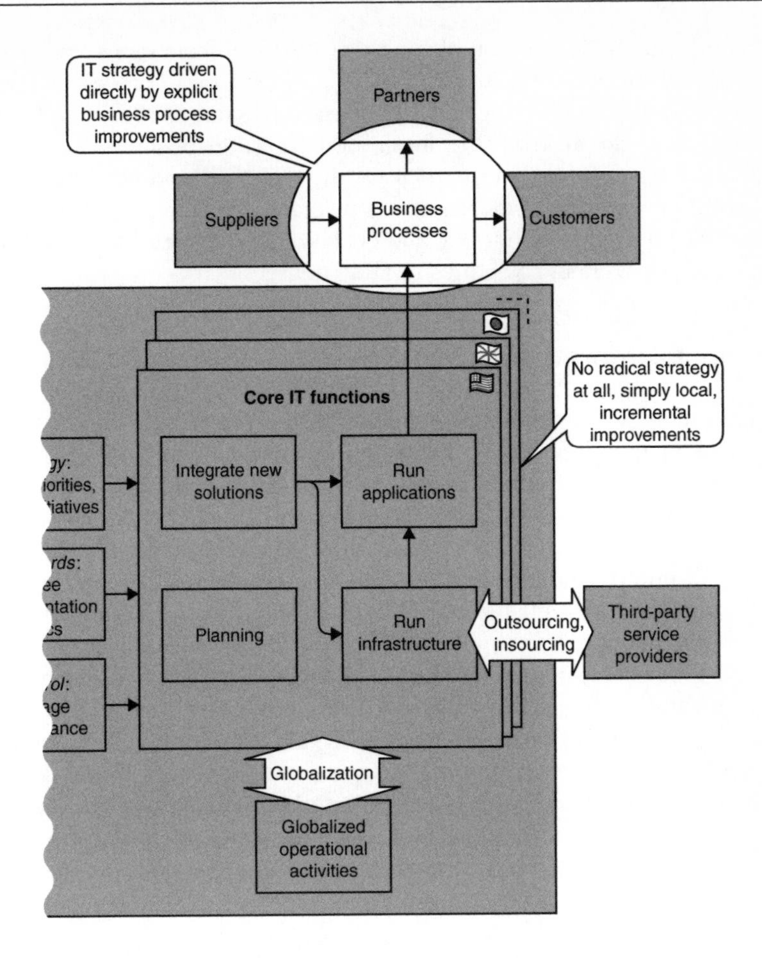

Figure 4.2—Candidate themes for global IT strategy

Business enablement

The ideal and clearest situation for defining global IT strategy is when elements of the current business strategy call for large-scale investment of particular IT resources. In this case, the IT strategy must directly support the business strategy. The most common case is when planned business process improvements dictate that ERP should take top priority in allocation of IT resources and figure prominently in the corresponding global IT strategy. One prime example is the GLOBE (Global Business Excellence) project launched at Nestlé in July 2000. This is a major business project to harmonize and simplify business process architecture across a traditionally decentralized company. The IT strategy is largely dictated by that project, but business strategy can also regularly require a concerted effort from IT in areas not dominated to date by ERP. Examples are customer relationship management, pricing and forecasting, and the integration of suppliers and customers more closely in the supply chain through e-business. Each of these business processes involves intensive information exchange and an aligned IT strategy is essential.

At least at a global level, the implication of IT in business strategy may not always be so evident. In these cases, the driver behind global IT strategy should still be business requirements, but more in the sense of the generic need to improve value for money and cut risk. This can lead to the following three, more introverted, categories of IT strategy.

Incremental improvement

Although strategy is most commonly associated with some type of radical change, in many cases it may make more sense to incrementally improve the status quo. Perhaps in principle a radical reorganization of IT would be beneficial, but business support for the idea is too limited or the IT community is simply not ready for major change. In such circumstances, a strategy of incremental improvement normally finds wide acceptance with business and IT communities, although this should not be allowed to degenerate into a "do nothing" strategy. The targeted improvements must be explicit. At a global level, the focus could be, for example, on setting up common benchmarking across affiliates for particular priorities such as IT user satisfaction, systems availability, or annual IT cost per user. Such transparency can help build trust between IT and business counterparts. On a functional level, IT efforts can be explicitly aligned with relevant line function objectives and, in the absence of the latter, efforts can focus on default objectives such as increasing top line sales for Marketing and Sales, decreasing cost of goods sold for Production, and cutting development time for R&D.

Globalization

Globalization has recently become a potent competitive force in business operations, with multinational firms aiming to compete better by concentrating certain activities at specific sites in the world wherever local conditions are most favourable. A car manufacturer might construct wheels in France, engines in Germany, and then assemble the car in the USA. The same principle applies to IT, but perhaps even more so because, in contrast to car components, the transport of information around the world is instantaneous and relatively cheap with modern telecommunications. The primary question becomes not so much whether to globalize IT, but rather which specific IT activities to globalize and how far to globalize them. The point of departure taken implicitly in this book is that architecture, strategy, standards and control should be globalized, but only to the extent that local activities are led and coordinated by lean central groups. But globalization can be applied to more operational IT processes and it can also be extended much further to include physical consolidation of originally local activities to regional or global centres. Considering the full scope of local IT activities, there are the following classic domains beyond strategy, architecture, standards and control, which lend themselves to globalization:

- To speed up integration of new solutions and avoid repeat development work, commonly required skills can be pooled into regional or global centres offering services from simple advice to delivery capabilities. Centres often focus on project management, solutions for particular business requirements such as customer relationship management, or use of standard technologies, say, for data warehousing.
- To meet business requirements for harmonized service, exploit economies of scale, or cut risk, common infrastructure operations such as networks, data centres, help desks and information security can be centrally managed or physically run at regional or global service centres. In some firms, service centres extend beyond infrastructure to include applications and business services, notably in financial accounting.

More will be said later about evaluating these options, but ultimately the choice to globalize an IT activity will be a balance between the diversity of requirements and intrinsic need for a service to be local, and any benefits of global alignment and pooling of activity. A popular and successful approach is to globalize core elements of generic IT infrastructure such as networks, telecommunications and information security. Whichever approach is taken, it should be borne in mind that IT employees play a particularly important role in globalization in two respects. They are directly impacted by any changes in location or reduction in local workforce, and furthermore the skills required in regional operations often extend beyond those needed for local activities. Given this, if globalization is to form a major part of the global IT strategy, it is an important enabling step to quickly establish human resources as one of the IT activities coordinated globally.

Outsourcing

Outsourcing is the process of transferring activities and associated assets out of a company into the hands of a third party. Companies already implicitly outsource IT to a certain extent by leaving development of commodity office tools and transaction systems to firms such as Microsoft and SAP. Few firms believe that developing similar systems of their own would be advantageous. The seed of top management interest today in outsourcing further areas of IT is usually irritation at a growing IT budget, exacerbated perhaps by some recent project failures or service outages and the belief that the IT organization is doing something poorly that other service providers would do better.

Certainly when applied to commodity activities such as desktop infrastructure provision or data centre operations, outsourcing promises to give greater service–cost transparency and allow management to focus on activities that are more specific to their business. But outsourcing deals that extend globally or encompass the majority of an IT budget are major projects with a high failure rate.[2] A precedent was set by the high profile global outsourcing of IT operations by Xerox to EDS in 1994, but even this deal could only be extended again in 2001 following litigation proceedings. Selective outsourcing deals which are restricted in geographic or operational coverage have a far higher success rate. Within global firms, whether a general policy on local outsourcing is defined or a more opportunistic approach is taken, it is important that overall global control is retained, as the degree and duration of obligations incurred in local outsourcing contracts can make any later global realignment of technologies difficult and expensive.

Exhibit 4 – global IT strategy in featured firms

Philips

Until 2001, IT strategy setting took place in annual meetings between corporate and division CIOs. Each party simply presented their own respective issues and priorities in a standard format, with presentations followed by general discussion and agreement on the way forward. A formalized process has now been introduced which aims to be more systematic and achieve better business support. The approach takes place annually in the four months leading up to budgets:

1) Corporate and division CIOs identify strategic issues and opportunities which are then compiled together by corporate IT.
2) The IT Policy Board (consisting of Vice-Chairman of the Board, corporate head of corporate core processes, and corporate and division CIOs) makes a preliminary decision on who investigates which options. Findings are then recompiled into a proposed portfolio of strategic IT initiatives which is then agreed by the same IT Policy Board.
3) A very high level IT Steering Committee (consisting of Vice-Chairman of the Board, divisional CEOs and the corporate CIO) ratifies the proposed strategy, which is then fed in to corporate and divisional IT programmes.

Two facets of this set-up are of particular interest. First, the level of business leadership involved in IT decisions reflects strong executive commitment to IT. Secondly, despite the split in organization between corporate infrastructure and divisional IT, the core work in the strategy process above is carried out by the corporate and divisional CIOs together in monthly meetings. This emphasis on collaboration between corporate and divisional activities is viewed as an essential enabler for further IT service improvement.

[2] Lacity, Willcocks and Feeney showed in 1995 that of 15 "total" outsourcing deals investigated, only two could be described as successful.

Nestlé

The IT strategy at Nestlé is almost entirely dictated by the business strategy of implementing a common business process architecture. This initiative sets a precedent at Nestlé and is driven directly by the CEO with a view to making Nestlé more responsive to a changing business environment and leveraging the scale and geographic spread of the company. The GLOBE initiative was launched by bringing together a team of several hundred key people drawn from throughout Nestlé worldwide. This team initiated work on the process model and all the ramifications of implementation, including changes to IT. A tight five-year deployment frame was set, aiming to cover the majority of core business processes in the first implementation, completed in two waves in late 2002 and early 2003.

Novartis

At a corporate level, IT strategy is agreed between the CIO and the Board of Directors. The strategy sets the mid-term financial framework and overarching priorities in those key areas that are common across business divisions. These mainly concern the underlying infrastructure and the organization and governance of the IT operation. The corporate IT strategy covers a five-year outlook and is updated on an annual basis. Most IT strategy activity occurs one level down in the respective divisions and business units. Here IT Steering Committees, composed of executive functional and regional leaders and their IT counterparts, integrate division-specific priorities with overarching priorities which in turn are formally cascaded down into the organization for implementation. The main emphasis is on building business support and drive for a few key strategic projects.

Toyota

The annual Global IT Committee summits run jointly by corporate business and IT planning form the focal point of dialogue on global IT priorities between executive IT and business leaders. The summits are part of an annual planning process whereby regional mid-term strategies, plans and expected costs are validated by corporate IT for alignment with global business and IT initiatives before being rolled up into a single strategic plan for approval by the Board.

Most IT strategy defining activity occurs however within the respective regions. Here the main trend is towards tighter integration or even merging of the distinct IT organizations serving the manufacturing and sales divisions. Operational efficiencies, for example through data centre consolidation, are expected, but the main driver is the need to support the evolving integration of supply and sales processes that aims to cut stock, shorten lead times and generally improve end-customer satisfaction.

UBS

IT strategy is prepared by executive IT management on the basis of business strategy and subsequently agreed through dialogue with the Group Executive

Board. Once agreed, the strategy is expected to remain stable for several years and only be updated in response to business changes. A key feature is the alignment of IT strategy with business strategy: despite the role that technology evidently plays in finance, IT is fundamentally understood and managed as a service to the business. Dialogue is, however, continuous between business and IT partners and takes the concrete form of "business technology centres" located within each business group. Each centre is a business department dedicated to managing the interface to the respective IT unit and ensuring effective translation of business needs into IT specifications.

While the IT strategy lays down a set of strategic directives, the practical side of implementation is in the corresponding execution of projects. Overall, projects are categorized as "run the bank" or "change the bank" and then sorted into portfolios according to which business stream of the banking value chain is concerned. Project portfolios are then managed in collaboration with IT by dedicated portfolio managers located in the business technology centres with business accountability for project success.

Managing strategy

Defining the right strategy and actually making that strategy happen is a non-trivial process which takes active and ongoing management. Two common approaches are the inclusion of strategy in a comprehensive IT planning process and the use of balanced scorecards for IT. When applied on a global scale, both show weaknesses. The more traditional planning approach often requires an inappropriate level of resources at head office for analysis and planning, but without producing a clear statement of strategy with which affiliates can work. In contrast, balanced scorecards are by default clear statements, but seen practically, the need to give a balanced view of priorities and set metrics for each renders scorecards a difficult tool for quickly establishing strategic priorities (nevertheless, the scorecard is an excellent tool for overall progress management and is described in Chapter 6).

The practical approach proposed here is simpler and adapted to a global environment, but admittedly exploits many of the ideas from traditional planning and balanced scorecards. There are three important elements to the approach. Element one is the instigation of an IT Steering Committee composed of top business and IT management to agree global IT strategy and ensure fundamental business alignment on priorities. Element two is the use of a simple mechanism to guide dialogue between the business and IT, articulate the strategy, and formally cascade the strategy down through the organization into affiliate plans. The last element is the need to go beyond strategy definition and make something happen by both launching initiatives and actively monitoring progress.

The whole process is moderated by a lean central strategy group and timed to provide clear, relevant priorities to functions and affiliates in time for local annual planning and budget submissions, but without going into detailed planning at a global level. The aim is to position global IT strategy as a unifying theme in local planning processes and to use IT strategy as an essential communications tool between IT and the business, both locally and globally. The next sections present the necessary organization and funding, followed by the main steps in the annual strategy process: agreeing strategy, aligning and communicating strategy, and implementing strategy.

Organization

One way of seeing strategy is to view it as a two-step cycle of putting the right organization in place and then getting that organization to focus activities on the right things. In the first step an IT organizational hierarchy is constructed which faithfully reflects the underlying demands of the business organization it supports. In the second step IT priorities and resource allocation are aligned with evolving business priorities.

Seen locally, both these steps are normally already an integral part of detailed IT planning activities that take place wherever concentrations of operative IT resources are to be found, usually in affiliates and line functions. The aim of the proposed approach to global IT strategy is *not* to replicate all these planning activities again at a global level, rather to focus just on the process for setting overarching priorities that are fed into the existing local planning processes and then launching specific global IT initiatives where appropriate. Figure 4.3 shows the main groupings involved directly in this process:

- CIO as champion of global IT strategy.
- Global IT Strategy Group responsible for moderation of the strategy process.
- IT Steering Committee responsible for setting and executing global IT strategy.
- Local IT Heads and Functional Information Managers (if present) responsible for local implementation.

The only resource explicitly dedicated to IT strategy at head office is the small Global IT Strategy Group. In every other respect, the strategic planning process builds deliberately on people already integrated within the IT and business communities, the aim being to leave detailed planning to locations where the main IT resources are situated.

CIO – champion global IT strategy

In most firms IT strategy will be inextricably linked with the CIO. The CIO's ideas are usually at the base of the IT strategy; people view it as the CIO's strategy, and irrespective of any strategic planning processes, the CIO will ultimately carry the burden of any failures in the strategy. So the CIO needs

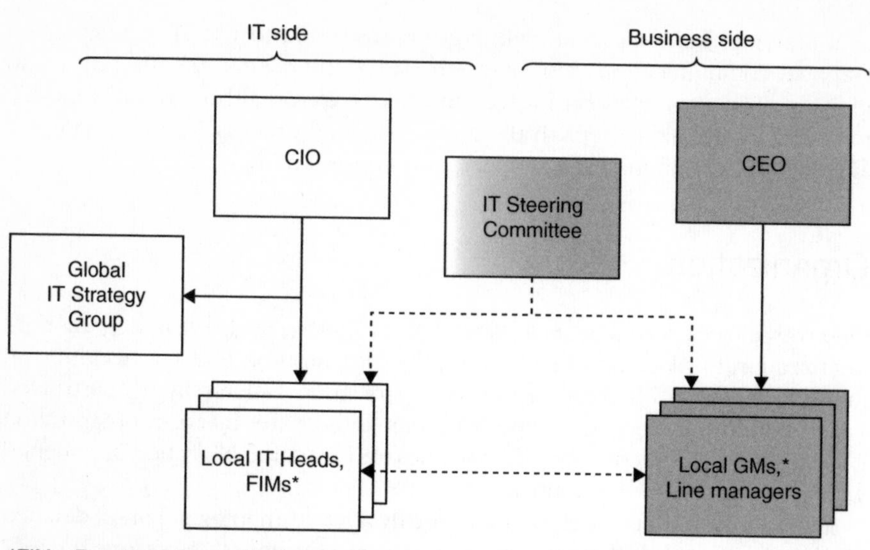

Figure 4.3—IT Steering Committee as focal point of global IT strategy organization

to actively support the processes being set up for managing global IT strategy and champion the agreed strategy.

Global IT Strategy Group – set up and moderate process

The Global IT Strategy Group is a small staff group or single person dedicated to supporting the CIO in establishing, maintaining and implementing global IT strategy. This is primarily a task of process moderation. The group does not set the strategy itself, rather its mandate is to put everything in place such that strategy can be agreed by the IT Steering Committee and subsequently executed in the IT community.

The group's main activities are divided as follows in about equal proportions among research, organization of IT Steering Committee meetings and communication of the agreed strategy:

- *Research*: Prepare the basis for decisions on global IT strategy by collecting input from relevant IT and business management on their respective priorities, integrating priorities revealed by the global IT architecture process, carrying out preliminary analyzes of the main options available and lastly condensing the often extensive material down into a format suitable for decisions.
- *Organize two annual IT Steering Committee meetings*: One meeting focuses on agreeing strategic priorities and launching initiatives and the other

focuses on reviewing operational improvement and progress of launched initiatives. Critical is that the right people are motivated to attend and that the timing of the first meeting should allow sufficient time for agreed priorities to be formally incorporated into local annual plans *before* budget submissions.

- *Communication*: Articulate, document and publish the agreed strategy in simple terms. Work explicitly with local IT Heads and any Functional Information Managers to ensure that the strategy is understood and to help them align their own planning with the strategy.

Two special skills in the Global IT Strategy Group are a prerequisite for the above activities. On the one hand, the group needs to be able to recognize and communicate the essentials in otherwise complex scenarios. On the other hand, the group needs to be capable of motivating senior management to take an active role in IT strategy, as ultimately the best IT strategy is the one with which business and IT management can identify and feel at least partial ownership for.

IT Steering Committee — set strategy

Despite the common overuse of committees, there are three good reasons for setting up an IT Steering Committee and explicitly making joint decisions on IT strategy. First, the impetus for IT strategy should come from business requirements. Secondly, the extent of business dependence on IT has grown and the potential impact of an IT strategy on the business community is large. Lastly, many current IT dependent initiatives, such as ERP systems, e-business and Customer Relationship Management, straddle functional boundaries and it makes sense for all affected functions to be involved in IT strategy decisions (Figure 4.4).

IT side	Business side
CIO (chair)	CEO
Head IT US	General Manager US
Head IT Japan	General Manager Japan
Regional Head IT EU	Regional Manager EU
FIM Production & Supply	Head Production & Supply
FIM Finance	Head Finance

Figure 4.4—Sample, heavyweight IT Steering Committee composition (optimal composition will differ in firms for example with several divisions)

The IT Steering Committee needs to be composed of a balanced functional and geographic mix of business executives and IT counterparts, chosen for their vested interest in IT and control of the affected resources. Securing commitment by local general managers can be difficult because of the travel imposed, but if meetings can be timed with other regional business meetings, this problem may be avoided. The size of the committee should be kept to 10 to 12 members and chaired by the executive intending to champion IT strategy, which most often will be the CIO, although the CEO would be preferable if prepared to take on this task. Delegation of committee membership by executives should be avoided, unless the delegate in question is similarly respected and empowered to make decisions and, where necessary, allocate resources.

The committee mandate is essentially threefold:

- *Set global IT strategy*: Agree global IT priorities on the basis of business priorities, potential opportunities, risks and current IT policies (for example on globalization).
- *Launch and resource strategic initiatives*: In some cases, it is sufficient for a particular priority to be effectively communicated and affiliates to align local resource allocation. In other cases, concrete initiatives need to be launched to accompany a strategic priority—and resource levels will need to match intentions.
- *Review progress*: The committee should review progress of launched initiatives, other business-critical IT activities and overall IT progress, for example through benchmarking with competitors.

Meetings can be held twice a year, with meetings dedicated respectively to initial agreement on strategy and then to subsequent progress review. The Global IT Strategy Group is responsible for ensuring that the best possible use is made of limited executive time through comprehensive preparation and follow up to meetings. The ultimate objective is for the committee to meet at the right frequency, to discuss the right issues, and lastly to have sufficient material and understanding to make the right decisions. Even before this is achieved, the IT Steering Committee essentially institutionalizes high-level dialogue between the business and IT on strategic issues, and initiates the mutual learning that is really the source of alignment between IT and the business.

Local IT heads and functional information managers – implement strategy

Once the IT Steering Committee has set direction and launched initiatives, it is key that priorities in local and functional plans reflect those decided globally. The Global IT Strategy Group works together with the IT management community to ensure that overall priorities flow coherently into local or functional resource allocation plans.

Funding

The funding requirements for global IT strategy can be divided between the cost of the process and the cost of launched initiatives. Concerning the former, the only significant costs likely to arise are those for the Global IT Strategy Group in terms of travel and external consulting fees, which can mount considerably if the scope of activity is not kept under control. Overall, these costs should remain limited and can be carried centrally by IT. The costs of launched initiatives is another issue. Fundamentally, the composition of the IT Steering Committee should be sufficiently empowered to be able to decide itself on how resources are allocated to launched projects and how the costs for these are accounted for. That will depend on the extent of involvement of business side personnel, but not being able to reach agreement on respective resource commitments is often symptomatic for insufficient support for the chosen strategy. Throughout, the costs of effectively managing and implementing IT strategy on a global level need to be compared with the potential business impact of neglecting global IT strategy.

This chapter has so far covered the range of strategic options available and the organization and resources required to manage strategy. The next sections present work templates for each of the four main tasks in the strategy process, that is, initial agreement, alignment of local and functional plans, implementation, and review. The unifying theme is the need to manage complexity, ensure top management support for a feasible strategy, and match planning and resource levels to intentions.

Agree strategy

Agreeing on global IT strategy is the key opening stage in the overall strategy process depicted in Figure 4.5. Naturally, agreeing on the right strategy is important and extensive literature is available proposing systematic methodologies for identifying the right IT strategy for any particular business. With or without an acknowledged methodology, two issues commonly arise in a global IT context:

- Agreement is held back by exhaustive analysis and the resulting strategy is not transparent, despite the number of genuine strategic options being limited.
- Insufficient business commitment is secured for the chosen strategy to tackle challenges that lie further downstream in global alignment of local IT organizations and strategy execution.

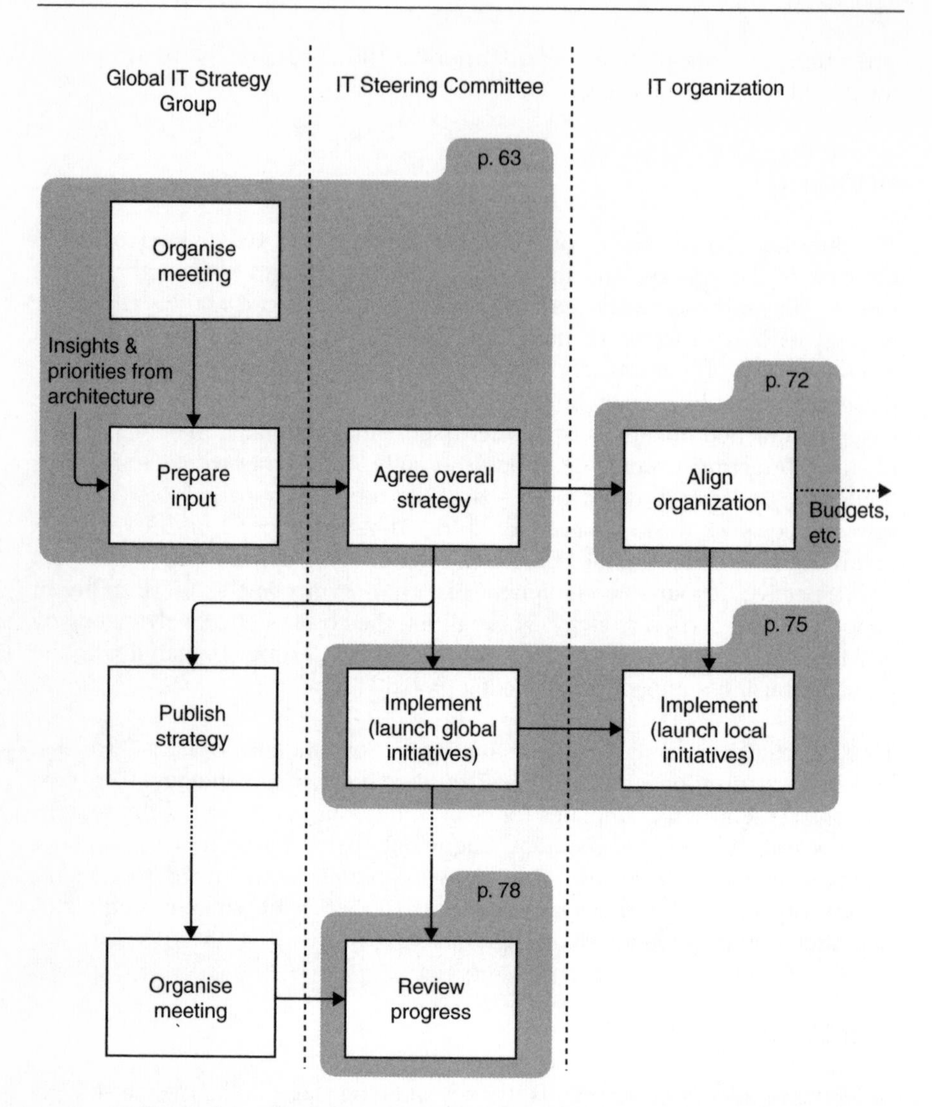

Figure 4.5—Overall work stream for managing global IT strategy

The following simple work template aims to address these issues by shifting the focus of activity from systematic analysis to systematic dialogue between business and IT, culminating in mutual agreement on global IT strategy.

Organize Meetings: the whole idea of an IT Steering Committee is to bring the right mix of business and IT management together to discuss and set IT strategy. Setting up this committee and identifying dates when meetings can take place should be a top priority in the strategy process. Members need to understand the committee mandate and be keen to participate both for the opportunity to discuss IT priorities in their own business terms and because of the potential impact of IT strategy on their operations. Finding dates when all members can be present and the output can be sensibly used in annual planning is not easy and has to be done well in advance, but at least once found, a ceiling is set for the duration and depth of preparation.

Meeting Preparation: preparation for the IT Steering Committee needs to cover both options and actions, the aim being to decide at the meeting on the strategic options to take and then to commit to the associated actions. As a backdrop to this preparation a simple situation analysis can document the status quo, detailing, for example, the business organizational structure and matching IT organization, perceived business priorities, current IT policies, and known strengths, weaknesses, opportunities and threats or risks.[3] The main effort of preparation needs to be individual discussions with committee members to establish exactly which strategic options such as business enablement or globalization need consideration and what form the options take. For example, perhaps a pending business strategy of multiple acquisitions requires IT to focus on rapid integration of new systems, or globalization of supply chain management requires harmonization of particular applications across sites. Once the focus has been set by management, some of the techniques presented further below can then be used to analyze and compare options in more detail. Preparation of each option then needs to be followed up with respective draft actions. This could be simple alignment of certain priorities in local organizations, or improved commitment to an existing project, or lastly the launch of a new initiative, in which case potential project leadership, investment, risk and return should be established. Preparing options and actions in this way provides the IT Steering Committee with a concrete basis for setting direction and extracting the necessary commitment involved.

Agree Strategy: given the level of management composing the IT Steering Committee, it is essential to extract maximum use of the little time available together at meetings. Beyond the preparation above, one method which can be very fruitful is to arrange for business leaders (not IT leaders) to present and champion the options and actions in which they have a vested interest. Whichever approach is taken, the ultimate aim should be agreement on the key relevant business priorities, the derived IT priorities and associated high level, but concrete, action plans which match resources with intentions. If the global IT strategy genuinely focuses on fundamentals, then with a little discipline it can often be articulated succinctly on a single page (Figure 4.6).

[3] Strengths, weaknesses, opportunities and threats are commonly depicted in matrix format and known as the SWOT analysis.

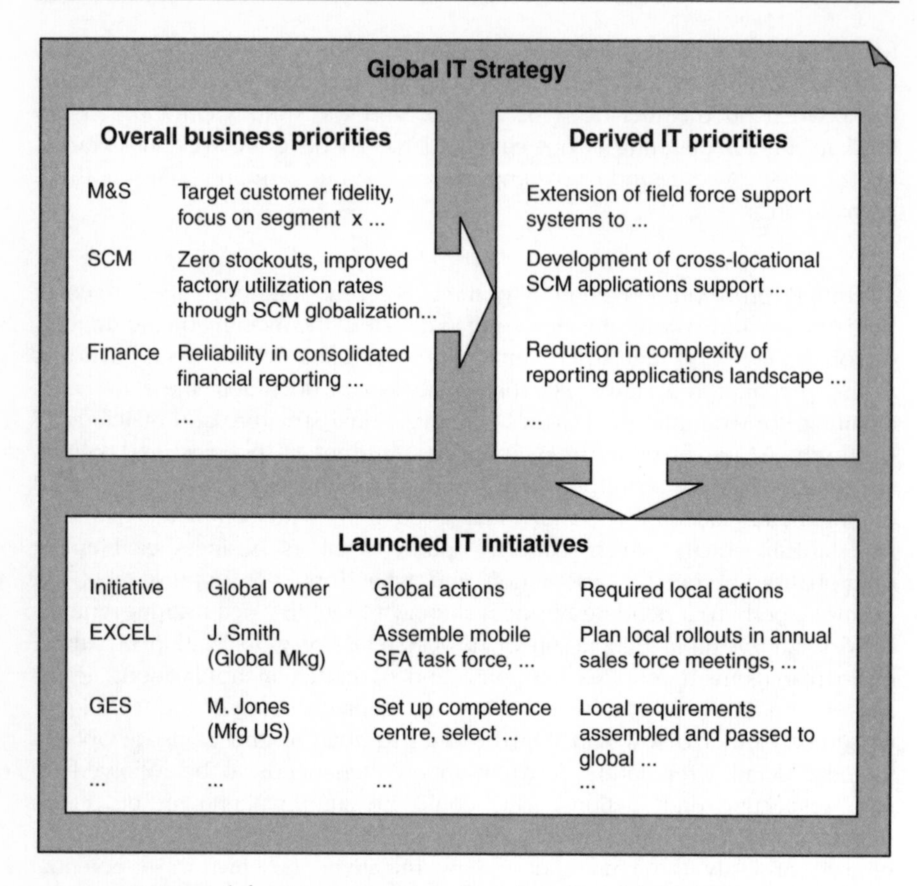

Figure 4.6—Sample template for articulating global IT strategy

While the above approach goes a long way towards achieving tangible business–IT alignment and the commitment of business support to IT strategy, one key issue may arise. On a global level, IT itself may not have any human resources to commit. With a decentralized point of departure such as that in Figure 4.1, the only IT resources at a global level are those for managing global IT architecture, strategy, standards and control, but none are present for resourcing global projects with project managers and expertise. There is no easy solution other than to borrow resources on an *ad hoc* basis from local operations and, if momentum grows behind globalization, to build up an explicit pool of global IT project resources.

The key message of the proposed approach to agreeing strategy is to focus on dialogue and internal management intuition, but, before concluding, the following sub-sections summarize some well-established techniques and considerations for providing support material in the domains of business enablement, globalization and outsourcing. Be aware that in global and normally complex companies, experience shows that these techniques are best applied to substantiate and communicate specific areas already identified by management; using them too systematically for fact finding can be time consuming, expensive and unproductive.

Identifying and evaluating business enablement options

The following techniques are essentially lines of investigation that can help either to position suggestions for strategic priorities made by line management, or check that opportunities enabled by IT are not overlooked. In some cases pre-projects may need to be started to investigate ideas to a sufficient depth for a concrete decision to be made. Even if no new opportunities are identified, there remains a very positive feature of this work. While line management may not be accustomed to viewing their own business in exactly the same way, the more IT learns about the business, the more IT is likely to be accepted as a viable partner for dialogue with line management. Here are four main techniques:

- Understand a firm's *current business strategy* and the contribution IT can make to it. The emphasis so far has been on deriving IT priorities and intentions directly from current IT related business priorities, but one can take a step further back and consider the business strategy as a whole as a source of impetus for agreeing IT strategy. Most global firms will have a defined business strategy and discussions with the corporate planning department should be fruitful. The case mentioned earlier of multiple pending acquisitions clearly has integration requirements that need to be reflected in IT strategy. In cases where the defined business strategy does not provide tangible priorities for IT strategy, priorities can be derived from the underlying way in which the business competes, which is basically limited to the three fundamental approaches to the market:[4] cost leadership through operational excellence such as at Dell, differentiation through innovative products or services such as at 3M, and focus through customer proximity such as at SAS airlines. While firms should strive to match competitors in each domain, market leadership is usually associated with excelling in one domain only. Establishing which domain that is in a firm and the potential role played by IT gives valuable high level priorities for IT. In the case of SAS airlines, IT systems, for example, played a strategic role in customer relationship management that enabled SAS to gauge customer requirements well.
- Assess the main *competitive forces* in an industry and where IT plays a role. M. Porter[5] introduced a concept in 1980 to characterize any particular

[4] M.E. Porter, *Competitive Advantage: Creating and Sustaining Superior Performance*, Free Press, 1985, 1998.
[5] M.E. Porter, *Competitive Strategy: Techniques for Analyzing Industries and Competitors*, Free Press, 1980, 1998.

industry based on five forces that shape competition: direct rivalry between competitors, the respective bargaining power of customers and suppliers, the damaging potential of new entrants to the industry and the threat of substitute products or services. Although the model aims primarily to give a flavour for how attractive a particular industry is as a whole, considering what impact IT could have on each of these forces can give useful pointers to genuinely strategic roles IT can play. For example, bundling remote IT driven maintenance with a commodity product can bring value and reduce customer bargaining power by introducing subsequent switching costs. Or IT automated bidding systems could reduce supplier bargaining power. Or building proprietary electronic monitoring systems into cars could exclude new entrants from the market providing car service. Thinking in this way beyond straightforward competitive rivalry can generate radical ideas, but be aware that these often lead into uncharted business terrain and need careful judgement.

- Learn what a firm's *critical success factors* are. If a business has particular objectives such as achieving a certain market share, then for each objective there are normally a number of things that must go right such as reaching specific standards of sales force productivity, product awareness and pricing. These are termed critical success factors. They can in turn form objectives for individual functions and be used to spawn lower level critical success factors for each function. Perhaps to achieve that level in product awareness, the marketing department may have to exceed certain levels in television advertising, journal articles and supermarket promotions. Some critical success factors are explicitly money orientated such as sales levels or cost of goods sold; others are orientated to variables such as employee turnover, customer fidelity or delivery times. For IT, understanding critical success factors is useful in two respects. To begin with, management information systems need to focus on reporting critical success factors, for example through balanced scorecards. Moreover, critical success factors give IT insight into what line managers really care about and where IT can have the best impact. Continuing the example above, perhaps customer relationship management systems can make a major contribution to achieving customer fidelity.
- Learn how a firm *generates value* for customers. This analysis is called value chain analysis and starts by tracing the various core activities that a business carries out, in general from inbound logistics for supplies, through manufacturing, into sales and outbound logistics for finished goods. The traditional high level picture is shown in Figure 4.7, although, to be useful, more business specific information is required on each activity and the interfaces with third parties. Process charts generated in the global IT architecture process can often be used as a starting point. Once the core activities are traced, the next stage in the analysis is to run through each activity, assessing how much the activity costs and how much value it effectively adds to the product for the customer. For example, in perfume,

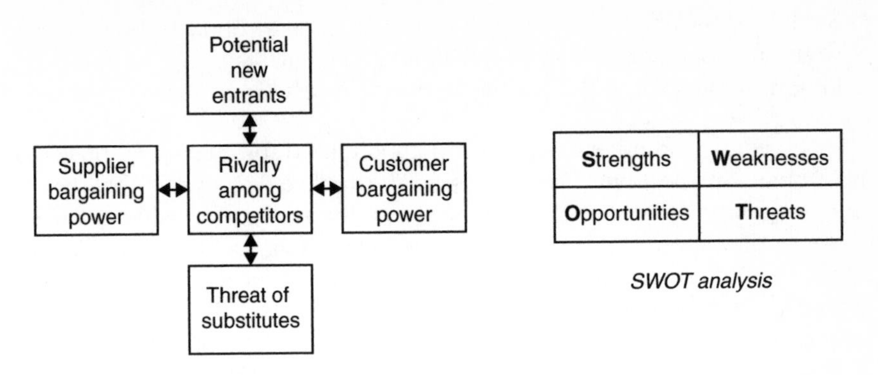

SWOT analysis

Five forces in industry competition[1]

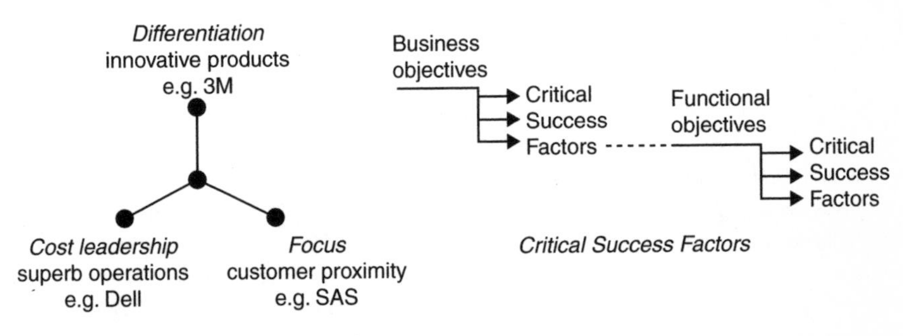

Generic strategies for competing[2]

Critical Success Factors

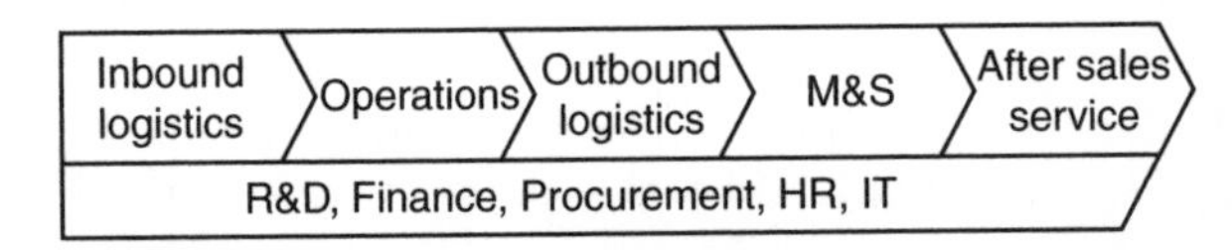

Value chain analysis[2]

Figure 4.7—Strategic analysis techniques [1]Adapted with the permission of The Free Press, a Division of Simon & Schuster Adult Publishing Group, from COMPETITIVE STRATEGY: Techniques for Analyzing Industries and Competitors by Michael E. Porter. Copyright © 1980, 1998 by The Free Press [2]Adapted with the permission of The Free Press, a Division of Simon & Schuster Adult Publishing Group, from COMPETITIVE ADVANTAGE: Creating and Sustaining Superior Performance by Michael E. Porter. Copyright © 1985, 1998 by Michael E. Porter

this could show costs and perceived value of, respectively, fragrance manufacture, packaging and logistics. The last stage is to pool net value and costs to give the overall value added (i.e. profit) and understand that suppliers, manufacturer and customers all compete for that profit. Changes to activities are then identified that increase the profit retained by the manufacturer. Important for IT strategy is to find out how IT can contribute, perhaps through automation of particular activities or improved information exchange at a particular interface between activities.

While value chain analysis is very commonly used for identifying business opportunities, the technique can just as well be applied directly to IT processes. For example, in desktop infrastructure service provision, the value chain, in the sense of value to the user, runs through ordering, delivery, installation, support, maintenance and disposition. On a global level, the focus when looking at the individual activities is effectively the extent that added value is dependent on an activity being local and how much costs can be reduced by moving the activity. This point brings us to the considerations for globalization and outsourcing.

Evaluating globalization options

Progressive globalization of IT activities is a major strategic option for IT, but while not as radical as outsourcing, the topic remains emotionally charged because of the direct impact on personnel. Seen at the highest level, pooled operations need less resources, handle demand peaks better, take advantage of preferential local conditions and potentially reduce risks through controlled best practices. Options can be evaluated in more detail with the following sequence of steps, which are best carried out with discretion and a certain sensitivity to employees:

- Identify commodity IT services that can, at least in principle, be globalized. Activities associated with a service must be able to be carried out remotely and there should be no significant differences in required service across sites. For example, desk-side support can obviously be excluded, whereas data centres and help desks, at least for commodity services, can be considered.
- Compare service and costs today with a globalized service run in particular locations. While assembling representative data for a future site may be straightforward, evaluating the current situation can be difficult. The main points of orientation are employees, equipment, materials, services, facilities, land, proximity to markets and telecommunication costs. In a global context, the impact of differing time zones, languages and local legal requirements also needs evaluation. For example, some nations specify that all data processing must be carried out within national boundaries.
- Assess feasibility in terms of the management skills available and the fit with the prevailing business culture, and estimate transition costs composed of direct project costs, personnel change costs and the additional costs of running both local and central services during an interim transition period.

- Assess whether improvements in service and reduction in ongoing costs outweigh the cost and effort of transition, and whether mid-term, a globalized service will be able to sensibly follow evolution of business requirements.

Evaluating outsourcing options

Each potential outsourcing deal needs to be evaluated by weighing up the service and cost benefits, the feasibility of separating out operations as opposed to carrying out improvements in-house, and the risk of mid-term project failure arising, for example, from mounting charges simply to follow technology evolution. Throughout, the overarching driver needs to be the conviction by general management that IT weaknesses are a business distraction and the best way to improve service is to outsource. IT organizations will rarely be the driver behind efforts to outsource themselves. The following considerations, which have a number of similarities to the issues in globalization, can form the basis of an evaluation:

- Establish which activities could be outsourced and assess the potential benefits. Some commonly sought benefits are refocusing in-house skills and management attention by transferring maintenance of legacy systems out of the company, or reducing costs by accessing economies of scale at an outsourcer, or budget smoothing of technology deployments through leasing.
- Assess the feasibility of a transfer. Are activities and budgeting already separated out and is the organization mature enough and ready for a bold move? Is the scale of activity sufficient to maintain an outsourcer's interest? Will the local legal framework actually allow the proposed transfer of human and material assets?
- Assess what needs to be done in terms of initial contracting, transitioning and ongoing management of the interface between outsourcer and customer. Each of these phases takes an organization and management of its own.
- Factor in the many risks, including the following. (1) There is a latent conflict of interest in outsourcing as an outsourcer may want to maintain the status quo, while the customer expects a service to keep in step with technology evolution. Although alleviated by a good contract, there is a real risk that outsourcers cash in on service changes required following unforeseen developments in business or technology. (2) Switching costs at agreement expiry can give the existing outsourcer considerable bargaining power to the detriment of the customer. (3) The role of the outsourced service can evolve to such an extent that it becomes strategic and better controlled directly within a business.

Align organization

The steps above described how to use the IT Steering Committee to agree global IT strategy. This section presents a model for the next stage in the strategy process which is to communicate the strategy and formally integrate the strategy into local plans. In a uniquely local context, this step is fairly straightforward, as the community is relatively tight and the same people lead local planning as agree on strategy. In a global context this is not the case, as the community is neither tight, nor are local planners accustomed to working with a remote IT Steering Committee.

The starting point for the alignment stage is the agreement reached by the IT Steering Committee and articulated, for example, as in Figure 4.6. Before any overt communications, the nature of the agreement needs to be reviewed, as it has an impact on the type of communication needed. In particular, any elements involving reorganization require a discrete, shuttle diplomacy style of communication, at least until the impacted communities are informed. Loudly declaring, for example, that outsourcing legacy systems maintenance is a strategic priority can lead to premature mass exodus of key personnel before any real arrangements have been concluded. Communications in such cases are best handled as an integral part of change projects.

In general, while people may appreciate that isolated elements of the strategy may not be for public consumption, it is important that the strategy as a whole is not perceived as secretive. After limited cleaning, the bulk of strategy such as specific mid-term priorities and initiatives should be subjected to a real marketing-style communication campaign. All traditional communication channels should be exploited to explain and reinforce the agreed strategy within the company. For the IT community to be aware of the strategy, the same consistent message needs to be broadcast repeatedly in meetings, conferences, newsletters, intranet and even local newspapers (which can have a great "take-home" effect). Company executives and, in particular, the CIO should also be seen to understand and actively support the strategy.

Launching such a communication campaign is an excellent way of reaching the IT community with key messages, but while awareness of global IT strategy is good, it is not enough on its own. Simple awareness is usually insufficient to make anything happen, and returning to the business and IT populations discussed earlier, a number of needs remain unmet:

- *Business managers*: While the IT Steering Committee institutionalizes alignment between IT spending and business priorities at a global level, there is a similar need for capturing alignment on a local scale within individual affiliates or line functions.
- *IT planners*: Viewed from head office, it is key that global IT strategy becomes an integral part of local plans. But from the perspective of an affiliate, local IT planners still need a simple mechanism for tangibly reconciling the few global priorities with the many local priorities.

- *IT community in general*: To the average IT employee, often struggling to secure a reasonable budget, global IT strategy can appear too remote and irrelevant to be able to impart a meaningful sense of purpose and vision.

The approach proposed here to meeting these needs is to complement traditional communication of IT strategy with a simple, non-intrusive method for each affiliate to build a strategy statement (see Figure 4.6), but adapted to be locally relevant. Exactly how an affiliate proceeds is left open: perhaps a simple meeting between local general manager and head of IT suffices, or a full local IT steering committee is established. The focus is on reaching a clear, coherent result. Constructed carefully, this local statement portrays a more relevant sense of purpose, captures both local and global business alignment and serves as a good guide for detailed local plans. The method also meets many of the COBIT® (see Appendix) standard auditing recommendations for mid-term IT planning without exaggerated local efforts and bulky reports.

The method is as follows. After IT Steering Committee agreement, the global IT strategy statement is handed down as "inherited" input to each of the respective IT organizations one level down from the CIO and they each carry out the following three short steps to derive an adapted statement of their own:

- Inherited priorities that are irrelevant are discarded, for example a priority concerning a research function not present in that organization. The remainder are localized, for example by being more specific to that particular organization's participation in global initiatives. Lastly, any further specific priorities and strategic initiatives of its own are appended.
- A localized strategy statement is assembled following the standard breakdown of business priorities, IT priorities and initiatives, distinguishing those which are inherited and those which are specific to the organization. To maintain clarity and keep down paperwork, the statement should still be constrained to one page wherever feasible.
- Business and IT management in the organization formally approve the statement and use it subsequently both within the organization and at budget and annual planning reviews.

Should substantial planning occur deeper in the organizational hierarchy, the newly derived strategy statements can be cascaded down further to serve as input for each sub-organization to work through the same procedure. Dialogue between business and IT counterparts on priorities becomes institutionalized at each level and the result captured simply in relevant strategy statements. The Global IT Strategy Group moderates the process, wherever possible physically participating in meetings, not only to instil coherence and discipline (organizations commonly insist their strategic priorities cannot be condensed to within five pages, let alone one page) but also to manage overall timing. While it is necessary to be conscious of strategy throughout the year the cascade itself should be completed within weeks to maintain momentum and ensure that statements are all produced in time to be useful in local annual planning and budget submissions.

Some organizational variants call for a modest adaptation of the cascade. The rule to bear in mind is that the underlying aim is to agree coherent mid-term business and IT priorities at key points in the organization based on original decisions made by the IT Steering Committee. The course of the

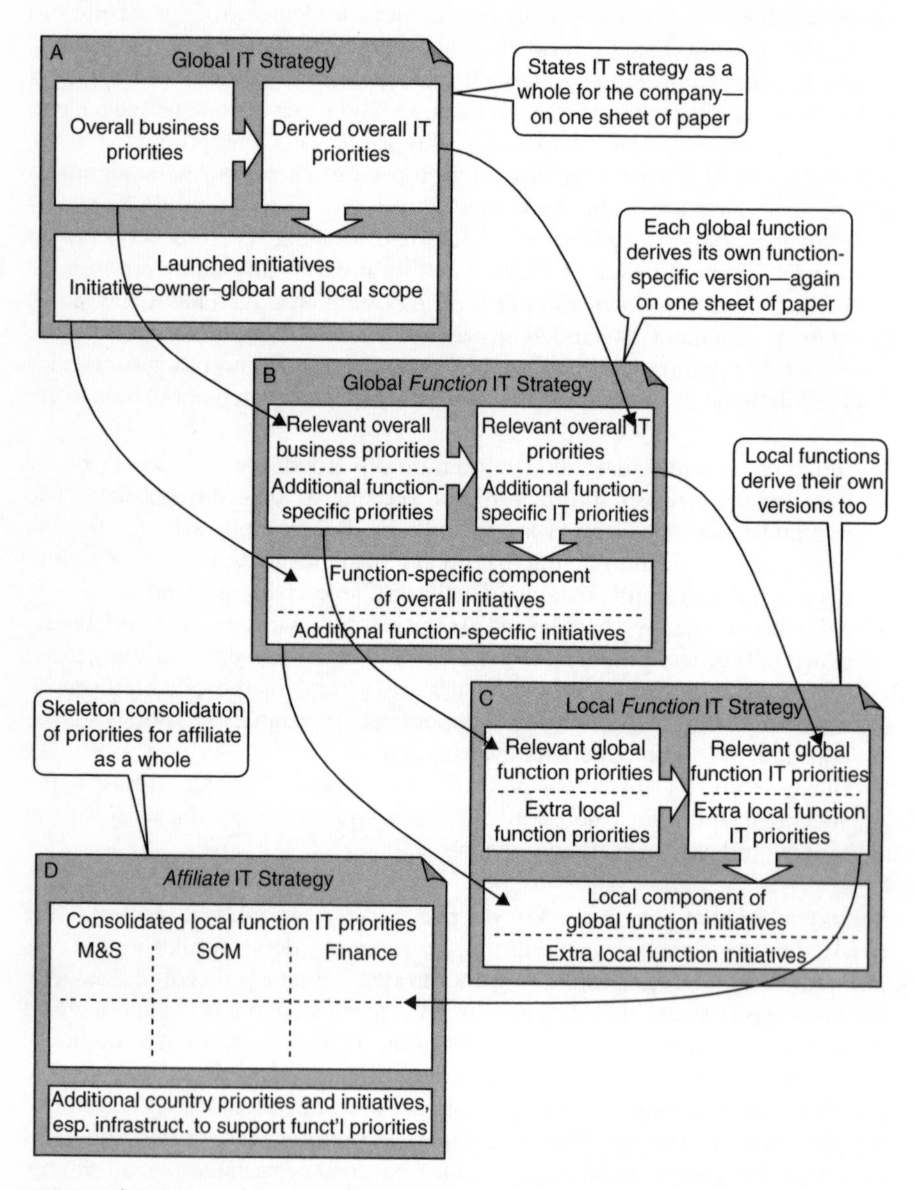

Figure 4.8—Example strategy cascade for matrix IT organization (easier in practice than it looks!)

cascade through the organization and the subsequent representation in strategy statements can be adapted to the business situation. Here are some examples:

- In organizations grouped into regions, for example Asia Pacific encompassing perhaps ten or more affiliates, there is only a need to cascade explicitly into individual affiliates if there are real differences in intentions across affiliates. There is no point in compiling ten virtually identical affiliate strategy statements.
- Infrastructure service provision and business applications may be distinct IT organizations. The applications organization usually mirrors the supported business organization, and linking business and IT priorities is straightforward. But the infrastructure organization may not mirror the business organization and provides a service intended to be generic. In such cases, it makes sense to cascade IT priorities down through the infrastructure organization, retaining throughout the same overall business priorities such as network availability.
- In matrix IT organizations where IT is organized across functions and locations, IT Steering Committee priorities can be cascaded initially down into global functions and local functions, and the latter can then be consolidated locally into summary statements for each affiliate. The fact that certain functions such as Marketing and Sales may be primarily local rather than global does not matter: only a few high level global priorities will filter down and local strategy statements will be dominated by local considerations. The overall approach is shown in Figure 4.8.

Implementation

Turning strategy into reality is the key objective and crux of the whole strategic planning process. This objective should be paramount in agreeing a strategy that is feasible and subsequently investing the necessary effort in implementation. It is true that a shared sense of direction and the alignment of local plans produced so far in the process is already an achievement, but most global IT strategies targeting non-trivial change on a global level require specific global initiatives to be launched and executed. Certainly, if they are to be implemented, the business enablement, globalization and outsourcing strategies discussed earlier require initiatives that go beyond simple adjustments in local IT plans.

The overall landscape for implementation can be set by picturing the scope and scale of transformation involved in an initiative using the "Seven S" model originally popularized by McKinsey & Company. This model characterizes a business using a set of seven distinct attributes: strategy, structure (organization and geography), systems (in the sense of both processes and IT systems), staff, style (for example dynamic versus bureaucratic), skills and lastly unifying shared values (such as respect for the environment and shareholder value)

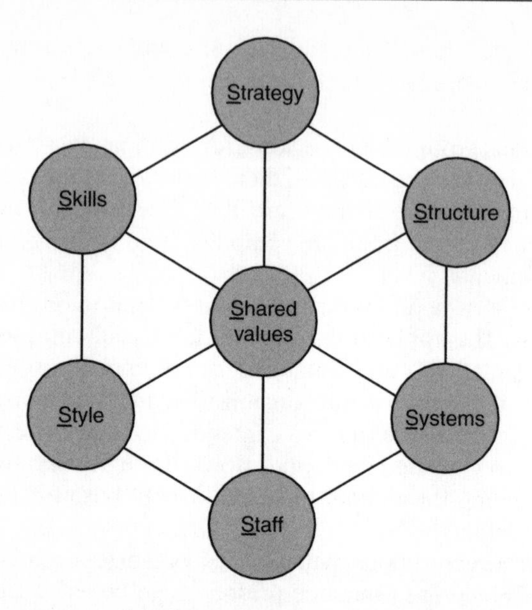

Figure 4.9—"Seven S" interdependent attributes for assessing scope in transformation projects. Reproduced with kind permission of McKinsey & Co.

(Figure 4.9). The fundamental message of the model is that the attributes are interconnected in a type of web and changes in one domain need to be matched by supporting changes in related domains. Neglecting to do so is a common cause of failure in change projects and this messages applies as much to IT as to any other branch. Applied at the level of the whole business, the model can highlight, for example, business staffing and skills changes required in conjunction with introduction of customer relationship management systems. The model can also be applied just to the IT community, treating IT as a business in its own right, for example referring to changes in IT staffing and skills implicated by a change in structure through regionalization of, say, help desk operations.

With the overall scope of transformation understood, the time for analysis is over. While acknowledged best practices for project management such as those described in the Appendix give guidelines on how to proceed, the ultimate success of an initiative can be traced back to the skills and capabilities of the people engaged and the extent of their empowerment. Without the right people, nothing will happen. If an initiative is strategic, then it needs an appropriate leader and matching team:

- Project leaders should be willing and able to challenge the status quo, whereas established managers often subconsciously want to retain the status quo.
- Teams need to be co-located and composed of dedicated representatives from each of the major stakeholder groups, including the main affected

affiliates. Other stakeholder groups can nominate representatives to be consulted in particular instances. Wherever possible, the alignment stage in the strategic planning process should be used to ensure that local or functional organizations explicitly plan for this resource allocation to avoid frequent obstacles such as "we didn't budget for that".

- Formal executive guidance and problem resolution capabilities should be provided on a regular basis either by the IT Steering Committee itself, or a project-specific steering committee.

Establishing the right team is key, but even given this, a number of more or less avoidable potential pitfalls can arise in implementation. One pitfall is that although the overall business case for a global initiative may be positive, seen locally the situation may appear negative in particular locations. Ensuring representation from such locations within the team and using a common approach to establishing business cases at both local and global levels should produce agreement on whether this is an issue. If it is, then an early decision needs to be made by the steering committee on how to deal with the situation. Another classic error is to concentrate too much on the clear technology challenges in many IT initiatives and to neglect the more implicit challenge of transforming an organization. The latter is the cause of most failures in major IT initiatives, not technology. Much can be learnt in this respect by investigations carried out by J.P. Kotter[6] on the progress of strategic business transformations in over 100 companies. On the basis of his findings, he established a basic recipe for success consisting of eight steps. To succeed, each step has to be correctly completed before proceeding to the next, and no steps can be omitted:

1) People must be really unhappy with the current situation and sense the urgency to do something about it, for example when faced with imminent insolvency of their current systems supplier.
2) A coalition of the main stakeholders needs to be formed that starts building momentum, for example through offsite meetings or retreats.
3) An explicit, simple vision of what needs to be achieved must be developed so that newcomers understand the essentials within five minutes.
4) Widespread, coherent communications must take place through all possible channels and be matched by executive behaviour. The vision must filter down to all those impacted.
5) Obstacles to the vision need to be removed. This could be, say, solving personnel issues or dealing effectively with local sub-optima in global initiatives.
6) Pressure must be maintained by planning rapid successes or "quick wins" and ensuring that these materialize. This is especially pertinent in complex, protracted and expensive projects which can otherwise lose momentum.

[6] J.P. Kotter, Leading change: why transformation efforts fail, *Harvard Business Review*, March–April 1995.

7) The temptation to declare victory too soon should be resisted.
8) Changes need to be anchored in corporate culture to ensure that they last. For example, changes should not be carried by one charismatic leader, as if he or she leaves, organizations can easily slip back into old habits.

Review progress

Running a second annual IT Steering Committee meeting that reviews progress is important in a number of respects. The review meetings themselves focus executive attention where problems in strategic initiatives lie and where corrective actions need to be taken. More subtly, knowing in advance that formal reviews will be carried out keeps agreements and commitments realistic and reinforces the IT Steering Committee as an effective, long-term institution.

The Global IT Strategy Group can organize the review meeting, and to avoid a perspective of IT that is artificially skewed towards strategic initiatives, reviews presented by respective leaders can be complemented with reviews and benchmarking of overall IT performance, for example using balanced scorecards (see Chapter 6).

Tool support

The emphasis of the proposed strategic planning process is on dialogue and resolute follow-through, and in this respect tools do not play a prominent role. Nevertheless, there is one particular domain where tool support can be very helpful, and that is for online publication of the resulting strategy statements such as those depicted in Figure 4.8. The Web site `www.gitm.biz/strategy` demonstrates one possible approach which combines online statements with a straightforward navigation system allowing the user to both view the statement relevant to his own unit and to skip easily to others to see how they are interrelated. This type of system brings a number of benefits:

- By default, receptiveness in affiliates to new planning processes from head office is low. Cutting out lengthy explanations and showing statements online helps local planners quickly understand the limited scope of effort required and appreciate the usefulness of the result to them, while at the same time seeing that the high visibility of statements means they must be taken seriously.
- Much effort has been expended on deriving strategy statements that are relevant to IT organizations. This relevance makes them of immediate interest to the whole IT community and business counterparts. The system allows everyone to look up and print out their IT strategy at any time.

- Alignment between business and IT priorities both on a global and local scale is rendered tangible for everyone.

Summary

Understandably, knowing the best IT strategy for a business is a top priority in many people's minds and some guidelines as to the basic options and respective business considerations have been given here. But the emphasis of this chapter is to take a step back from the strategy itself and to establish a simple overarching process that manages strategy effectively in a global context from agreement through to implementation, meeting the demands of business managers, IT planners and the general IT community along the way:

- Top-down IT and business agreement on IT strategy: the range of basic options is business enablement, incremental improvement, globalization and outsourcing. The use of an IT Steering Committee is important to enable joint decisions and commitments by business and IT executives.
- Straightforward articulation of strategy and cascade of priorities into local and functional planning: a simple approach to alignment of priorities without significant intrusion into local planning processes was proposed.
- Avoidance of well-known pitfalls in execution: it is key in major IT initiatives to populate the projects with quality representation from the main stakeholder groups and to treat initiatives as change projects, not just technology projects.

5 Standards

Introduction

Global IT standards are often the first and frequently unpopular point of contact between affiliates and head office, and can range from commodity standards such as the mandatory use of a particular model of PC, to process standards such as the industry best practice ITIL for service management. Throughout, the aim of global standards remains essentially to improve service or achieve cost reductions in any one of the core IT functions, namely integration of new solutions, running applications and operating infrastructure (Figure 5.1).

Viewed by the user population in affiliates, IT standards can be perceived quite differently. Most IT users have had contact at least with local IT standards at some stage, even if it has only been a guided choice in the PC that they and their colleagues may use. Although they may know why a standard is required, all too often an element in the IT value chain fails, leaving the user dissatisfied. Perhaps the advantages of the chosen standard are clear, but it appears just too expensive compared with local alternatives. Or it is good value, but delivery is too slow.

The aim of this chapter is to not to say what you should standardize, rather to show on what basis to choose standards and how to manage them, so that head office and affiliates can *both* appreciate the promised improvements in service and cost. To see how close your organization is to achieving this ideal, try answering the following questions as a simple standards health check for your firm:

- Do IT, users and procurement know what the standards are?
- Is each standard really current and at a useful level of detail?
- Is it clear why each standard is selected?
- Are the standards mandatory?
- Is it clear how standards are defined and maintained, and exceptions handled?
- How good is the acceptance and adherence locally?
- Have the standards really achieved something?

The challenge is to be able to answer each of these questions positively, and the simple model presented here for managing standards goes a long

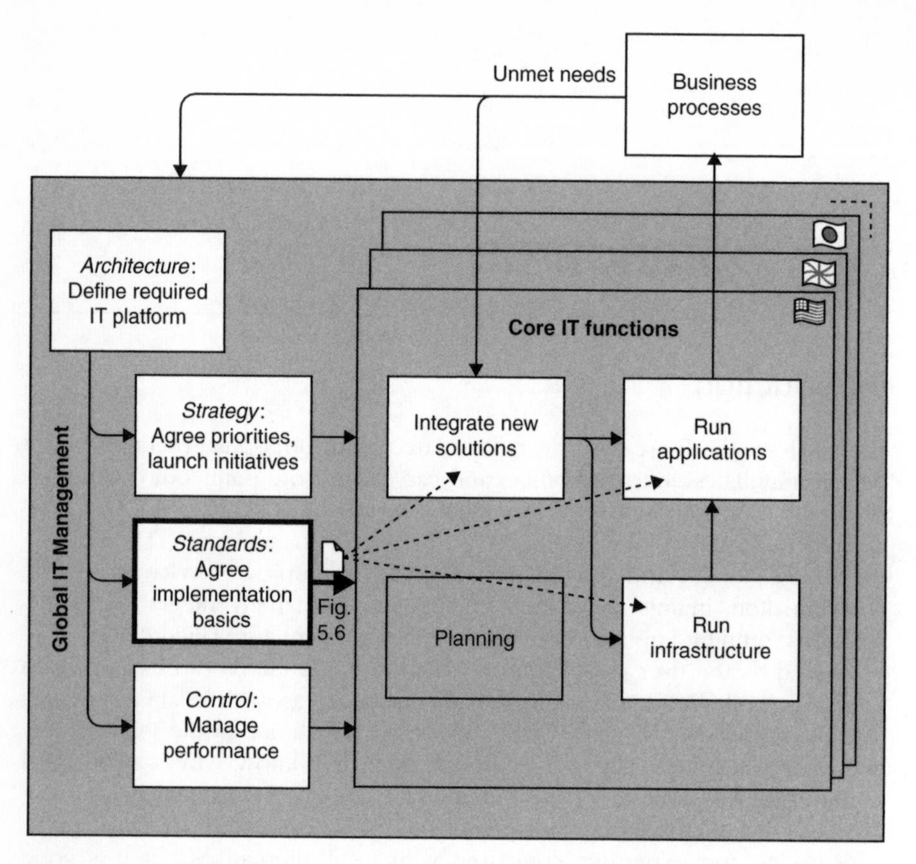

Figure 5.1—Overall positioning of global IT standards

way towards achieving this goal—ensuring that standards are justified, have the management support required, and actually work. The principles of this model are:

- Justification of each global standard by an individual business case.
- Decentralized management of standards led by a small central group.
- Straightforward processes for standards definition, maintenance, and exception handling.

Options and expectations

In principle, there is an extensive pool of potential options for standardization on a global basis. Figure 5.2 shows the classic areas in which firms regularly standardize, presented in the context of the basic IT value chain. Note how the field is not confined to technology standards, but can also encompass standards for the IT processes used to integrate new solutions and run

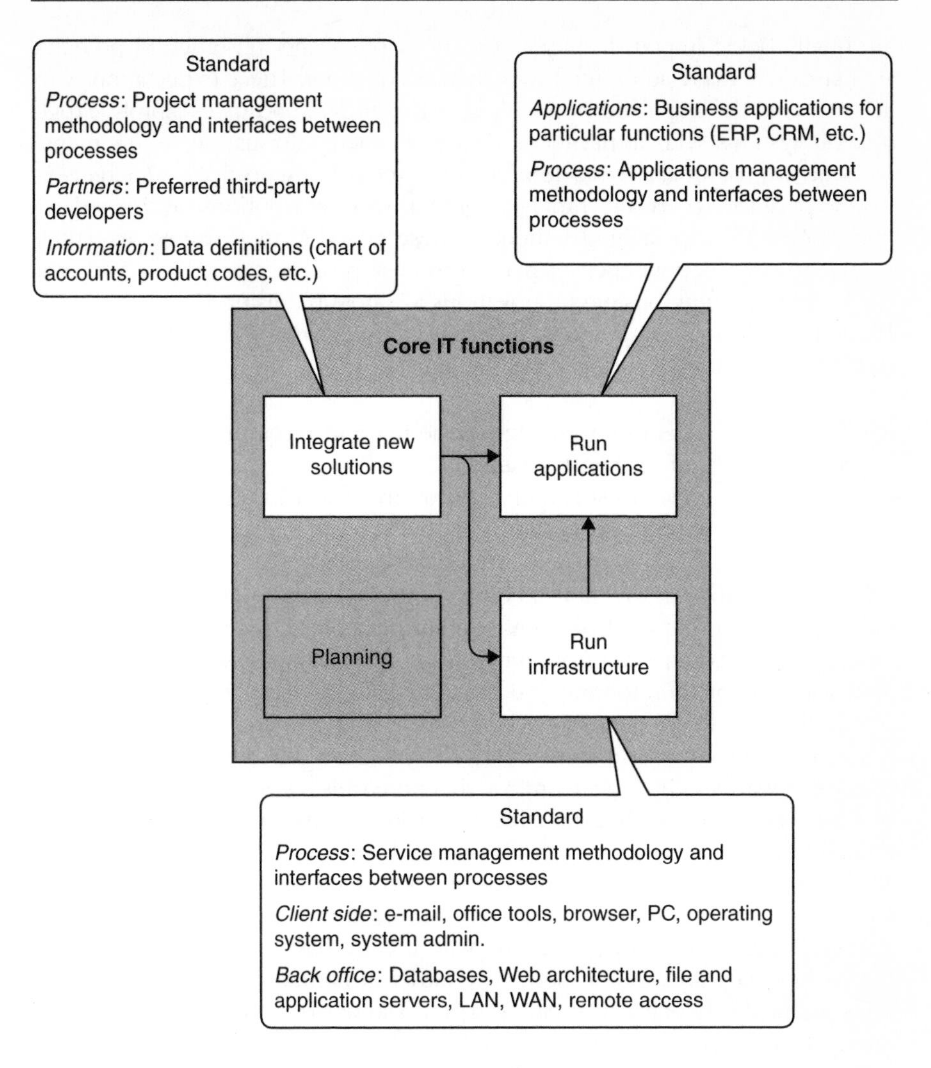

Figure 5.2—Common candidates for global standardization

them. Given the notoriously high failure rate for IT projects and the level of business dependence on uninterrupted operation of particular applications, focussing on a standard recognized approach in these domains is often a necessary complement to the judicious selection of basic technology standards. Fortunately, a number of best practices for project and service management have already been established in industry, and these do not need to be re-invented. The essentials of these industry best practices are summarized in the Appendix.

In practice, standards do not exist in a vacuum and must fit with the expectations of the receiving business community on which the standards are finally being imposed: only a certain subset of the full range of potential standards will make sense for any particular company. These expectations vary according to the impacted population. For example, end users simply expect reliable systems with applications that meet their information requirements, without any particular consideration of standards themselves. Managers in turn expect low costs and rapid integration of new solutions, and standards may appear to help or hinder them in these goals. At the business executive level, the clear dependence of many business processes on IT support, and the feeling that new business innovations are possible using IT, have brought IT as a whole to the attention of business executives. Two expectations in particular arise concerning global IT standards:

- Resolve problems in information gathering and reporting across locations caused by use of disparate systems.
- Take opportunities to streamline operations, cut risks and reduce IT costs, for example through economies of scale.[1]

The IT executive or CIO at head office needs to meet the above expectations globally, but is often confronted as a point of departure with a patchwork of different systems inherited from mergers, or from a time when affiliates operated with complete autonomy. Successfully introducing a few, well selected standards globally is one way for a CIO to bring value: progress towards reducing complexity and containing IT costs can be demonstrated, while moving towards achieving many of the prerequisites for supporting global business requirements. But the effective distance between a CIO and end-user community can be large in global organizations, and it is worth considering at this point how global IT standards are perceived by local IT organizations which carry the burden of standards implementation.

Many large local IT organizations will already have spent time and effort establishing IT standards of their own, and will naturally have some reservations about the benefits to them of global standards. If the latter are poorly handled, there is plenty of opportunity to damage both global IT standards and the relationship between global and local organizations. Key from the start is to treat such organizations not as a nuisance, rather as a key source of expertise in decisions on standards.

By contrast, perception of global IT standards by smaller local IT organizations can be ambiguous. On the one hand, local IT forces can feel in common with their larger counterparts that global IT standards are imposed on them, but do not correspond to those used by their favourite local service provider, cost more and constrain their ability to respond rapidly to mundane local business requirements. On the other hand, globally set standards free up local resources from evaluations that have already been carried out elsewhere, and

[1] Line managers who lead functions across locations will already be familiar with similar challenges, albeit in the context of their own functions.

can often facilitate local financial approvals for IT infrastructure investments by carrying the label "Global IT Standard".

From the many options for standardization available, the aim remains to choose and manage just those that will best meet overall business expectations. The next section presents the business case principles that can be used as a valuable tool to choose the right standards, and subsequent sections propose a model for managing global standards effectively together with local IT organizations.

Choice of standards

Viewed generally, it is the impact that global complexity in IT has on a business that determines whether a business will gain from global IT standards. Even locally, within a reasonably sized IT organization, the cost of developing and maintaining interfaces between disparate systems consumes a significant proportion of an average IT budget and slows down deployment of any new solutions for the business. Certainly one element of the attractiveness of ERP systems such as SAP is that they internalize these problems within one monolithic application.

In a global context, merely consider the impact of complexity one level higher up, i.e. across locations. Think about the extent that business processes extend across locations and national boundaries. For example, does the supply chain source from factories or suppliers in different countries? If a firm already has or is moving towards such cross-boundary processes, then in the interests of being able to support smoothly the corresponding information exchange requirements, global IT standards for the respective business applications will generally need to be developed. On the down side, this traditionally meets with significant organizational resistance; on the up side, it is something that should really be championed and owned primarily by the business itself, not IT. The role of IT is "simply" to deliver the technology solutions, and run the supporting infrastructure. This business requirement to deliver standard, or at least harmonized, solutions has a consequent effect on the level of standardization required in the supporting infrastructure. Throughout, the pressure to establish global IT standards is the need to meet direct business information requirements, i.e. provide immediate business value.

However, in many multinational firms, business processes are run neither globally nor even regionally, and pressure from line managers to provide global IT support is minimal. Nevertheless, there can still be an excellent case for global IT standards, although the drivers for them will be different. This is the time to take a fundamental step back from business driven applications and instead to focus on using global IT standards to improve the underlying IT infrastructure both in terms of service and costs. If, for example, there is a basic requirement to be able to support generic communication across units, then there will be at least tacit business support for the global introduction of standard e-mail, groupware, wordprocessing, spreadsheet, presentation programs and other utilities—if these are not already present. Following that, the further standardization is applied in the realms of application servers, file servers, PCs and systems administration, the more valuable opportunities are simply being taken to streamline operations and reduce IT costs, in general through some form of volume synergy or economies of scale.

The impact of global complexity in IT sets overall priorities in choosing domains to standardize and provides background justification for global IT standards as a whole. Business environments are sufficiently varied that, in addition, each individual standard chosen requires a business case of its own to be sure that the standard is actually contributing value: standardization is not an end in its own right. The business case does not, however, need to be complex, and can basically be composed as follows of an analysis of the benefits versus costs for the standard in question.

Benefits

The ultimate motivation behind establishing any particular standard forms the foundation of the respective business case and needs to be concrete, generally falling into one or more of the following categories:

- *Business*: The business may require a particular service to be harmonized globally. If, say, a large proportion of the employees in a consulting firm travel internationally and require the same access to company networks wherever they work, then a global IT standard for remote access (RAS) will need to be established.
- *Savings*: Here the spotlight falls on both procurement and operational costs. Concerning procurement, pooling demand globally and negotiating once with a supplier cuts down overall time spent on local negotiations and leverages the consolidated volume in a global company. In contrast, the bulk of operational costs are generated by the cost of skilled personnel, for example support engineers trained in a particular flavour of operating system, or programmers maintaining a web of intersystem interfaces. Standards reduce the range of technologies to support, and firms can move towards a leaner workforce, or free up resources to focus on activities closer to the business. Be aware though that procurement and operational costs are often interdependent: it is not the aim to pay a low initial price for a particular product only to suffer later from elevated maintenance costs. An effective concept for protecting against this and communicating cost generation in general is the Total Cost of Ownership model (TCO) which takes a holistic view of all the various points of cost generation through the lifetime of a product. For example, the TCO of a PC is composed of costs from each of "forecast–procure–deploy–support–dispose". Note how over the lifetime of a PC, the original procurement price only accounts for ~15% of the total cost.

- *Responsiveness*: Delivery of new IT solutions to the business can be notoriously slow and laborious, and in an era of accelerating business change, projects need to be speeded up if they are not to be obsolete by the time they are deployed. A number of overarching models revolving around "adaptive IT" address this challenge, and one key component to these models is establishing a set of clear technology standards. These should form the framework or platform into which all new solutions are integrated. For example, affiliates regularly innovate using the Web, which by default has global reach, and it makes sense to establish global standards for how these Web sites should be built and run. The focus of these "architectural" standards is to introduce discipline in solution delivery and ensure solutions fit the overall environment, enabling IT to handle effectively a continuous flow of incoming projects. Always dealing with the same foundation technologies speeds up the projects, ensures they are scalable, and avoids accumulation of complexity in downstream operations.
- *Risk*: IT-related risks fall into a number of categories, not least of which are breaches of information security, project failures and exposure to dependency on particular suppliers. Any one of these can mushroom into a serious problem, and global standards can be an instrument for reducing risks, for example by establishing a common platform for protection of networks against outsider intrusion. Note, however, if risk reduction is the primary motivation, care needs to be taken concerning the definition of a *global* standard for a particular product. The standard definition needs to be narrow enough to exclude unsuitable suppliers, but generous enough to allow the local choice between at least two main suppliers. This maintains overall supplier competitivity and keeps a fall-back solution should one supplier later prove problematic.
- *Flexibility*: Although information systems are usually not a major force in considering business growth, restructuring, mergers, and acquisitions, global IT standards can accelerate how rapidly IT can react to and support such changes. This, too, is very much in the spirit of "adaptive IT", and focuses on standards in the underlying infrastructure such as PCs, tools, servers and networks.

Costs

For any particular standard considered, one or more of the motivations above will drive the respective business case to implement the standard, but there are important cost factors to add to the business case. First, where the overall business case for globalizing a standard may be clear, locally the situation may still be disadvantageous to isolated units. The politics of forcing a way through need to be considered or a solution must be found, either by diluting the standard to allow a certain amount of flexibility or instigating globally financed incentives to support such units. Secondly, to reap the value of standards, activities both upstream and downstream of the core standard definition need to be carried out, and the resources for this should feature in the business case. Neglecting this effort risks missing out on the majority of benefits, and undermining the credibility of global IT standards through a superficial approach. The following activities are the bare minimum for ongoing support for each standard:

- Problems and adherence to the standard in the field need to be monitored and the standard maintained as business requirements and available technology evolve.
- Relationships with technology suppliers need to be maintained, including negotiation of global framework contracts and management of price freshness.
- Exchange of skills and knowledge concerning the standard needs to be actively organized throughout the firm.

In special cases where declaration of a new standard needs to be accompanied by migration of the installed base (as opposed to waiting until a change needs to be made), a migration project will need to address this migration. More generally, the larger-scale benefits of global standardization come to fruition when the same activities are pooled globally or regionally. Global standardization forms an essential stepping stone or vehicle to being able to carry out this organizational transformation. Here are some common examples:

- *Competence centres*: pooled consulting capability, perhaps in data warehousing or project management.
- *Development centres*: pooled implementation capability, for example in developing Web sites.
- *Pooled operations*: pooled operational capability, for example in data centres, regional help desks, shared service centres.

Each of these pooled options implies non-trivial organizational changes, and the definition of the underlying standard is usually a smaller sub-component of a larger change project. Some of the issues that can arise in such projects were discussed in Chapter 4 on strategy. The overall corollary is that when it comes to standards, benefits in simplicity and initial procurement costs are fairly easy to achieve, whereas benefits further downstream, where much of the costs are generated, are a quantum leap harder to realize.

Exhibit 5 – global IT standards in featured firms

Philips

Corporate IT standards are kept to a minimum and almost all relate to implementation requirements for services run by corporate IT, namely WAN, desktop and local infrastructure, e-mail and groupware, Internet technology, security, and IT purchasing and contracting. Each service core team is responsible for proposing respective standards for subsequent ratification by the IT Policy Board consisting of the Vice-Chairman of the Board, the corporate head of corporate core processes, the corporate CIO and divisional CIOs. Ratification of a standard basically imposes the standard as mandatory on all parts of the organization, including acquired firms and services delivered by third parties. While the range of standards is fairly restricted, exception handling is tight. Requests for exceptions can in principle be raised to the responsible divisional CIO, but most standards qualify as "policy" and must be implemented, with any ensuing costs absorbed locally.

Nestlé

Business and IT standards are understood to be a key part of the GLOBE initiative to implement common business processes. One central competence centre defines and maintains the GLOBE "solution", and setting global IT standards is an integral part of that activity. Each individual project, for example concerning networks or desktop infrastructure, is responsible for working with stakeholders from the impacted community to agree on relevant standards, which are then approved by the respective project steering committee before being passed on to regional operational centres for implementation. In a way, IT standardization is driven directly by the wave of business standardization.

Concerning exceptions to standards, the complexity of the GLOBE solution or package is such that local exceptions to individual components of the solution are very hard to justify, although escalation paths do exist for handling such requests. Flexibility, is however, allowed in the current systems during the period leading up to deployment of GLOBE. Here businesses have free choice as in the past, but it is understood that when the time comes, everything will be replaced by the standard GLOBE solution.

Novartis

Until recently, beyond a common e-mail system, corporate IT standards were restricted to a few isolated, commercially orientated standards for which preferential corporate contracts had been negotiated. Most standards were set at a divisional level. In a major shift, the comprehensive standards maintained within the pharmaceutical division were promoted to apply to the company as a whole. A decentralized ownership model for managing standards is used and has proven successful in addressing the controversies that often beset standard setting. The domains chosen for standardization are primarily technology and infrastructure standards motivated either for architectural reasons or cost reductions in procurement and operation. Application standards are managed lower in the organization within divisions or functions, although where there is a common choice of application, contract negotiations and expertise are pooled. Overall, in managing corporate standards, the emphasis is placed on maintaining completely up-to-date standard definitions; the onus of implementation (and coverage of ensuing costs) lies with individual IT units. Over time, commitment to corporate standards has grown considerably, as demonstrated by the recent implementation of single desktop and laptop standards throughout Novartis.

Toyota

Toyota maintains a well-defined standards framework which charts each technology domain and documents whether the respective standard is set locally, regionally or globally, and what degrees of freedom units may have in implementation. Those standards that are set globally are agreed directly by the Global IT Architecture Committee which is chaired by corporate IT and composed of IT architects from each region. The emphasis in setting global standards is on consensus and adequate up-front involvement of stakeholders to ensure that potential issues in implementations are identified before any decision is taken. There are follow-up mechanisms to foster adherence to standards, but the general policy is that while exceptions are not permitted in cooperative environments, local exceptions in isolated environments can be simply approved by regional IT management on the basis of the local business case.

UBS

The IT landscape in the finance industry is particularly complex and implementation of standards to reduce complexity is viewed at UBS as key to improving reliability and security of service. This commitment to standardization is an explicit part of the IT strategy and framework standards such as operating systems are specified directly in it. One step further, the focus of standards effort is on projects that physically implement the standards laid out in the IT strategy. Where necessary, these projects may propose additional technical specifications within the overall standards framework for approval by the central IT Committee, composed of IT heads from each IT group and additional selected IT professionals.

The handling of standards in the field depends on the domain concerned. Underlying technology standards such as those for networks or anything influencing information security are applied rigorously across the board. By contrast, handling of applications is driven by the respective business. The requirements set by business functions determine the selection of applications and the timetable and policies for migrating the installed base of legacy applications. In general, local businesses implement the standard applications, but, ultimately, local general managers are responsible for how requirements are met and bear ensuing costs, so they can choose, for example, to develop systems of their own, provided they adhere to the underlying technology standards and are in a position to justify their decision when escalated.

Managing standards

An intuitive approach to managing global standards is to set up a large central standards group which is uniquely responsible for setting and maintaining standards. Although adopted by many firms, such an approach commonly suffers from being resource intensive through the range of skills required in the group, and being out of touch with the local realities of standards implementation.

This book proposes an alternative approach, whereby a *lean*, dedicated central corporate standards group has overall responsibility for leading and coordinating definition and maintenance of global IT standards. However, responsibility for each individual standard lies with a respective "owner". An owner can work anywhere in the organization, but will always be a key stakeholder for that particular standard and directly impacted by its definition. For example, the owner of the standard for office tools could be the IT manager accountable for desktop services in the largest affiliate.

Through the careful separation of responsibilities between central group and owners, just enough resources can be dedicated to ensure that standards as a whole are always established following strict minimum business case requirements, whereas the expertise for deciding on the choice of standard is drawn directly from the sharp end. Separate approval and stakeholder groups are used to retain overall standards governance.

The following sections present details on the organization and processes for the proposed model: enough to accomplish the bare minimum activities highlighted earlier. Activities reaching significantly beyond definition of the standard, such as pooling of operations, should be handled in distinct organizational transformation projects separate from the core standards group, although these projects should nevertheless adhere to the same core process for the actual standard definition.

Organization

The presentation of the lean model for managing global IT standards has been divided into organization and corresponding processes. The suggested roles, responsibilities and resource requirements are covered first, while later sections explain the main processes for defining new standards, maintaining existing standards and handling exceptions. The priority in approaching global IT standards should be to get the organization in place and IT standards on the executive agenda—processes can always be fine tuned later (Figure 5.3).

The aim of the proposed organization is to dedicate sufficient resources to make standards a success, while neither building up a large head office overhead, nor demanding too high a contribution from local affiliates. There are four prime groupings:

- Global Standards Group responsible for management of standards as a whole.
- Standard owners bringing material expertise and responsible for individual standards.

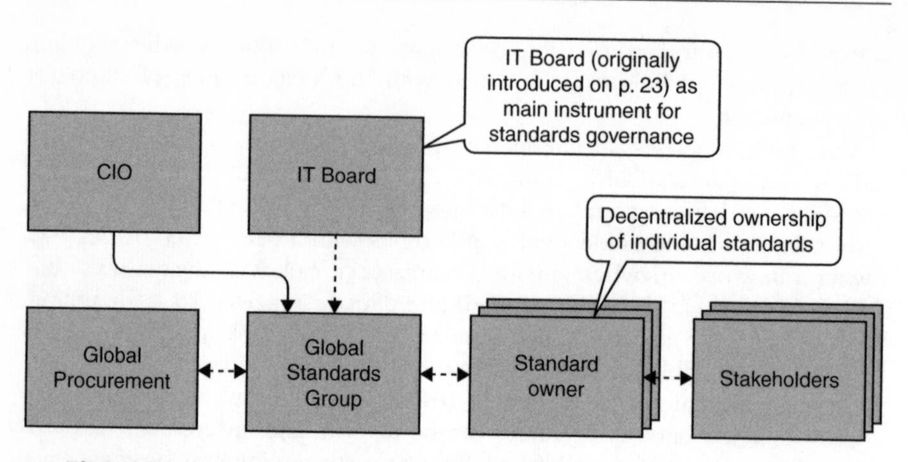

Figure 5.3—Organization for decentralized management of global standards

- IT Board responsible for guidance and governance.
- CIO responsible for championing standards.

Notice the absence of a strict hierarchy. Reporting lines do not feature strongly here, as ultimately the challenge for the Global Standards Group of overall responsibility without authority over owners largely reflects the realities of business in a global firm, and reporting lines do little to change that. However, as an effective confirmation of executive commitment, the Global Standards Group should report where possible directly to the CIO or Head of Global IT Infrastructure.

Global IT Standards Group – overall responsibility

Although named the Global IT Standards Group, this could be a slight misnomer, as depending on the scale of a firm, the global role might be accomplished by a single person, even if some affiliates have larger groups dedicated to their own local standards. It is important to appreciate the group mandate, activities and skills required at a global level.

The group mandate is to set up and maintain processes for defining new standards, maintaining existing ones, and handling exceptions should they arise. The recurrent foundation of these processes is the need for each standard to be well defined, justified by a transparent business case, and last, but not least, to have executive approval and general buy-in with affiliates.

In practice, activities are divided in about equal proportions across the areas of executive communications, moderation of processes carried out mainly by respective standard owners, and communication of standards to the larger affected community:

- *Executive communications*: Executive commitment is a prerequisite for success in standards; however, in practice, access to executive time is limited. Significant effort needs to be made by the group to establish standards as a regular agenda item in IT Board meetings, to prepare decision material at an appropriate level, and lastly to follow through on IT Board decisions. Finding the right level of dialogue is not always easy, as technical issues in standards are not uncommon. However, if the group works well with owners and stakeholders, much of the technical controversy should be resolved in advance of IT Board presentations for approval.

- *Moderation of processes*: A key facet of the lean approach is to use standards ownership to capitalize on *in situ* expertise distributed around the firm. Whereas a designated owner might know all the intricacies of, say, systems administration software, he may well be unaccustomed to viewing applicability beyond the realms of his own local unit, or to running a formal tender process and assembling a business case for his choice of technology as a standard. It is the responsibility of the Global Standards Group to accompany the owner through each step in definition and maintenance of a standard, paying particular attention to the business case and achieving buy-in through a representative global stakeholder group. Similarly, in handling exceptions, although the responsibility lies with the applicant to provide the business case for an exception, it makes sense for the Global Standards Group to provide unbiased assistance, which can both reinforce relations with affiliates and keep the group up to date with evolving requirements concerning a particular standard.
- *General communication*: Two factors make general communication of global standards important. First, in a global context the population affected by a standard usually extends well beyond the circle of stakeholders and decision makers involved in defining and maintaining the standard. Furthermore, the emphasis is on ongoing maintenance of standards, and particular standards (often dictated by market availability) will evolve on a regular basis, independent of a firm's desire to hold them constant. The Global Standards Group must publish standards, actively notify changes and generally promote standards, ensuring that local IT support organizations, local purchasing organizations and local IT investment approvers are in touch with current standards.

Viewing the mandate and activities above, it is clear that the Global Standards Group requires the much sought after combination of skills in high level management, technology and people management.

Standard owners — expertise

Whereas the Global Standards Group is accountable for standards as a whole, each individual standard is managed by a standard owner with ongoing responsibility for the definition and maintenance of the respective standard. In contrast to the Global Standards Group, which is dedicated to standards, the task of ownership should remain a role that is assigned to someone as a logical extension of what she already does. If particular standards are interrelated, such as Web technologies, one person can own those standards en bloc.

The essential mandate in owning a standard is to provide the specific business case and buy-in for initial approval of the standard and then to maintain the standard as requirements and available technology evolve. This is a dual role of both material expert and decision maker: after initial IT Board approval, the owner is authorized to update the standard without further escalation. Note that the mandate focuses on the definition of the standard and does not extend beyond that to include, for example, operative services in related developments or supporting end users.

To preclude working in a vacuum, the owner must be supported by a representative group of stakeholders drawn from across the company, including for instance counterparts from other affiliates. If standard-specific stakeholders prove hard to find, default nominees delegated by the IT Board can be used as proxies. Either way, this institutionalization of consultation between owner and stakeholders greatly facilitates IT Board commitment to the principles of delegated standards ownership.

The activities as a standard owner can be viewed as establishing the expertise underpinning the standard, intermittent revision of the standard definition, and tracking success of the standard:

- *Establish expertise*: The credibility of a standard stands or falls with the reputation of the respective owner among the IT community. The owner pools and maintains knowledge around the standard, for example global requirements within the firm, options available from technology suppliers, and industry benchmarks or best practices.
- *Maintain standard definition*: The nature of the definition lies in the hands of the owner. For example, it may make sense simply to name the manufacturers from which to source a particular product, or to specify vendor, model and version. But the choice should be driven by the business case and the latter must be maintained by the owner. If there is a significant commercial component driving the standard, then the owner should also actively engage procurement in negotiations to ensure that the promise, for example of volume synergies, is realized. Throughout, the owner needs to draw on the assigned stakeholders, who can really help the owner weigh up requirements beyond the boundaries of his own unit.
- *Track success*: As frequently occurs with business cases in general, once approved, they are forgotten. A key, and often neglected, step in standards is to keep track of how successful the standard actually is. Without being directly accountable for the success of their standard, each standard owner must nevertheless remain in touch with progress towards delivering the benefits promised in the business case, and be able to report on this at least at a high level.

It is clear that each owner must be a material expert in the standard in question, but, in addition, each owner must be willing to tackle communication in two senses, albeit with support from the Global IT Standards Group. On the one hand, owners need to be prepared to extend their horizon beyond the scope of their primary duties and to work with other stakeholders to reach global agreement. On the other hand, owners need a feeling for the business side of technology, and to be able to work with procurement and suppliers towards beneficial commercial conditions supporting their standard. Note that although ownership is intended primarily as a role, the task and associated skills remain non-trivial and the IT Board should make its backing of the owner explicit.

IT Board – governance

It is important that the highest level of IT management shows commitment to global IT standards. The most appropriate body to do this is the IT Board, introduced originally on p. 23. The IT Board can contribute by establishing standards policies, setting priorities in targeting standards and backing individual owners. For the policies, the IT Board basically dictates the boundaries within which owners are authorized to handle their respective standards. For example, the IT Board can set the following:

- *Vendor policy*: In product orientated standards, setting a standard to a single vendor can appear ideal, but brings implicit dependence on that vendor and the ensuing risk of falling mid-term competitivity. For such cases, a vendor policy can be agreed that stipulates, say, that affiliates must have a choice between two vendors, or that the maximum duration of exclusivity contracts can be fixed.
- *Adherence policy*: A clear policy on required adherence is a necessary complement to well maintained standards. While a popular model segregates standards into "mandatory", "recommended" or "optional", a tighter policy that adherence is always mandatory has the advantage of being clear to all concerned and resources can be focused on the essentials. Throughout, it is important to complement the adherence requirement with a fair exception handling process.
- *Control policy*: The tenet "What you don't measure, you don't get" appears prominently in Chapter 6. Nevertheless, the lean model presented here does not recommend introducing formal systematic control for local adherence to global standards. Doing so can lead to significant administrative overhead and basically undermines the credibility of original agreements made by the IT Board.

With standards policies set, it remains for the IT Board to set priorities and back respective owners. Throughout, their main contact and working body remains the Global IT Standards Group.

CIO – drive

At the risk of stating the obvious, a CIO's job is to meet global business demands for information and take advantage of all global opportunities in his own organization to improve overall IT performance. With a steady evolution away from proprietary systems development and the high rate of technology obsolescence, much of this role involves selection and procurement of technologies that meet business requirements. Setting up appropriate management of global IT standards is a large step towards meeting this challenge. But the soft elements should not be neglected. Having a CIO prepared to demonstrate commitment to global standards and possessing sufficient charisma and powers of persuasion to bring business and local IT managers on board is half the battle. The need for this combination of management and leadership should not be neglected, especially in cases where isolated local units suffer from introduction of a certain standard.

Funding

The funding required for standards can be considered on two distinct levels as funding for management of standards as a whole, and funding for the implementation costs of individual standards. For standards management, beyond central funding for the Global IT Standards Group and umbrella market research contracts, the main investment is in effect made by affiliates in freeing up their experts' time for contributions to global initiatives. Ironically, those affiliates with such expertise are usually the large ones with well-tuned local operations that often have the least to gain from global standards. All the same, no central compensation is proposed for this investment by affiliates, but the extent of contribution to global initiatives can be included among the metrics appearing in the balanced scorecards for the unit. Contingency central funding can be made available for special primary costs that a standard owner may have in maintaining standard definition, although in practice this can become more of an administrative overhead.

The other, more significant, funding requirement is for the implementation costs of standards. Where changes are big enough to give rise to significant costs, the latter should be covered within respective migration projects, but they remain a difficult issue which is well worth understanding. One recurrent issue is that the geographic distribution of benefits may not match the distribution in implementation costs. No matter how well standards are defined globally, genuine local problems can arise either because of specific geographical considerations or historical reasons and poor timing. For instance, excellent commercial conditions may have been negotiated for a new server standard, but a particular location may be in the middle of a three-year lease obligation on other equipment. These are local "sub-optima" or situations where the local business case is negative despite a positive global business case. If local exceptions can be made without jeopardizing the global business case, exceptions can be approved, but in other instances some form of central funding or compensation for the unit can be instigated, perhaps through adjustment of local management result. More generally, two mechanisms can be put in place to smooth implementation of a particular standard, but note that cross-border accounting concerns render execution on a global scale problematic:

- Incentive schemes can encourage migration to a new standard. For example, when Eastman Kodak introduced a new PC standard, they arranged for Dell PCs delivered to branches in the first four months of their migration project to be paid for by head office.
- Disincentive schemes can discourage deviation from a standard. For example, IT help desks and support organizations regularly charge out double rates for supporting equipment not appearing in the standard catalogue.

So far, this chapter has covered the choice of standards in a firm, and the organization and resources required to manage them. The next sections focus on work templates for the proposed organization in the classic three processes of defining new standards, maintaining existing ones and handling exceptions. The key driver behind their design is the need for simplicity and transparency at a global level but, in common with the other principles in this book, they can be replicated at a local level: often, large affiliates will want both to add local specifics to global standards and set standards of their own for technologies not covered globally. For example, where the global standard for PCs may specify the operating system and choice of models from two vendors, an affiliate often selects just one of the given vendors, and may want to add a local standard for the corresponding choice of monitor. Wherever the scale of the local operation justifies it, local equivalents of the organization can use the same basic processes for managing their own standards.

Defining new standards

While the ability of IT to enable radical business improvements attracts significant attention, there remains an underlying expectation that the value and costs of existing IT operations should first be improved. Global IT can go some way to meeting this expectation and justifying its own existence by both simplifying systems across locations and pooling activities regionally or globally to bring down consolidated costs. A key prerequisite for this is the definition of global standards, and the proposed process is shown in Figure 5.4, with further notes following below. The aim is to document the essential tasks to be carried out for those few standards that are to be implemented globally, not to build a process that produces a multitude of new, but ineffective, standard definitions.

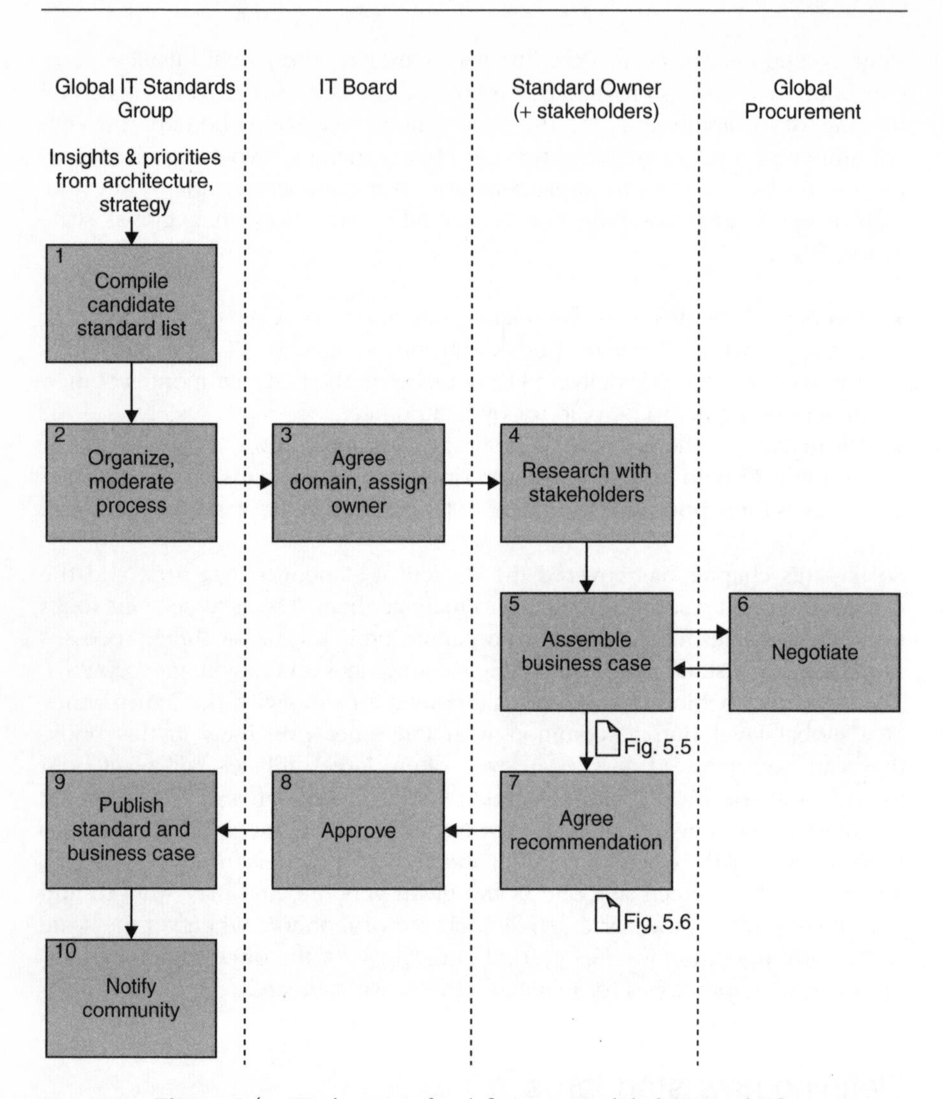

Figure 5.4—Work stream for defining new global IT standards

Initiation (Steps 1–3): With a little dialogue across the IT community, the Global IT Standards Group can produce a target shortlist for standardization by combining their understanding of any standards already established, the current business environment, and the level of resources required for implementing and maintaining standards. A major source of input is insights drawn from the global IT architecture process. Note, however, that by default, head office employees are in favour of global standards, and affiliates are against global standards, but experience shows that the real difficulty is identifying a suitable owner prepared to champion a particular standard. As experts, they are normally busy and often not receptive to additional, global responsibilities.

Convincing them is very much a task of persuasion with them and their managers that their contribution will be appreciated and recognized by the IT Board. Each owner needs to be supported by a stakeholder team, and the earlier they can be identified, the better. Certainly anyone in the field who has raised serious reservations about the standard should be included, as half the challenge is to ensure that all representative views have been heard.

Research (Step 4): The stakeholder team can be used to draw together an understanding of the requirements a firm has across locations, and discover which potential standard each location favours or already has in place. To this foundation, independent research from companies such as Gartner, Forrester and Meta Group can be added. In most of the technology domains likely to be standardized globally, comprehensive market evaluations will be available. Finally, any information on the preferences of a firm's direct competitors can also be valuable. Throughout, it is important to objectively research each viable alternative, as later the question "Why didn't you choose X?" will be asked, and acceptance of the chosen standard is reinforced if it can be demonstrated that X was at least researched thoroughly as a possibility.

Business Case (Step 5): The standard owner, supported by the stakeholders and Global Standards Group, needs to distil the results of research and understanding into a business case justifying global selection of a particular standard. Using a high-level template is often a good starting point for assembling the business case, and the same template can be used later for explaining the findings to others. Figure 5.5 illustrates an example in which the business case is taken to be any combination of motivations (business value, cost, responsiveness, risk and flexibility) together with eventual project migration costs. Altogether, the key elements of the business case are there and it just remains to compare these across alternatives, not neglecting that "do nothing", i.e. do not establish a global standard, should be treated as a viable alternative.

The example template gives a panoramic view of a standard's business case that does not focus exclusively on financials, but does guide everyone to the differentiating factors between alternatives. Whatever is really important should be stated directly in this table; everything else is in essence mere supporting material. Discussions on the business case for a standard often end with this table, but a prerequisite is confidence in the table entries. One contributor to that is carrying out the foundation research described further above, the other is that necessary negotiation has taken place in parallel.

Negotiate (Step 6): Attention always needs to be paid to cost figures, which should in general be substantiated. For example, if a reduction in procurement price through global volume is the motivation, then volume reductions should be explicitly negotiated to give concrete numbers in the business case. Even if

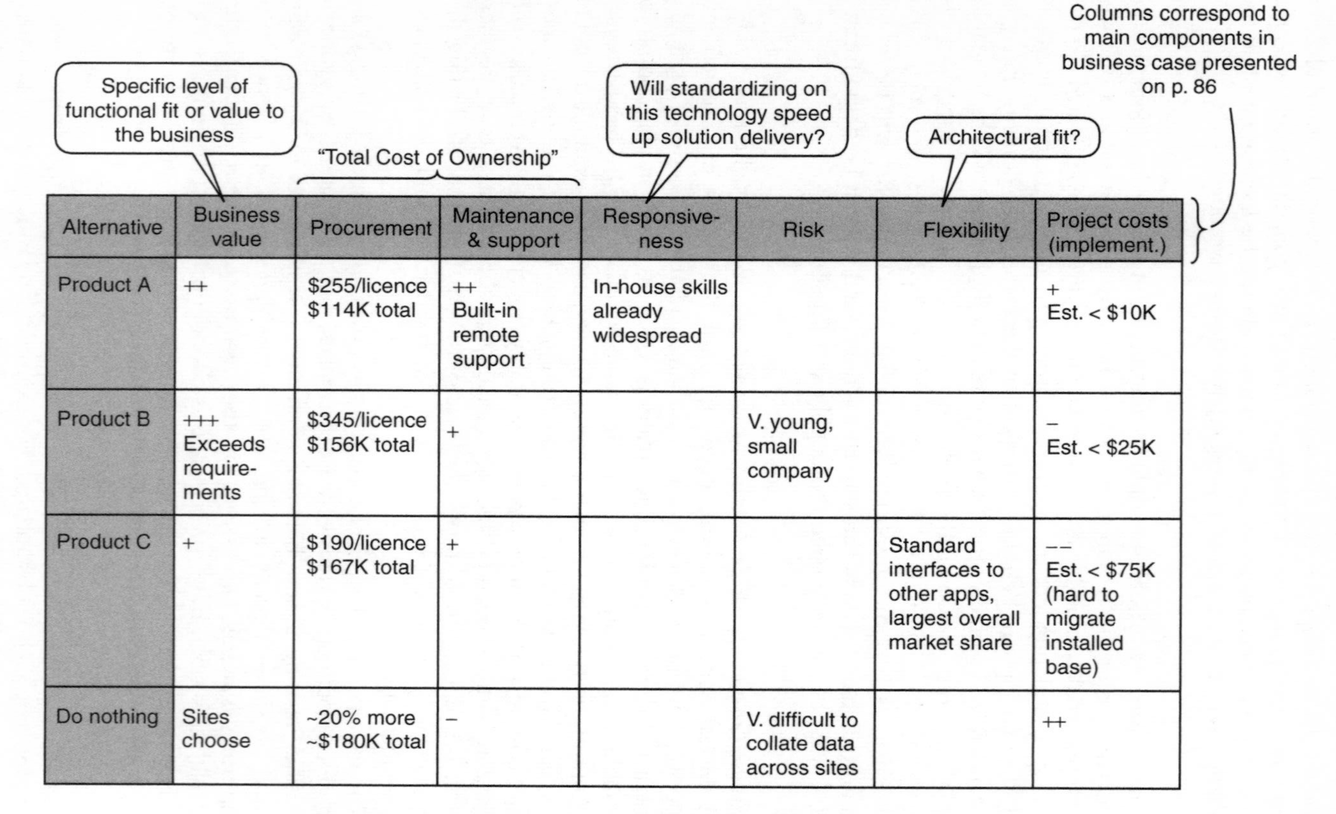

Alternative	Business value	Procurement	Maintenance & support	Responsive-ness	Risk	Flexibility	Project costs (implement.)
Product A	++	$255/licence $114K total	++ Built-in remote support	In-house skills already widespread			+ Est. < $10K
Product B	+++ Exceeds require-ments	$345/licence $156K total	+		V. young, small company		– Est. < $25K
Product C	+	$190/licence $167K total	+			Standard interfaces to other apps, largest overall market share	–– Est. < $75K (hard to migrate installed base)
Do nothing	Sites choose	~20% more ~$180K total	–		V. difficult to collate data across sites		++

Figure 5.5—Example business case template for standards

a standard is architectural in nature, and there is no large commercial element to the business case, if a vendor or partner is involved, negotiations should be carried out *before* the definitive choice of standard becomes public knowledge, otherwise it will be the vendor in a strong bargaining position.

Quite what form the negotiation takes will depend on the standard, but the technology supplier will usually be presented with the incentive of a potential sourcing deal which is then used both to improve overall conditions and cut time wasted on local negotiations. While this work stream should be led by corporate procurement, its success depends on good cooperation with IT, and it is well worth understanding the various approaches that can be taken. With this in mind, two particular negotiation techniques are presented further below. Irrespective of any technique used and the format of corporate agreement targeted, the ultimate aim remains to secure the best global commitment on the essential parameters by each potential vendor involved.

Definition (Steps 7–8): The definition of the standard should follow directly from the business case, extending just far enough into detail to be useful and no further. Any degrees of freedom present in the global business case can be used to give local units latitude in implementation. For example, if the motivation behind a standard is only price and a flat rate reduction on list prices has been negotiated with a vendor, then choice of model can be delegated to the affiliates. One further, critical point of flexibility is the policy on timing. Does the new standard just apply for new purchases, or does the installed base need to be migrated and, if so, when? Beyond the obvious up-front costs of the latter, there is a cultural element to be aware of, especially when commodity hardware items are owned by line functions. Asking units to replace equipment before it appears to reach end-of-life costs money and, more importantly, is commonly resented as outside interference.

The owner should use the business case and the degrees of freedom at his disposal to reach and document buy-in from the expert stakeholders, but should avoid diluting the standard to such an extent that the benefits cannot be realized. With stakeholder buy-in and a succinct recommendation to the IT Board, approval will be forthcoming and standards will stay on the IT Board agenda.

Publication and Notification (Steps 9–10): assuming the standard definition is ratified by the IT Board, the last step is to make sure that the new standard is understood at key points throughout the organization and in particular in affiliate IT planning and purchasing units. Much effort has been dedicated to adhering to a methodical approach to defining the standard from the outset, and it makes sense to extend this transparency to the rest of the company by publishing not only the standard, for example as shown in Figure 5.6, but also the business case[2] and background research. Overall, experience shows

[2] Carefully clean quantitative or sensitive data that could compromise relations with third parties.

IT Standard	Domain, e.g. database
Scope	Global
Standard	Vendor/model/version/product number or other definition
Owner, stakeholders	J. Bloggs, K. Smith, P. Monk, H. Miller, etc.
Timing	E.g. only for new purchases, no migration of installed base
Business case	Widespread in-house skills in this product, for further details see full business case, for example in table similar to Figure 5.5
Notes	Any further degrees of freedom such as local choice of vendor. Any acknowledged conditions for exceptions
Contract	Reference for contracts, contact details
Last reviewed	11 August 2003 (should be within last six months)

Figure 5.6—Example standard definition template

that effort invested in presenting standards visibly and clearly to the impacted community contributes greatly to their acceptance and perceived usefulness.

The next paragraphs present details on two negotiation techniques that can be applied to the negotiation phase in step 6. Readers not interested in these details can skip to the discussion on p. 108 on maintaining standards.

Tender process based on the Request For Proposal

A common incentive for establishing a global standard is lower procurement costs that can be realized if a company uses the same product globally to attain corresponding volume-related reductions with the respective supplier. Reductions can be particularly high if there are a number of viable alternative suppliers on the market that can be brought to compete against each other on a global level. However, negotiations are exposed to several pitfalls, such as difficult comparison of supplier offerings, unnecessarily protracted negotiations and, worst of all, accusations of lack of objectivity in final supplier selection. Adhering to a formal tender process based on the concept of the "Request For Approval" (RFP) greatly cuts the risk of such failures in selecting a standard. The following paragraphs present the essentials of the RFP, which is now the *de facto* standard for multi-supplier IT negotiations. Extensive literature is also available on the market for readers wishing to learn more.[3]

[3] For example, Bud Porter-Roth, *The Request For Proposal: A Guide to Effective RFP Development*, Addison-Wesley Professional, 2001.

The cornerstone of the RFP is a single, clear statement of customer requirements that need to be fulfilled. This statement shifts initial attention away from market offerings towards an understanding of in-house needs, covering, for example, both technical specifications such as product performance and the supporting service required. Potential suppliers are subsequently given the customer requirements and invited to offer solutions that meet them. These bids are submitted by suppliers within a certain time frame, and have a common format allowing straightforward cross-checking of pricing and requirements met by suppliers. A single, pre-agreed evaluation framework is then used to give objective valuations of each bid and allow selection of the best supplier.

While the RFP does carry some administrative overhead, it also has clear advantages over an ad hoc approach to initiating multi-supplier negotiations:

- Using in-house requirements as the basis for negotiation provides an excellent point of departure.
- Following the formal procedure leaves an auditable trail and cuts the risk of missed timelines.
- Results are improved by early identification of which elements need most negotiation effort.

The RFP procedure essentially starts with a clear statement of requirements, in this instance requirements concerning a standard. Compilation of these requirements should be led by the standard owner drawing on the expertise of the delegated stakeholder team. The requirements may need to be compiled from scratch, or, if the selection of a standard is a sub-component of a larger change project, requirements should be assembled as a matter of course within the scope of the overall project, and these can be inherited as a starting point. Either way, the final document should accurately express the needs that are to be fulfilled. For the sake of clarity, these can be ordered into distinct categories such as technical specifications and service requirements. For example, for a PC hardware standard, the technical specifications section might include a requirement "Processor speed must be at least 1.6 MHz", and the service section might include the requirements "At least 95% of PCs must be delivered within 10 days of ordering" and "No more than 5% of PCs delivered may be defective on arrival". As a general rule, requirements should be kept meaningful, measurable and succinct. Finally, requirements should be complemented by statements on the overall scope, e.g. which countries need to be covered, and any overall constraints in solutions delivered, e.g. solution must be in place by July.

In the context of global standards, the particular challenge arises of reaching a balance between varying local requirements. Although one common approach is to consolidate requirements submitted by each unit, experience shows that this can lead to an endless list of partly contradictory requirements which cannot be fulfilled by any supplier at an advantageous price. One alternative approach is for the owner to draft requirements, invite stakeholders to give input at particular points in the draft, then to redraft the requirements at a final agreement workshop with all stakeholders present. Whichever approach is taken, it is important to resolve any fundamental differences between units at this early stage. The final result should be a meaningful requirements document that is formally agreed and signed by both owner and stakeholders.

With requirements accurately documented, the RFP can be carried out following the simple sequence of steps shown below. This should be a joint effort between IT and the purchasing department, but throughout, there are two distinct levels on which to focus attention. On an underlying level, the quality of RFP and evaluation documents is naturally important. On a higher level, care needs to be taken to identify and involve the right people from the beginning in preparation and decision making.

1) *Notify bidders*: The standard owner should work with procurement to identify those suppliers that are to be invited to bid. If potentially viable suppliers are excluded, then the reasons for their exclusion should be documented. Ultimately a compromise needs to be reached between inviting enough bidders to ensure competition, and inviting so many that resources are insufficient to allow a fair evaluation of bids. Bidders should then be informed of the firm's intention to carry out an RFP, explaining the subject of the RFP and the main schedule, in particular when bidders will receive the RFP, when responses are due, and when decisions are to be made. Bidders should confirm their intention to submit bids.
2) *Agree RFP document*: Procurement should work with the standard owner to draft this document, which needs to articulate everything that a bidder needs to know to be in a position to submit a sensible offer. Although the document may have several standard sections, those that require real attention are requirements, legal conditions and response format. The requirements may be incorporated directly from the agreement made between owner and stakeholders. In the legal section, it must be clearly stated to what extent supplier bids are binding and, likewise, to what extent the customer commits, for example, whether global volumes are guaranteed. Lastly, the response format section is used to specify a particular format that the bidder must use for submitting its bid, with the aim to facilitate later assessment and comparison of bids across suppliers. This should cover, for example, checklists confirming which requirements are met by the solution offered, and particular schemes for specifying pricing. With the RFP drafted, care needs to be taken with document approval. In principle, and in line with the concept of the IT Board simply ratifying recommendations made by the owner, it should be sufficient to have signatures from owner, procurement and stakeholders. In practice, if there is a likelihood that higher level management will want to take a more active part in the process, then the IT Board should sign the RFP. It is key to have continuity throughout the process in approvals for RFP, evaluations and decisions.

3) *Agree evaluation framework*: An important measure in assuring objectivity of bid evaluations is to agree an overall bid evaluation framework at the same time as the RFP document itself is approved; doing so also provides a safety check that elements that appear prominently in the evaluation are actually requested in the RFP. One recommended approach is to construct overall scoring by weighting the importance of each requirement met and pricing offered. Note, however, that room should be left for other objective input, such as the overall business case for each bid, which may include components beyond price such as migration costs and risk. Once drafted, the evaluation framework should be approved by the same people that approved the RFP.
4) *Send RFP to bidders*: The RFP document should be sent to each bidder. If the RFP is complex, then a formal mechanism can be put in place to provide for further explanations and avoid uncontrolled communications. For example, individual question and answer sessions with bidders can be carried out a few days after RFP emission, with subsequent distribution of a consolidated list of questions and answers to all bidders. This mechanism ensures that all bidders can place their bids on the basis of the same information supplied by the customer.
5) *Receive bids*: Bidders should submit bids by a particular date. In some cases, the customer may wish to investigate soft factors in the bids, and invite bidders to formal bid presentations. This can provide bidders with the opportunity to explain their bids and demonstrate organizational commitment, for example through active participation of company executives.
6) *Preliminary evaluation and shortlist*: With the bids received, the owner and stakeholder team can proceed to carry out a preliminary evaluation on the basis of the originally agreed evaluation framework. This evaluation can give a rough ranking of bids, identify where further clarifications are required, and recognize bids that can be totally discounted. Bidders should be informed immediately whether they are shortlisted or not. Note that suppliers knowing they may be rejected on the basis of the initial bids alone and without further negotiation puts pressure on them to submit their best bids in the beginning.
7) *Final selection*: Preliminary evaluations can form sufficient basis for a decision, but, in general, a fixed period for clarifications and negotiations should be scheduled to improve individual bids. In some circumstances, the reverse auction mechanism described in the next section can be used to accelerate these negotiations. At the end of this period, the team should draft a finalized evaluation (still based on the original evaluation framework) and recommendation for approval or ratification by the IT Board as part of the overall approval for the global standard, as shown in activity 8 of Figure 5.4. A formal letter of intention should be sent to the selected supplier, and rejections to the remainder.

The steps above present a systematic method for approaching supplier selection that can be applied to global IT standards that have both a significant commercial component and several viable suppliers. The next section looks more closely at a new, specialized tool for negotiating one particular parameter (normally, but not necessarily, price) in competing supplier bids.

Reverse auctions

In a traditional auction, a single supplier offers a product for which potential buyers compete by offering ever increasing prices. A reverse auction is similar, but the roles are reversed, with one buyer declaring an interest in a particular product or service, and potential suppliers offering ever decreasing prices in a bid to receive the contract to provide the product. In a simple example, a company might decide to single source office supplies and run a reverse auction for pencils, granting the contract to the supplier making the lowest bid. Such reverse auctions can also be used in selecting certain global IT standards. For example, a reverse auction could be run to select a single supplier for a particular category of PC monitor. In practice, the situation may not be so clear, and consideration needs to be made of the following:

- Does a reverse auction make sense for a particular standard?
- If so, how should the auction fit into the overall tender process?

To answer the first question, there must be several viable suppliers which all provide products that potentially meet customer requirements, and the products themselves must be comparable in the extent to which they meet those customer requirements. Answering the second question is more complicated. If the standard is a true commodity, then the only distinguishing factor between suppliers is price and a reverse auction can be run in place of an RFP. On the whole though, decision criteria for standards are more multi-faceted and there will be a number of factors that differentiate supplier offerings, for example, financing conditions, service levels and extent of geographical reach. While these may remain different across suppliers, they still have to be negotiated and fixed in advance of entering a reverse auction. In such circumstances, the reverse auction can be placed as an integral part of the RFP process, run as soon as RFP bids have been clarified and negotiations on non-price elements have been completed.

In cases where a standard does prove suitable for reverse auction, the sequence of steps to take to run the auction is relatively uncomplicated, but the amount of effort that needs to be invested in preparation for the auction should not be underestimated:

1) *Communication with vendors*: As with the Request For Proposal, potential vendors should be invited to participate in the reverse auction and informed of the proposed schedule as soon as possible.

2) *Complete secondary negotiations*: The auction should be the final step in competition between suppliers, and all other variables, such as service levels, should be fixed in advance so that attention can be focused on price. For example, if the auction is for a standard PC, then the particular model offered by each respective vendor must be defined on the basis of the requirements and then fixed. This reassures suppliers that they are all competing in the auction on the same basis, and it avoids manipulation during the auction, for example through undeclared substitution of models.
3) *Prepare auction*: Most large vendors will already be familiar with reverse auctions, however, three key features need to be clarified. First, an online "e-auction" system should be used as the tool for carrying out the reverse auction, and vendors will require training and support in using the system. Secondly, there must be a common understanding of the bids themselves. In the simplest case, this will be unit price, but in some cases it makes sense to use another parameter such as monthly leasing rate. In any event, the basis for the bid must be tangible and unambiguous. Lastly, the legal framework for the auction must be established, including, for example, whether the customer is obliged to grant the contract to the lowest bidder or not—depending on whether the auction is being used as the definitive method of selection, or as a simple negotiation tool for one aspect of the tender process.
4) *Run auction*: Exactly how the auction is run will depend on the system in use, but, in general, the customer has a complete view of bids being placed by suppliers. The latter can place their own bids online, but have partially restricted views of competitor bids. For example, they may not see the identities of other suppliers, or they may only see the current lowest bid. Recommendations vary on the time frame to allow before closing the auction, but the most active bidding invariably occurs just before close, irrespective of how long the auction is open, so there is little advantage to leaving the auction open for an long period: auction times are generally measured in hours or minutes, not days.[4]
5) *Final selection*: The final selection of the chosen supplier should be able to follow fairly rapidly after the auction, as any other factors contributing to the choice between suppliers will have been defined before entering the auction.

This simple approach has a couple of features to be aware of. On the positive side, the transparency in bidding can accentuate competition between suppliers, and the set time frames accelerate negotiations on price itself, and set a limit on negotiations in other fields. On the negative side, the pressure exerted on price alone can remove all supplier margin for manoeuvre and lead to unforeseen service deterioration in other areas.

[4] To avoid suppliers using the tactic of last second bidding, auction close can be automatically extended if bids fall within a certain minimum delay before close.

Maintaining standards

Ideally, once defined, standards could be left alone for several years before further revision, and this would allow maximum stability in the IT infrastructure. In some cases, for example policy style standards such as computer naming conventions, standards can be left as originally defined. However, both the ongoing evolution in business requirements and, to a greater extent, the rate of technology obsolescence on the market, essentially dictate the need to review IT standards on a more frequent basis. Unfortunately, neglecting to invest modest, but regular, effort in maintaining a standard can undo all the original effort expended in setting up the standard. For example, affiliates

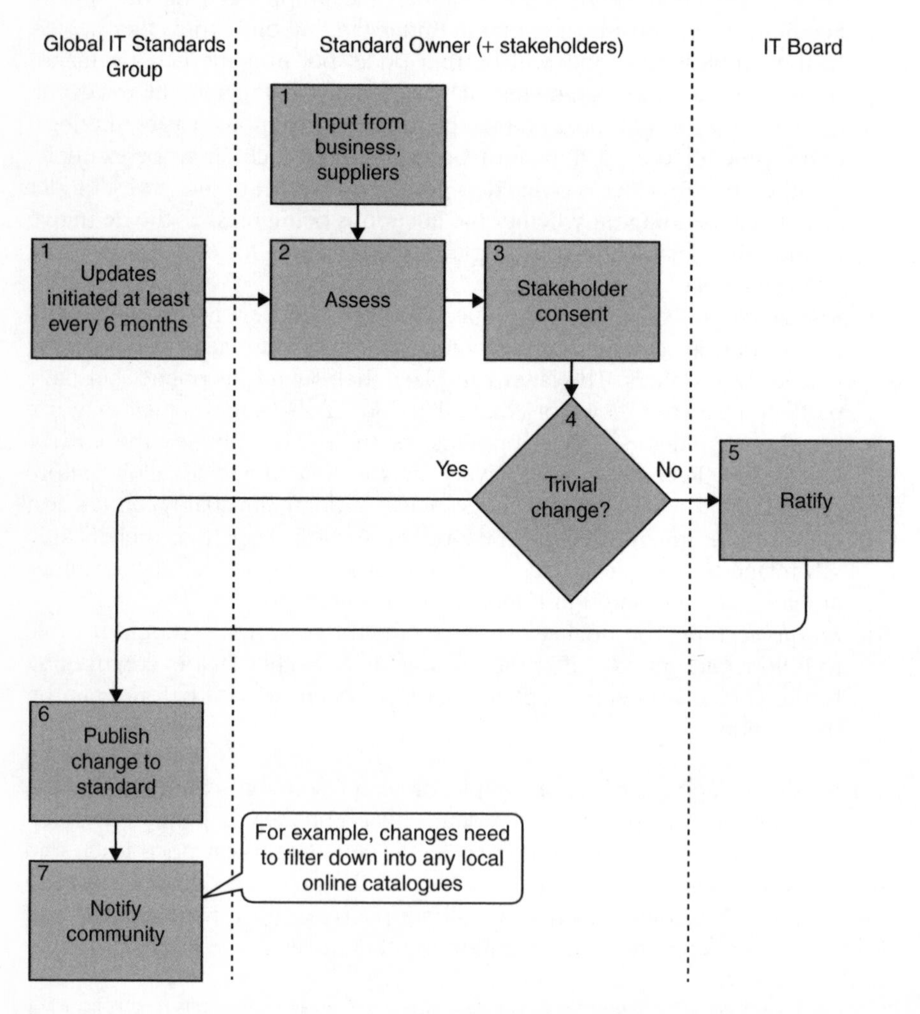

Figure 5.7—Work stream for maintaining existing standards

ordering a standard printer, only to find that the defined model is no longer available, largely negates the usefulness of the standard and undermines the credibility of global IT standards as a whole.

The foundation of the approach to standards maintenance proposed here and shown in Figure 5.7 is that each standard owner has ongoing personal responsibility for ensuring that the definition of the respective standard is kept up to date. The owner must be aware of evolving business requirements and available technology, and whenever a revision of the standard is required, the owner is empowered with the consent of the stakeholders to change the standard. Only controversial changes need to be escalated to the IT Board for approval. Accompanying this event-driven maintenance of standards, the Global Standards Group coordinates six-monthly reviews of all standards. In most cases, this can be a pro forma confirmation by a standard owner that the standard definition is up to date, but this is also an opportunity to research whether the benefits indicated in the original business case for the standard are being realized. Beyond fostering standards ownership and keeping standards updated, the approach develops goodwill throughout IT organizations in affiliates because, without needing to know anything about the maintenance process, they see that each standard has been reviewed within the last six months.

Handling exceptions

The emphasis of the model for managing standards presented so far has been on establishing a few, well-defined and well-maintained global IT standards. Explicitly engaging standard owners from the field and formally involving stakeholders takes a significant step towards ensuring consensus on choice of standards. Inevitably though, the need for local exceptions will arise. Handling this need effectively reinforces the dialogue with affiliates and ensures that the best approach is taken on a case-by-case basis, whether an exception is approved or not. Neglecting to handle this need effectively can seriously undermine global standards by both losing contact with affiliates and developing an undercurrent of undeclared exceptions to standards.

Viewed from the perspective of an affiliate, two questions need to be clear. First, how are solutions under development checked for alignment with global standards? Secondly, what steps need to be taken should an exception be required? Concerning how alignment is checked, one common approach is to build in a formal checkpoint to the purchasing or IT solution delivery processes. For example, no project execution approval is given without an official stamp of approval by the standards group. On a global scale though, this approach is often impractical, as processes requiring checkpoints prove too diverse, and the administrative overhead of official project checks is too high. Under such circumstances, a less bureaucratic approach is to delegate alignment checking to affiliates, for example to the solution architects engaged in projects, stipulating only that the checks should be made as early as possible, *before* momentum accumulates behind a particular choice of solution.

However alignment with global standards is checked, the second question arises of the procedure to follow when alignment is not present. While some firms expressly incorporate bureaucracy and delays into exception handling to discourage potential exceptions, the approach proposed here is the opposite. The process for handling exceptions should be transparent, fast and unbiased, for example, as shown in Figure 5.8. Here the responsibility for preparing the request for approval of an exception lies with the unit requesting the exception. The request itself is based on a business case analogous to the original business case for the standard itself, such as in Figure 5.5, but demonstrating how the requested alternative is superior locally to the standard and documenting to what extent the benefits of the standard in other affiliates is compromised if the exception is approved. For example, a certain affiliate may well have access to an apparently inexpensive local application, but using that application locally could reduce global volume discounts on licences for the standard application in other affiliates.

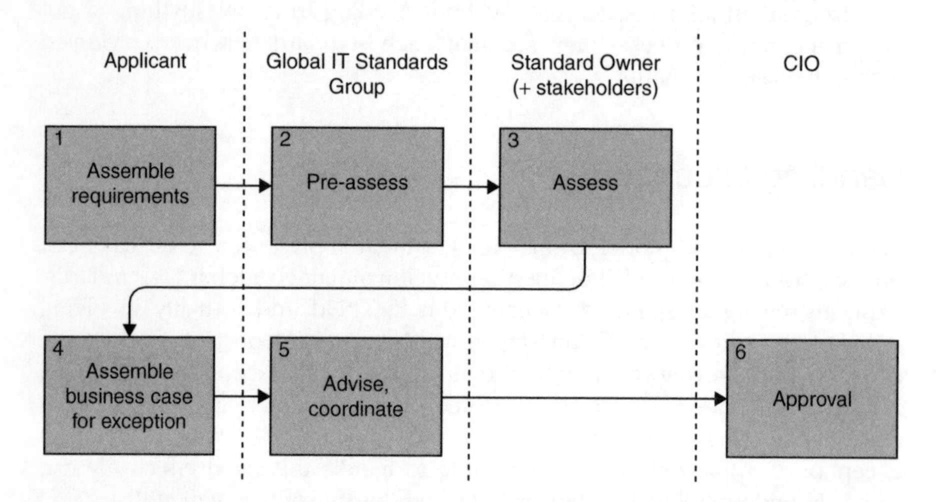

Figure 5.8—Work stream for handling exceptions to standards

The Global Standards Group works with the respective standard owner to moderate and support the request, ensuring a rapid response. The approval decision lies with the CIO: keeping decision making at such a high level reaffirms executive commitment to global standards and also implicitly cuts down on the number of requests that are presented. Should a multitude of minor requests start to accumulate, either an investment cut-off point can be set, below which exceptions can be approved locally, or decisions taken to date can be documented as precedents and used to automatically block or accept requests which arise with similar reasoning. Should several requests stem from the same standard, it may be time to have a review of the usefulness of the current standard definition or to consider introducing adherence incentive schemes as outlined on p. 97.

The process above aims to manage approval or rejection of exceptions whenever new solutions are being developed or existing infrastructure updated. Much of its success depends on the growth of dialogue and trust between Global Standards and the affiliates. Nevertheless, there may be a complementary need for more general control of adherence to standards in affiliates, one method being site visits and official internal audits. A softer, less intrusive approach is for affiliates to report an overall metric for adherence to standards as part of regular balanced scorecard reporting. For example, considering the annual investment on those technologies covered by global standards, the proportion expended on the standard technology or approved exceptions can be reported. This figure should in general be 100% and will only be lower if non-standard investments are made without approvals. Being in a position to commit to 100% means that local IT managers will need to track and promote local adherence to standards and the exception handling process.

Challenges to standards

One common occurrence associated with requests for exception approval is that the respective standard definition is challenged as being flawed. Although there may be an expectation within affiliates of a particular process for challenging standard definitions, the best approach is generally to avoid too much formality and establish a flexible dialogue between affiliate, owner and stakeholders to ensure that the justification for the standard is understood, and to decide on whether any revision is necessary.

Tool support

A consequence of the proposed active style of standards management is that the consolidated list of standards is updated regularly, if only in minor ways. As such, keeping standards documented in traditional paper form is inappropriate, and it makes sense for standards to be published and maintained online. The priority is to both publicize the local responsibility to check solutions compliance and clearly document the current reference list of global IT standard definitions, owners and last revision dates. Links to secondary pages can present additional details such as stakeholders, contract references, business cases justifying each standard, and other background material. Short e-mail notifications can be distributed whenever changes to the standards are made: the distribution list should include at least local IT planners, controllers and purchasers,[5] but also allow for others to add themselves to the distribution list online.

[5] Beyond needing to know standard definitions, local purchasing units may maintain online catalogues, and entries may need to be updated to match changes in standards.

One of the persistent themes of this book is the need to bring value to affiliates; an example in this chapter was negotiation of global volume discounts on chosen standards. The tool support for managing standards is another opportunity to bring value. Affiliates can use the same set of tools for managing their own local standards. The latter can be either standards not covered globally, or local details for global standards which leave certain choices open for affiliates. The system can present users working in a certain location with a locally relevant list of standards consolidated from global and local standards. The example Web site `www.gitm.biz/standards` demonstrates one possible approach.

Summary

This chapter presented a simple model for defining and managing global IT standards:

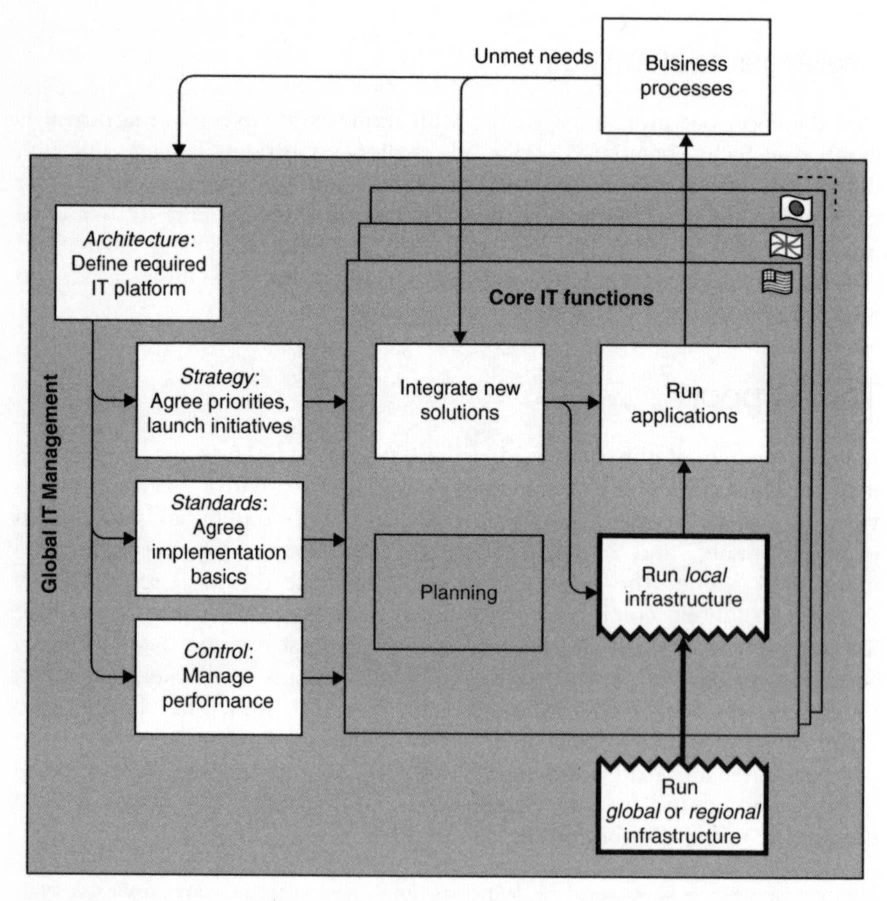

Figure 5.9—Standardization enables regional or global pooling of activities

- Justification of each global standard by an individual business case.
- Decentralized management of standards led by a small central group.
- Straightforward processes for standards definition, maintenance and exception handling.

Because of the accessibility of commercial benefits in standardizing commodity technologies globally, much of the focus has been on quickly achieving buy-in with affiliates for these items and carrying out single negotiations for global volumes with suppliers. These types of benefit can be achieved with the lean organization proposed, but they remain *tactical*.

Looking further ahead, it should be borne in mind that the greatest potential benefits of standardization lie with the *strategic* reorganization of standard activities, such as the regional consolidation of help desks or data centres as depicted in Figure 5.9. In such cases, the lean organization should still retain responsibility for the maintenance of the definitions of the associated standards, but the organizational change itself needs to be carried out by separate, fully blown project teams.

6 Control

Technology makes it possible for people to gain control over everything, except technology. J. Tudor

Introduction

The traditional role of the average controlling department is to tightly monitor and control the use of scarce and expensive resources in a firm. The focus is first and foremost on money, although people, too, are increasingly being recognized as a scarce resource and headcount is controlled almost as tightly as money. Management attention is drawn to IT controlling because of disproportionate growth in internal IT costs and headcount requirements, despite technology costs on the market appearing to be falling. Managers are naturally suspicious of this evolution. The reasons will depend on the firm, but are generally a mixture of expanding requirements due to business growth, exponentially increasing use of existing applications such as e-mail, and lastly accumulating running costs for new applications. In the latter case, the investigations made to ensure year 2000 compatibility showed clearly how many applications remain in operation well beyond their originally expected lifetime.

Even if the controlling department can trace the reasons for the rise in IT costs, the next challenge for IT managers is to show that the investment is worth it. Understandably, accountancy orientated IT controllers may shrug their shoulders at this stage, knowing that whereas an individual business has clear earnings to balance investment, no such financial measures of the value of IT can be taken. However, a key message of this chapter is that, while direct financial measures of the value of IT to a business remain difficult, other forms of value can still be measured, for example the extent of user satisfaction with applications or the reliability of networks. Controlling the value side of IT is important because the cynical expression "what you don't measure doesn't happen" applies to IT value and, furthermore, because presented together, costs and value are a better measure of IT performance than cost alone. It is this combination that can help managers answer the question whether IT expenditure is really worth it (Figure 6.1).

Especially when enthusiasm for IT tends to be sporadic, effectively controlling IT performance both in terms of cost and value over time forms a

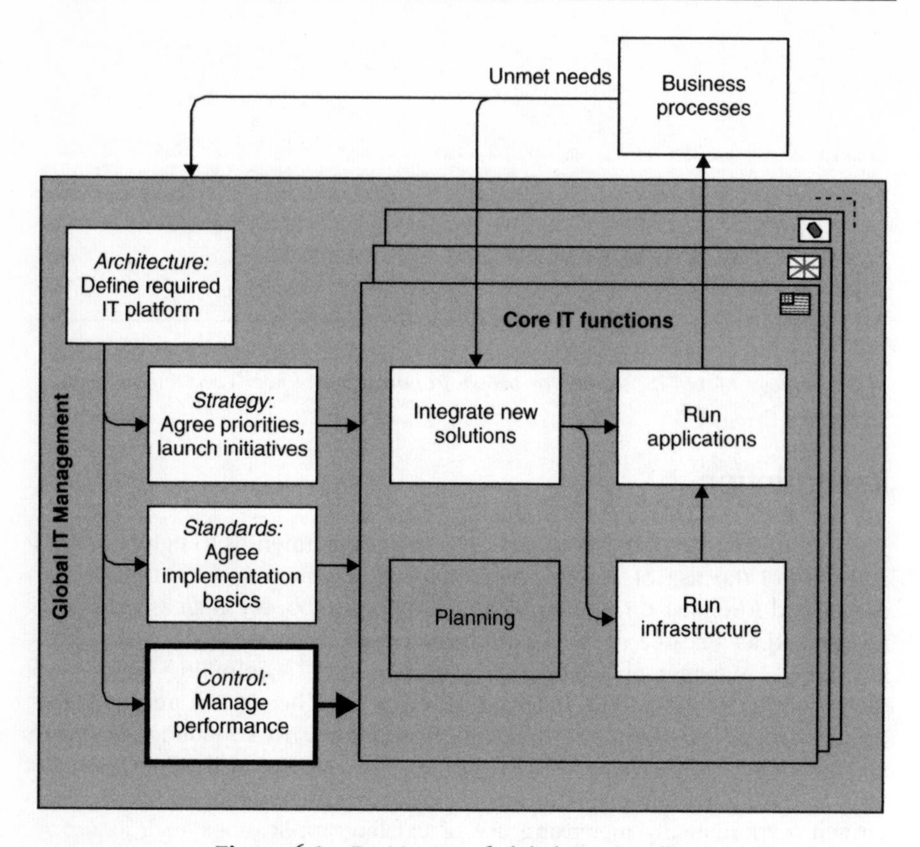

Figure 6.1—Positioning of global IT controlling

key foundation for correctly managing IT. Try applying some of the following questions to IT controlling in your enterprise:

- Is there credible control of both IT value and cost?
- Is the split across core IT activities such as new solutions integration or running infrastructure clear?
- Is the interface between global and local controlling clear and constructive?
- Can IT performance be compared across similar affiliates or organizations?
- Does control give useful insight into how to improve performance?
- What has been achieved by global IT controlling to date?

Introducing global IT controlling of costs and headcount will be a challenge in many companies, and combining this with value control makes this task admittedly more complex. If handled carefully, acceptance in affiliates can be good as the transparency offered in IT performance gives affiliates an effective tool for justifying and defending their IT budgets. This chapter proposes the following staged approach which aims to establish just enough control at a global level to be constructive, without being too intrusive and controlling activities which are best managed locally. The approach is as follows:

- IT accounting through partially allocated cost centres.
- Improved investment approval criteria for IT projects.
- Balanced scorecards in each major IT organization to manage performance.

Options and expectations

Managing most operations consists fundamentally of investing funds in people and machinery, following a particular process, and finally producing a certain result. Controlling aims primarily to provide the quantitative background to investments and results with a view to being better able to improve performance. The main parameters are money, headcount, risk and value, as depicted in Figure 6.2. Two factors, however, implicitly render control challenging. Factor one is that employees are directly impacted by headcount and budget constraints, and factor two is that control is usually imposed on a department from the outside, often by head office. Given this climate, it is worth considering the expectations the main stakeholders commonly have concerning IT control in a global company:

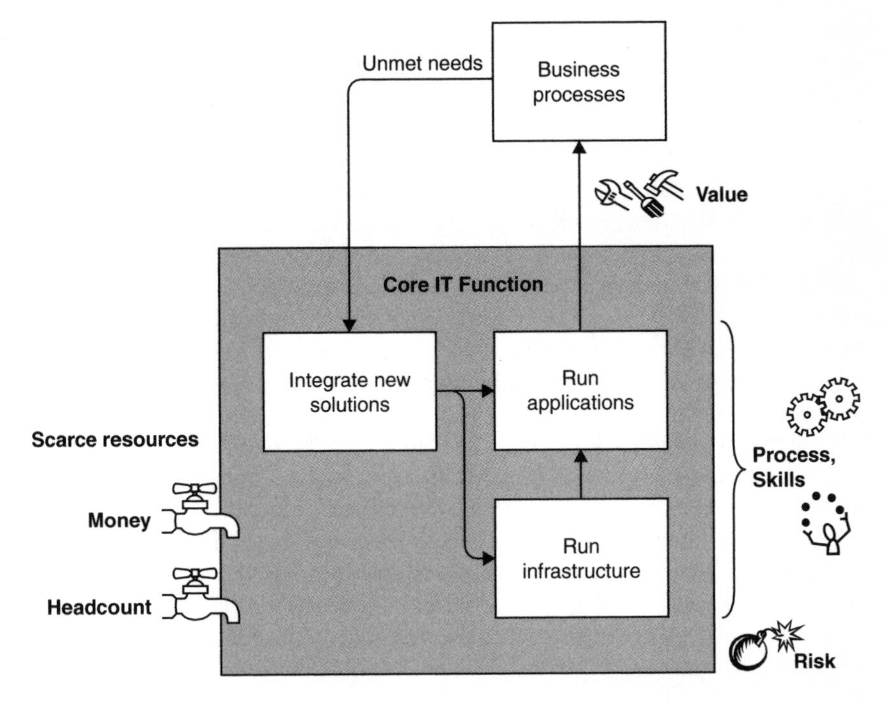

Figure 6.2—Conceptual view of the main IT control parameters

- *CEO*: One motivation behind the original creation of the CIO position can be the desire by the CEO to have a global counterpart for IT, following either visible local failures in IT, or the perception that IT costs are out of control locally. The main control expectation is to meet budget objectives and give a consolidated, quantified view of IT performance, benchmarked wherever possible against similar firms, if only to be reassured that performance is no worse than at the competition.
- *CIO*: In principle, a CIO would like to have all data on affiliates and functional IT organizations at his fingertips. In practice, the challenge is to isolate those few metrics which can reasonably be harmonized across units and yet faithfully represent IT performance and ultimately help justify IT budgets. While benchmarking non-financial value measures against competitors will always be hard, comparing performance internally across affiliates can be an excellent lever for improvement.
- *Local IT heads*: Most local IT heads feel closest to the affiliate they serve as they meet that business's information requirements, and that business essentially approves and finances the local IT operation. Additional controls imposed by head office are perceived as a further intrusive administrative hurdle and the value of comparisons across affiliates may not generally be appreciated initially.

In this environment, finding a working compromise in global IT controlling is not easy. Beyond the potentially conflicting demands of global and local units touched on above, two further issues make implementing truly effective control difficult. The first issue is that the point of departure in most organizations is a tight set of existing, mandatory financial controls. These are often institutionalized and changing them is rarely feasible, so new controls will usually be in addition to the existing ones. The second issue is that there is a large range of value controls that could potentially be beneficial to establish, but with the danger of simply increasing bureaucracy over and above that already associated with financial controlling. Experience shows that, as a result, global IT organizations commonly sacrifice the ability to control real performance by falling back to focusing just on financials, or at the other extreme, head office IT controls more aspects of local operations than it is really in a position to actively manage, slowing down local operations in the process.

Traditionally, control falls into the categories of overall annual financial planning in terms of budget approvals and progress tracking, and complementary specific approvals for individual investments exceeding certain threshold levels. Taking this as the initial control foundation, the main degrees of freedom open to global IT controlling are to be found in the way in which IT costs are accounted for, improvements in control in IT projects, and lastly the extension of controls to cover overall performance. The following sub-sections present each theme.

Cost accounting

While the greatest need today may be to extend control to include IT value, that is not to say that IT costs are already controlled perfectly, and there are a number of fundamental options for improving IT cost control. Foremost is the question of how IT cost accounting between IT and the business is set up. This is more than just a paper exercise when managers' performance assessments are potentially impacted by the choice in IT accounting. It is also an important reflection of the underlying relationship between IT and the business and can take one of the following three generic architectures:

- *Unallocated cost centre*: In an unallocated cost centre,[1] IT costs arising from service provision to the business are simply accumulated and funded as a separate function. IT services appear to business users as essentially free, and IT costs are not incorporated into line management appraisals. This set-up has the advantage of being transparent with low administrative overhead, but the lack of mutual accountability can lead to extravagant over-use of IT by the business or reduced business pressure on IT to be competitive.
- *Profit centre*: The profit centre is the exact opposite of an unallocated cost centre. Here IT is seen as a distinct business within a company, providing services at a profit to internal or even external business users. The belief must be that the information services provided are of more value to business users than the costs incurred providing them. Given the difficulty in directly measuring financial value of information services, this can only really apply to those particular services for which there is a general market and where a certain market price has been established, for example, payroll accounting. In such cases, IT as a profit centre can make sense provided that it fits the company culture and the business user has the opportunity to take alternative offers from the market and IT may serve other customers. The situation to avoid is where IT profits at the expense of the served business community.
- *Allocated cost centre*: An allocated cost centre is a form of hybrid between profit centre and unallocated cost centre. At its foundation is a cost centre where primary IT costs are accumulated, but IT can charge business users internal rates for certain well-defined services such as provision of desktop infrastructure. These "charge-outs" do not need to correlate exactly with the genuine points of cost generation arising from a certain service, in fact the most successful charge-out schemes allocate simple flat rates for something that the end user can identify with, for example a fee per transaction or a monthly fee for a certain help desk response level. It is important that there be mutual agreement that the charge is fair. The

[1] Unallocated cost centres may also be referred to as service centres.

allocated cost centre architecture takes a step towards commercializing IT by formalizing service in a number of areas and passing representative costs on to the served community, but without going so far as to replicate a free market situation with a profit centre approach.

In principle, the architecture should be selected that leads to optimal setting of IT resource levels in the budget negotiation process. In practice, the IT organization in a large global company can use a combination of these architectures according to the location, for example, using unallocated cost centres for small affiliates, allocated cost centres for large affiliates, and perhaps profit centres for specific regionalized commodity services. Be aware though that charges across business units, and more especially across national boundaries, will be viewed by the authorities as transfer pricing and be open to some scrutiny, so the charges need to correspond to the service implemented.

The choice of cost accounting architecture provides the overall framework for the business–IT relationship and provides the basis for consolidated cost information on IT globally. At a more granular level within IT costs, financial control of the distribution in cost between the core IT activities of new solutions integration, running applications and running infrastructure is an option. This is especially important when budget pressure tends to cut off new solutions integration, suffocating IT's response to evolving business requirements. Locally and globally, a decreasing proportion of investment in new solutions is an effective red flag in budget negotiations. Partly to avoid this scenario, some firms split the IT organization and budgeting between applications provision and infrastructure.

Control of IT projects

While the choice of accounting environment for IT costs forms the backdrop for the overall relationship between IT and the served business community, the warmth of the relationship is more directly affected by the value delivered by IT, and in particular the success or failure of IT projects. It is individual projects that historically over-run cost, under-deliver value and run high risks. In principle, acknowledged best practices in project management, such as those summarized in the Appendix, should address these issues. In practice, there are a number of worthwhile options for improving the investment approval process to explicitly control project performance:

- Methods can be institutionalized for drawing up cost, value and risk analyzes for use in investment approvals.
- Relevant decision-making bodies can be set up with the right people to judge each element, for example including not only financial representation, but also qualified personnel from IT and line management.

- Decision-making levels can be aligned appropriately to avoid unnecessary micro-management of local projects by head office which in some cases may already control overall project performance with other metrics.

Management of overall performance

Demand for IT evolves with the available technology and, as such, control based on historical cost alone does not always provide the best allocation of resources to IT. An analogy can be drawn with a police department. In the face of rising crime, it makes sense to combine department cost control with the volume of prevented or resolved crimes and popularity of service with the public. Likewise with IT, cost control can be combined with measurement of, for example, user satisfaction, service reliability and responsiveness. Such metrics can be incorporated directly into budget planning and interim reporting but, especially at a global level, this approach can deteriorate to a long list of incoherent metrics which take significant effort to gather, but on which little action is taken.

A far-reaching concept called *balanced scorecards* has proven more effective.[2] This simple but powerful concept is a combination of a standard performance representation in the form of scorecards and a mature methodology for implementing control on this basis. A scorecard normally displays about 16–25 business-specific controls, distributed evenly among the groups financials, customers, processes and learning as depicted in Figure 6.3.

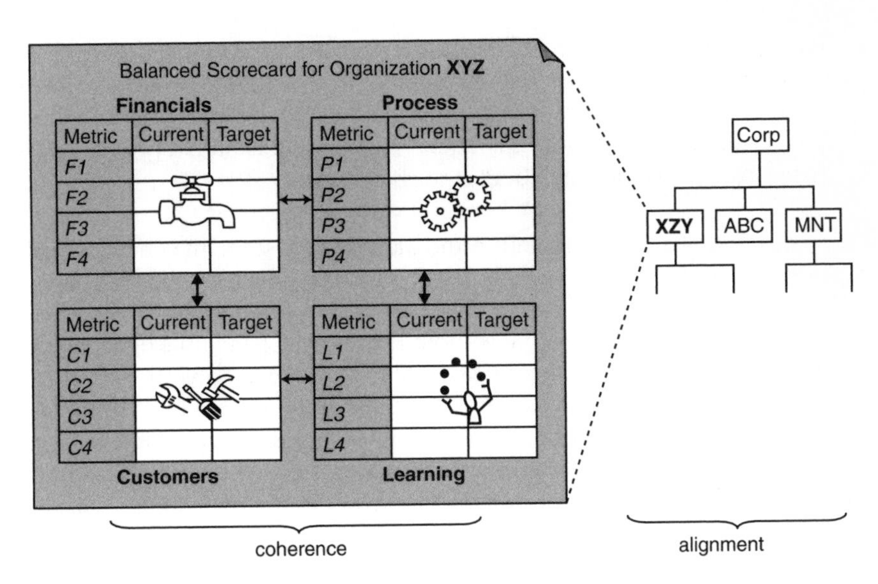

Figure 6.3—Balanced scorecards concept—for examples of metrics, see Table 6.1

[2] R. Kaplan and D. Norton, *The Balanced Scorecard*, Harvard Business School Publishing, 1996.

Together they render on a single page a balanced perspective of an organization's most important objectives and progress to date. Sub-organizations can also have their own respective scorecards. The scorecard methodology ensures that the metrics appearing in a scorecard will together lead to genuine performance improvement, and that the scorecards for respective parts of an organization are aligned with each other as a whole.

Balanced scorecards are usually seen in the context of performance management for entire businesses, but the very fact that they are "balanced" and include explicit customer views of value, makes the scorecard representation all the more attractive for cost centre management, and in particular IT. The real question is to what extent the scorecard methodology is applied to managing IT performance, and although it is more of a sliding scale, the following basic options are open in order of increasing sophistication:

- *Diagnostic tool*: The concept of balanced scorecards can simply be used carefully to extend budget planning and interim reporting to include a balanced set of non-financial controls summarizing operational performance. The main objective is to identify performance problems early.
- *Marketing and benchmarking tool*: As above, but the visibility of scorecards within a company can be widened to a larger audience, so that, for example, both business and IT communities have easy access to the scorecards either in paper form or online. The main objective is to use the transparency and compactness of scorecards for widely communicating operational priorities and demonstrating progress over time or across IT units.
- *Strategic change tool*: In the fully fledged scorecard methodology, the scorecards themselves are one component in a process to radically change an organization. The scorecard forms the fulcrum of activity and control, going well beyond simple operations to focus on strategic priorities. The main objective is to bring about strategic change.

The maturity of an IT organization and ultimately its strength of ambition will dictate the most suitable approach, but there are a number of further aspects worth considering. The low profile diagnostic approach requires affiliates to do all the effort of data gathering, but without reaping much tangible benefit. Local managers' degrees of freedom in managing local operations are cut down, and they may feel that this is simply one further burden from head office. The marketing approach requires the same effort, but sends a strong and welcome signal to the community that IT is measuring performance, and although the transparency can expose weaknesses, it can also support commercialization of IT service. Lastly, while the strategic change approach can be radical, many strategic priorities (for example those identified in the strategic planning process presented earlier in the book) do not lend themselves to meaningful metrics, and the demotion of financial control institutions implied by the focus on scorecards can prove difficult to realize.

Exhibit 6 – global IT control in featured firms

Philips

Beyond the high level committees for overall governance introduced in the section on strategy, several best practice mechanisms have been set up to maintain basic IT control. A common, transparent chart of accounts for IT costs is in place and costs are reported from over 1000 administrative units worldwide using a single reporting system. Consolidated costs are reported to the Board, with infrastructure accounting for about half of the costs, and of that about one third is dedicated to services run explicitly by corporate IT. For each corporate service, local service level agreements have been agreed and implemented, with adherence and customer satisfaction now monitored regularly. Sophisticated balanced scorecards for IT have likewise been implemented and linked explicitly to performance appraisals for personnel. Perhaps the most striking feature of IT control at Philips is a well-established system of peer reviews. These reviews are carried out both for major IT projects and IT operations in different parts of the organization, covering value, costs and risks for the IT activity in question. Review teams are drawn together from genuine peers taken from comparable units in the organization, for example including the head of IT at one location in the team to review IT value at another location.

Nestlé

Traditionally, IT spending levels and performance were managed solely by local, market-specific general management. This did, however, lead to uncontrolled increases in consolidated IT spending. In contrast, when deploying GLOBE to businesses, the IT budgets for expenditure are set centrally by the GLOBE initiative and, as a result, consolidated IT spending is expected to come rapidly under control. Concerning more general performance, the GLOBE solution includes a number of key performance indicators to enable performance management over time and across units. However, until the GLOBE solution is implemented, control concentrates absolutely on adherence to IT budgets and the timelines set for solution deployment. IT solutions must meet the deadlines to support planned business process changes.

Novartis

There are two distinct aspects to corporate IT control at Novartis. The first is the need, as in other companies, to effectively manage IT value and cost at an appropriate level of detail. The second aspect is more specific to the pharmaceutical and aerospace industries, and that is regulation. On the topic of value and cost, Novartis runs monthly cost and headcount reporting for all IT units to achieve tight cost control. This process is complemented by balanced scorecards run on a quarterly basis for each major IT unit and which are linked directly to manager performance appraisals. The scorecards all have the same basic composition and focus on establishing high level performance and business satisfaction in solutions delivery and running applications and infrastructure. The scorecards avoid unit-specific details and concentrate on key performance indicators that can be compared across units. The other important control aspect is regulation. Because of the potentially deadly impact in pharmaceuticals of system failures or errors, changes to critical systems are very tightly controlled and require compliance with a complete regulatory framework. For this purpose, a single, standard project methodology which meets all regulatory requirements has been established and is managed on an active basis at Novartis to ensure top project quality.

Toyota

Toyota practises full IT cost reallocation, including costs for global IT initiatives run by corporate IT. Regional IT costs are rolled up with plans globally and monitored by corporate business and IT planning. However, objective benchmarking across regions of overall costs, for example using the IT cost per car as a metric, remains challenging because of the fundamental differences in local market and dealer structure. More generally, the culture of conservative investment to date has kept overall IT expenditure under control, and today cost effort across regions focuses on opportunities for reducing primary IT costs through informal cooperation in vendor negotiations. Given that *ad hoc* comparison of vendor prices has shown divergences as high as 1 : 4 around the world, leveraging IT buying power globally is seen as a high potential opportunity to cut costs. Explicit value controls such as customer or user satisfaction are only implemented on a project-specific basis, as this is where the real business value is generated and where it is best measured.

UBS

IT control at UBS features the following three complementary approaches:

- Balanced scorecards have been implemented within each of the four IT units to control overall IT cost and value performance.
- Operative project steering committees with mixed executive business and IT membership are used as a tracking and monitoring mechanism for strategic IT projects and portfolios.
- Third-party companies are occasionally engaged to carry out objective health checks for strategic projects that carry significant inherent risk, or to benchmark specific aspects of overall performance in project delivery and operations.

Managing control

At its core, most global IT controlling activity is about collation of local IT performance data and focusing management attention on particular weaknesses or strengths. The challenge is to find a constructive level of control for head office to impose on affiliates. This is a judgement that needs to weigh up the potential benefits of wide-ranging performance information against the fact that most of the effort in collecting information lies with affiliates. The real test of success will be whether performance is genuinely improved as a result of insights drawn from global IT controlling.

The practical approach proposed here aims to extend affiliate controls to include value accountability in the complementary domains of cost accounting, project control and consolidated performance management. First, in cost accounting, the partially allocated cost centre architecture is used implicitly to help line management balance demand for IT with a feeling for the corresponding costs. In project control, basic value control practices for projects are established for use by local IT controlling. Finally, for performance management, the balanced scorecard is utilized as a marketing and benchmarking device, focusing especially on the core IT activities of new solutions integration, running applications and running infrastructure.

Overall, in all but the most advanced firms, coherently managing both cost and value for core IT activities across locations will be new, and while perhaps not welcomed locally, the service transparency and tangibility introduced will help develop trust between IT and line management, even before any performance improvements are made. What the lean approach does *not* do is explicitly control progress in execution of IT strategy. This remains the task of the IT Steering Committee, with global IT controlling concentrating, at least initially, on drawing up a realistic overall picture of core IT performance across affiliates.

The following sections present the organizational elements to the approach and the main steps to take for each of the themes of cost accounting, project control and balanced scorecards.

Organization

The proposed organization for global IT controlling builds almost entirely on the existing network of IT managers or respective controllers, with the exception of a small head office group dedicated to global IT controlling. The idea is to avoid unnecessary head office overheads, and at the same time to ensure that the extent of global intervention in local operations and controlling remains discrete and constructive. The following are the main groups involved:

- CIO responsible for leadership of global IT controlling.
- Global IT Controlling Group dedicated to managing the overall control process.
- Local IT heads and functional information managers responsible for local control.
- IT Board as a forum for acting on insights drawn from global IT controlling.

While the very act of controlling can lead to avoidance of potential performance aberrations, the target for global IT controlling is more proactive:

to move beyond mundane measurement and reporting towards bringing concrete insights to IT management, and in particular to the IT Board, on how to bring about performance improvement in terms of either cost or value (Figure 6.4).

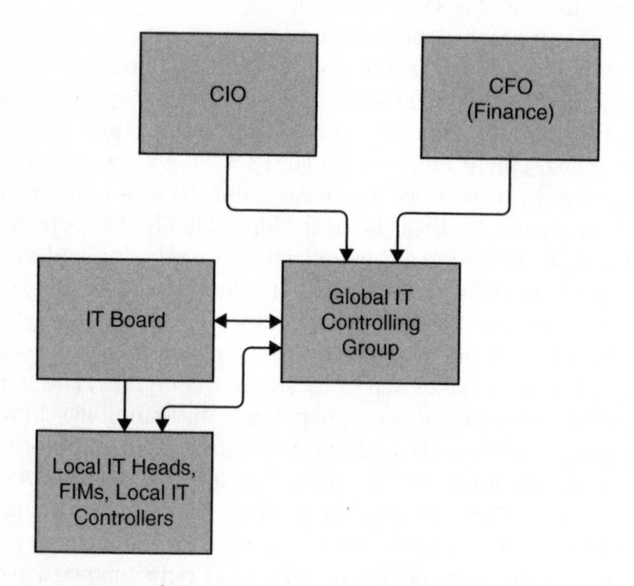

Figure 6.4—Global IT controlling organization

CIO — lead global IT control

The CIO inevitably plays the lead role in global IT control. Ensuring maximum effectiveness in use of scarce resources across affiliates is one of the CIO's prime responsibilities and encompasses three main tasks. Task one is to sell the chosen level of global control of affiliates to local IT heads, for whom the benefits of altering their existing controls simply to be in line with other affiliates may not be apparent. Task two is to sell the principle of taking a holistic view of IT performance including non-financial or headcount measurements to the CEO and local general managers, for whom the approach will usually be new. Lastly, the CIO needs to show sufficient midterm commitment to ensure follow-through on insights resulting from new controls.

Global IT Controlling Group — set up and moderate process

The Global IT Controlling Group is a small group dedicated to management of IT control on a global basis, reporting directly to the CIO. Depending on the alignment of IT controlling with overall business controlling, the group may have dual reporting to IT and Finance. In any event, while the extent of authority delegated to the group lies in the hands of the CIO, their main mandate remains to define and implement a set of global IT performance controls that are both useful locally and comparable across affiliates.

The group's activities are divided in roughly equal proportions across the task of bringing about a global change in controlling, actually running the global part of the control processes, and finally making something happen as a result:

- *Change*: The difficulty of establishing a simple, harmonized set of balanced controls to which affiliates adhere is not simply a matter of diplomacy. In most cases, any existing local reporting that takes place will be on the basis of information produced as a matter of course by their own systems, for example, help desk response times. Switching in the interests of global alignment to an alternative metric, say help desk resolution rates, may not be feasible without significant local effort to adjust systems and processes. The Global IT Controlling Group must lead the process to reach consensus and mutual commitment to a meaningful set of harmonized metrics and control procedures that still have sufficient bite to be of use to both affiliates and head office.
- *Operation*: Once global IT controls and procedures have been agreed, while much of the effort in information provision lies with affiliates, collecting, cleaning and analysing information globally still demands significant human intervention if the results are to be credible. In parallel, the Global IT Controlling Group still has to fulfil all the ongoing demands of the financial planning, budgeting and reporting processes.
- *Communication*: The Global IT Controlling Group needs to complement the challenging, but rather dry, task of global measurement with equal effort in effective communication of goals and results, both to those providing the information, and up to the CIO and IT Board. The aim is to widely communicate performance goals and for findings on progress to date to be sufficiently specific that real action can be taken to redress performance lapses or capitalize on revealed opportunities. Ultimately the group must ensure that global IT control of IT performance as a whole remains firmly on the IT Board agenda and progressively grows in strength *vis-à-vis* traditional cost control.

The skills required for these activities are wide-ranging. While the foundation still needs to be financial and accounting skills, there are two further prerequisite skills for success. One lies in being able to think beyond the security of a well-documented accounting framework to also consider the business environment, IT value and risk. The other skill lies in being able to communicate and persuade affiliates to adopt and act on the same notions. It is this combination of finance, value and change skills which can lead IT out of a regime of pure cost control.

Local IT heads and functional information managers – local control

The IT management community needs to work with the Global IT Controlling Group towards agreement on establishing and running at least a subset of globally harmonized controls, often in addition to any metrics they already use which may be more specific to local or functional requirements. While larger units may have dedicated IT controllers, needing to hire new local controllers simply to meet global IT controlling requirements is an alarm signal that either local control to date has been poor, or that too many new global reporting requirements are being imposed on local units.

IT Board – forum for learning and action

Introducing IT control globally and at the same time developing overall IT performance management alongside traditional financial constraints is not likely to be something a firm gets right first time, and should in general be regarded as an iterative learning process, correcting weaknesses and responding to new demands. The IT Board can be the ideal forum for both guiding evolution of global IT control and responding to findings from performance to date.

Funding

Requiring extensive funding for global IT control would be a slight, though not uncommon, contradiction in terms. For the proposed model, the explicit resource requirements should be funded by head office and are restricted to the Global IT Controlling Group and system requirements such as those for handling balanced scorecards and integrating these with existing systems. Note, however, that systems and consulting costs, especially in the balanced scorecard domain, can increase rapidly with the sophistication of system and process. Costs arising locally should be of an order of magnitude that they can be absorbed locally.

So far this chapter has covered the main domains in which global IT controlling can monitor and influence consolidated IT performance and proposed a lean organization model for implementing global IT control. The next three sections concentrate on presenting practical details for execution in each of the areas of cost accounting, project control and balanced scorecards. The recurrent challenge in each area is to identify and implement meaningful controls beyond cost and headcount that both IT and business counterparts recognize as representing particular aspects of IT performance.

Managing IT costs

Harmonized accounting for primary IT costs

In accounting for IT as a cost centre, the objective is to pool and control primary costs for IT, i.e. the money for IT that physically leaves the company, in the main as salary payments for IT employees, asset acquisitions, licence payments and other bought-in IT services. In a global context, for cost figures to be comparable across sites and consolidated figures to be useful, the same principles for recording IT costs need to be applied everywhere. This means adopting a common cost account structure and accompanying definitions. Without this, overall IT spending estimates may be inaccurate and misleading, and the basis will be missing for any consolidated budgeting for planned expenditure. Figure 6.5 shows one possible cost structure, adapted from a model used by Gartner Group.

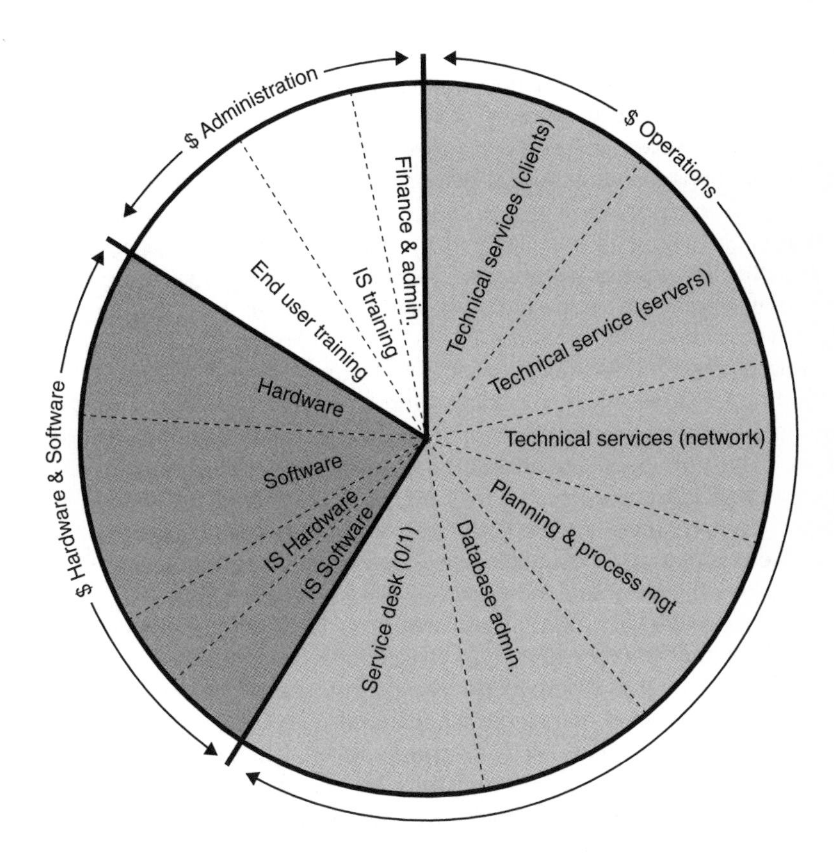

Figure 6.5—Sample cost account breakdown for controlling primary IT costs across sites (adapted from *TCO Manager for Distributed Computing, Chart of Accounts*, Gartner Group Inc., 1999)

Whichever cost structure is adopted, it is important that there is agreement on the scope of activities in a firm that fall within the domain of "IT". For example, are control systems for manufacturing tools, or home office systems for remote workers included? In such instances, one straightforward guideline can be labelling an activity as "IT" only if systems are connected directly up to the company networks. Within the agreed scope of IT activity, every effort should be made to bring residual primary IT costs still hidden in line function budgets out into the IT cost structure. For example, line functions may purchase their own PCs and simply require the IT department to run a service on that PC. This type of situation is not uncommon, but such accounting contributes to understatement of IT costs and, more subtly, the sense of ownership and the costs for mid-term management of the PC as an asset lie erroneously with the business function, not IT.

Allocating IT costs

Internally reallocating some or all primary costs back to the business functions within the firm receiving IT service is an administrative option, proposed here, for retaining business awareness of the cost of IT services they use. Incorporating these secondary costs in functional costing boosts line budgets for which line managers have to compete, and on which basis their performance is usually appraised. As a result, there is (intended) business sensitivity to the extent of use of IT services and the respective levels of cost allocation, and much management attention is commonly devoted to securing equitable allocation schemes. Nevertheless, it should be borne in mind that it is primary IT costs that impact business results and, at least within affiliates, handling of secondary costs in cost allocation does not impact overall results. Analogous to the budgets themselves, the temptation should be avoided to invest more time on internal negotiation or wrangling than actually providing the required service. The option of reallocating IT costs remains, like transfer pricing, a business policy decision.

Seen globally, there are two levels to view cost reallocation. At a global level, there is potential cost-reallocation by Global IT Management to IT organizations in affiliates or global business functions at head office. At a local level there is cost-reallocation within affiliates from IT to served functions. In the case of Global IT Management, cost reallocation or "charge-outs" to affiliates should remain more of an exception than the rule. Certainly, none of the global planning activities shown in Figure 6.1 warrants reallocation, but should particular infrastructure services, such as desktop systems administration, be offered globally, such services may meaningfully be charged out, similar to transfer pricing for products between head office and affiliates. For such services, the key used for determining the distribution of charges between affiliates will normally be the number of users profiting from the service in each affiliate.

At the local level of cost reallocation from IT to served business lines within an affiliate, local IT departments need to set up, if they have not already done so, cost reallocation. This should be the product of local dialogue between IT and business counterparts and encompasses the following main tasks:

- Confirm that primary IT costs, assets and headcount are accounted for properly within IT.
- Establish what services IT runs and how associated costs are generated.
- Agree which services should be charged out, and what the allocation mechanisms should be.

The question here is the extent to which head office needs to be involved in what are primarily local issues, but there are drivers in favour of head office involvement. For example, there may be pressure, generally from global functions, for harmonization in particular services across affiliates. Furthermore, the development effort required for service definitions can be substantial, and yet the basics are normally similar across affiliates. In this instance, Global IT Controlling can lead transfer of best practices across affiliates, irrespective of whether service definitions are subsequently harmonized. Important in both cases is the contribution of Global IT Controlling more in the sense of assistance than control and intervention. The next paragraphs present the main issues that need to be covered and that relate directly back to the tasks highlighted above.

Once the scope of IT activities has been defined and all associated primary costs are handled by IT, the focus moves towards identifying the range and nature of individual services provided to the business. Mature IT organizations may already have taken this step; for the remainder, the functional structure of the local IT organization is one starting point together with the interface to the served business community, as illustrated in Figure 6.6.

With services broadly identified, the task begins to reach agreement with business counterparts on which services can be charged out and on what basis, i.e. a service catalogue. Seen by the business community, the charge-out levels should appear reasonable in relation to the value of service, and the charges should be equitably distributed across the user populations served. Seen by the IT community, charges should simply recover costs incurred. But a number of challenges arise in finding a compromise:

- Dissecting out IT costs incurred in provision of a service can be difficult.
- The real end value of a service to the business user cannot normally be quantified.
- Free market prices cannot normally be used as a benchmark, as service scope is seldom the same and potential service providers often artificially depress prices to secure an initial contract.
- While IT costs experience peaks and troughs, business users want predictability in service costs.

Although many systems are available for calculating allocations, their sophistication makes them suffer from being less transparent and, as a general rule,

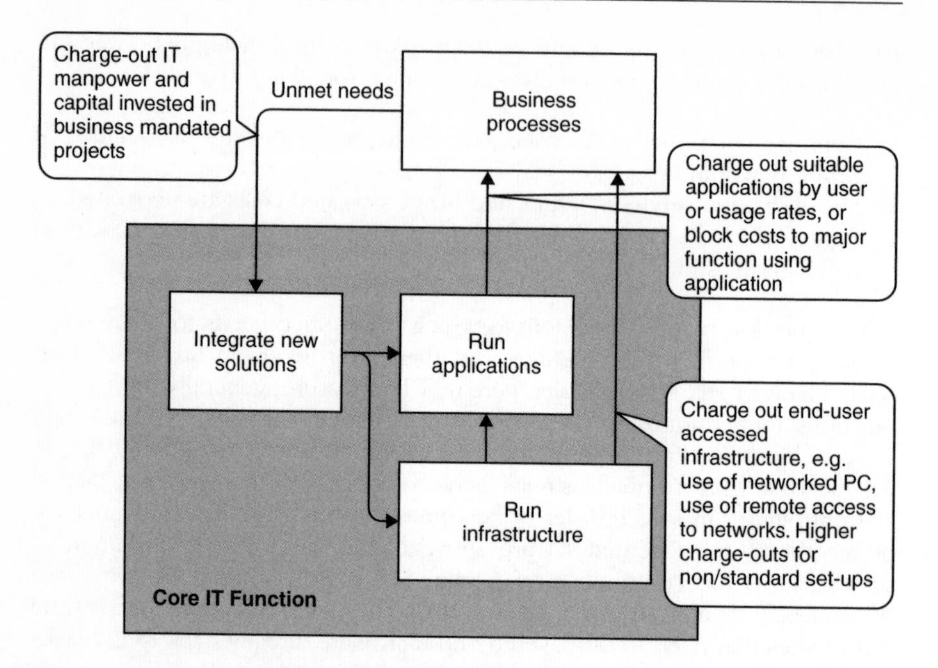

Figure 6.6—Example IT service cost reallocations

the more successful allocation schemes take a simplified approach which both IT and business users can understand and agree to, independent of whether the scheme truly relates to underlying cost generation. The issues that arise depend on the category of service in question:

Integration of New Solutions: Handling of charge allocation in integration of new solutions is relatively straightforward, as it is fairly clear that costs are generated primarily through time and capital employed. However, particularly with infrastructure upgrades and similar projects, although required as a result of overall volume growth, there is no particular business customer there to pay for the project. If costs for such projects are to be reallocated, then this can be covered by a contingency block within general charge-out for use of basic infrastructure and networks. For those projects mandated explicitly by the business, an agreement between IT and business needs to be set up defining the internal cost recovery rate for hours employed, and estimates of both the expected hours and capital required. If these costs are fixed, then it should be clear who absorbs any later variance. In any event, the criteria, such as scope change, for interim cost reassessment need to be agreed.

Running Applications: Running particular applications and providing application specific support should in general be charged out. The classic example is ERP systems which together with related costs can account for up to 50% of the IT budget. One issue is that the user population may not be well identified in an early stage, which makes flat per user rates difficult, but even where the population is clear, the volume of usage can increase dramatically over time. In the latter case, agreeing on a flat rate for example per transaction can circumvent problems with the population size and usage, although the charge-out is not directly related to what generates costs. Another choice that needs to be made is how to deal with increases in user population. Charge-outs for new users can be made at the same original rate, or marginal cost, i.e. just that extra cost incurred for every new user, or full cost plus which essentially demands a premium for using a well-tested, risk-free system. Independent of the allocation scheme used, it is important that well-founded estimates of ongoing application running costs are included from the beginning in the project business case. These are often underestimated, and yet the steady rise in consolidated IT operational costs despite falling market prices for technology is a testament to the longevity and magnitude of application costs.

Running Infrastructure: Flat rate per user charges for infrastructure services such as desktop infrastructure provision, maintenance and help desk operations can be agreed. These costs will, however, be harder to reach initial agreement on, as the sources of IT cost generation are complex and less transparent to the business community. As with applications, expansion of service volume can be charged at original rates including perhaps some overhead, or marginal rates. Both in infrastructure and applications agreements, the definition of cost allocation schemes occurs in conjunction with a defined service level, for example the time windows when the help desk is available, or systems maintenance windows limited to particular times at weekends.

Overall, it should be remembered that the whole idea of cost reallocation is to pass back representative costs to business users in the interests of motivating both IT and business counterparts to extract the best from IT. Nevertheless, the temptation to spend too much time on over-refining allocation schemes should be avoided (that only becomes a real necessity in outsourcing), and any subsequent end-of-term variances between primary costs and recovered costs need not be charged out. Doing so provides an unwelcome IT sting in the tail to line functions.

Project control

The implementation of cost reallocation provides an overall accounting environment which fosters attention to IT cost and value by line functions, but it is far from guaranteeing the wisdom of individual IT investments. IT project costs have been shown to be underestimated by an average of 30–50% and the frequency of conspicuous project failures is an indicator of the extent to which project risks are likewise underestimated. At the same time, beyond the growing dependence of businesses on IT, the cumulated benefits of deployed systems are not closely monitored.

So who is responsible for taking care of projects? Considering the life cycle of an average IT project, running from planning, resourcing and development through to deployment and operation, it is clear that the bulk of the responsibility for a project lies with project management or, for large projects, with the respective project steering committee. The proposed approach to global control aims to leave this in the hands of local IT organizations and to concentrate solely on improving the framework for the original investment approvals for projects. The exact approval or sign-off processes vary from firm to firm, with some IT departments having dedicated controlling of their own, and others using the business controlling processes. However, they usually share an implicit escalation of decision making that can make good judgements on IT projects difficult. The reason is that with difficulties in the quantification of costs and benefits, decision makers really need to understand the whole context, and yet they are often too far removed from the project to genuinely appreciate the issues.

A preliminary step that can be taken is to ensure that an objective mix of representatives from finance, line functions and IT is used for major project investment approvals, with each party contributing its understanding of cost, value and risk to the discussion. The follow-up is to extend standard guidelines for IT submissions for approval to require specification of project boundary conditions that have proved to be recurrent weaknesses. The following are the main elements that can sensibly be controlled at the investment approval checkpoint:

- Where the scale or impact of the project warrants it, an objective project steering committee should be defined that takes ownership of the project.
- The business case for the project should be clear, specifying business impact and projected costs, benefits and risks. More will be said below about the IT specific factors to consider.
- The proposed solution should be compared with rejected alternatives, in particular the "do nothing" scenario covering the situation today and expected evolution, for example in operational costs, if the project is not undertaken.
- Interim review points for the project steering committee should be agreed, and basic criteria specified in advance for stopping the project.
- The main project deliverables and metrics by which promised benefits can be subsequently confirmed should be specified. The project plan must correspond feasibly to these objectives.

Most of the points above are fairly routine, but constructing the core business case usually remains a real challenge. The temptation should be resisted to rely solely on vociferous business support for the project, and a genuine attempt made to crystallize out a coherent business case from the projected project costs, benefits and risks. There is no single method for carrying out this analysis and the approach will need to be adapted to the project circumstances, but there are some basic starting points for projecting costs and benefits. The following apply to tracing project costs or required investment:

- Direct or tangible costs can be established for software, hardware, development, deployment, training, operations, maintenance and overhead. In some cases such as major hardware acquisitions, costs may be capitalized, although rules depend on location.
- Costs can be measured as marginal costs or full costs. In marginal costs, only those extra, incremental costs resulting directly from the project are reported, for example the purchase of assets, but not salary costs for involved employees which need to be paid anyway. In full costs, the latter are included, as while the salary will in any event need to be paid, those employees could have been dedicated to some other, potentially more worthwhile, project.
- The evolution of costs over time throughout the life cycle of a system until retirement needs particular attention. Experience shows that transition and mid-term running costs with increased usage are easily underestimated.
- Further indirect, often intangible, costs are the business impact of disturbance and distraction during transition, and business side effort patching up weaknesses in project delivered training and support, for example, peers regularly helping each other out on how an application works.

The counterbalance to the above costs in the business case are the expected benefits. These can be evaluated using the following considerations as a starting point:

- The most straightforward tangible benefits are cost displacement or cost avoidance. In the former, existing costs are reduced, for example by automation of a manual task. In the latter, impending costs are avoided, for example by upgrading systems to avoid year 2000 incompatibility costs.
- A wider and normally business driven class of tangible benefits is profit enhancement. This refers to more generic improvements in productivity, efficiency, reliability or effectiveness of business operations, for example introducing a new computer-aided design system for use in product development. Of prime importance is to identify the immediate change made by the project and trace the ultimate impact on operations and express it in a meaningful way; in this particular instance it could be a certain expected reduction in product development times.
- Rendering the benefits of infrastructure investments tangible remains difficult. In general, tangible benefits can be sought in application-specific requirements, reduction in operating costs, replacement of obsolete technology, and coping with increasing volumes and peaks in information processing. Intangible benefits can also sometimes be identified, for

example the impact on sales force image from being seen to be equipped with a modern laptop.

In theory, it should be possible to analyze every distinct cost or benefit and express it in financial terms, but be aware that doing so can involve making so many assumptions that the end result lacks realism and undermines the credibility of the business case as a whole. In such cases, a more pragmatic approach is simply to identify cost and benefits, quantify those that can be quantified (although not necessarily in financial terms), and finally wherever the result will be meaningful, translate costs and benefits to financial terms. As a consequence, any summary financial approval criteria such as payback period or net present value which can only be based on financial inputs, will need to be complemented by statements on non-financial costs and benefits.

Risk assessment is the third ingredient to the business case. Risks need to be assessed on two levels. The first is technical and consists of reviewing each cost or benefit and considering how likely it is that each is going to occur. A best case, worst case and most probable case can be drawn up to render the risk and variability of the business case more plastic. The second level looks beyond the promised costs and benefits and concentrates on the high impact risks of failure due to a variety of circumstances often related to the complexity or novelty of the project. These risks need to be anticipated and a risk mitigation plan set up. Together, the identified costs, benefits and risks then form the core of any IT project business case.

The role of Global IT Controlling in the project control landscape needs careful definition. On the one hand, the best place to control projects is where they occur, i.e. locally, but on the other hand, every local project failure is also a failure of global IT as a whole. This given, the best role for the Global IT Controlling Group is to work together with affiliates to enhance investment approval decisions for projects to include the key boundary elements introduced above, such as advance definition of project termination criteria.

Implementing balanced scorecards for IT

Accounting for IT costs using partially allocated cost centres and tightening IT project control fosters joint awareness of cost and value for individual IT services. For example, each time a line function envisages a new IT application, the potential business value of the application will be weighed up against the costs and expected charge-out. But this link between cost and value remains fine grain and at the level of individual investments. It does not provide any overall view of the relation between cost and value of an IT organization as a whole. This is the role that balanced scorecards can play for IT.

A balanced scorecard is intended to be an instant picture of an organization's intentions and performance. Scorecards have a certain form, consisting of four standard quadrants, each dedicated to summarizing performance in one of the following perspectives:

- *Financial*: This perspective focuses on financials, such as profit and sales growth. For IT as a cost centre, the focus is on investment levels of money, people and any other scarce resources required for meeting information needs of the served business community.
- *Customer*: This perspective focuses on how well customer needs are met, for example, value for money, ease of interaction and customer fidelity. For IT, the customer is usually the business community served, and the focus is on how well that community is served and how positively they perceive service.
- *Process*: This perspective looks within the operations of an organization, and focuses on how well the organization works internally. For IT, this may be the processes for producing reliable service, or the quality of project management.
- *Learning*: This perspective captures how well an organization is equipped to respond to opportunities and adapt to the future. For IT, which is dominated by evolving technology and a fluid job market, the emphasis may be on how well skills are developed and qualified staff retained.

Experience has shown that this particular group of perspectives best summarizes organizational performance. Although quadrants may be superficially renamed to reflect business–specific nuances, say from "Learning" to "Innovation", overall, these four quadrants should all be present in any scorecard.[3] The contents of the quadrants are, however, more flexible. Each quadrant may contain four to six business-specific controls or metrics that dictate a certain direction and measure some distinct aspect of performance in that perspective, for example the annual personnel turnover rate in the learning quadrant. More candidate IT metrics are shown in Table 6.1.

What distinguishes scorecards from any other list of controls or key performance indicators is the balance and discipline of scorecard composition together with established best practices for managing an organization on the basis of scorecards. In IT, scorecards are the opportunity of using an industry best practice for formally presenting IT value directly alongside cost. That given, one of the prerequisites in considering scorecards is to be clear on the overall objectives, as despite their straightforward appearance, scorecards have (in common with any other performance management approach) as many potential objectives as there are consulting companies providing corresponding services.

The target assumed here is to meet the immediate needs of a globalizing IT community composed of a number of historically autonomous local IT organizations which largely perform the same information service for their respective business communities. Note that while strategic priorities can be incorporated into scorecards, here this is not a prime objective: managing

[3] Scorecards for certain businesses, such as oil exploration firms, include an additional "environment" quadrant, but this should not be necessary for IT.

Table 6.1—Example base performance metrics for each balanced scorecard perspective or quadrant

Financial metrics	Notes
Annual budget, #IT headcount, #users served, #networked seats	Best expressed in ratios for comparability across different sizes of organization
Annual budget as percentage of sales	May substitute functional budget for sales in IT organizations serving cost centre functions. Contains many factors beyond IT's influence
Proportion of budget expended on integration of new solutions	Need unambiguous definition of what a business driven project is and distinction to upgrades to existing systems
Annual budget per 100 served users	General impression of cost levels by population
Annual running cost per networked PC	Care required when users have more than one PC, or several users share the same PC
#IT headcount per 100 served users	Need to define whether external personnel included, and criteria for defining who is within IT, e.g. at least 50% technical IT related activity
Customer (business user) metrics	**Notes**
Average #days to bring new employee online from notification	One measure of responsiveness that makes initial impression on new employees
Proportion of helpdesk calls resolved on first call, or proportion of calls resolved within x hours	Parameters used in help desks vary widely
Proportion of top x projects delivered according to plan, i.e. time, budget and quality	Hard to define margins for adherence to commitments. Projects selected by affiliates and details available if required
Business satisfaction index concerning quality of IT staff in integration of new solutions	Preferably on scale 0–100, harmonized scope and approach across affiliates

Table 6.1—*(continued)*

Customer (business user) metrics, Cont'd	Notes
User satisfaction index on infrastructure and applications service provision	As above. Need to specify which applications and service levels promised. Measure satisfaction on extent these promises held
Internal process metrics	**Notes**
#critical outages over x months	Need to define threshold business interruption time, e.g. more than 4 hours is critical
% projects adhering to project management guidelines such as Prince2	Need to define threshold criteria for projects to qualify, e.g. project budget
% services conforming to service management guidelines such as ITIL	Need to define threshold criteria to qualify, e.g. service budget
% availability of infrastructure within committed window, e.g. five days a week from 06-20 : 00	Normally produced as part of service management
% availability of top x apps within committed window	Applications need to be defined by affiliate and details available if required
Learning metrics	**Notes**
#international job rotations	Only feasible for large affiliates
Average #days training per annum per IT employee	May need to define focus for training, e.g. best practice project or service management
IT employee satisfaction index	Preferably on scale 0–100, harmonized scope and approach across affiliates
% annual IT personnel turnover	Optimum depends on country and company culture but is rarely zero
Average #days to recruit new employee from opening of new position	Need to define from when to start counting and when to stop, e.g. contract signed
Proportion of external IT personnel	For example by external headcount over total headcount

global IT strategy lies in the hands of the IT Steering Committee. The objective of the described approach is to use scorecards as a vehicle for securing baseline IT performance:

- Use scorecards as a tool for communicating transparent baseline priorities and marketing progress to IT and business communities.
- Implement benchmarking across units to learn from best and worst performers and improve consolidated performance over time.

These objectives form only a subset of the more strategic ambitions of scorecards, but be aware that implementation is still faced with the same challenges as other scorecard initiatives. Seen practically, there is a real danger that the objectives remain unmet and that scorecards become another paper exercise for head office. Overall, industry experience shows that a sequence of five key tasks needs to be followed for scorecard initiatives to be successful,[4] and while the original focus of the methodology is on strategy, there are some relevant messages for IT scorecards:

- *Translate strategy to operational terms*: Fundamental business aims need to be expressed as practical and measurable targets which essentially form the corporate level scorecard.
- *Align the organization to the strategy*: Each organization within the business needs to be aligned with the corporate level scorecard by having its own set of measurable targets which contribute tangibly to overall success.
- *Motivate*: Individual goal setting, incentive and appraisal systems need to be aligned so that everyone is genuinely motivated to meet scorecard targets.
- *Learn and adapt*: Scorecards need to be linked in with the budgeting process, and regular dialogue established both to act on information and adapt targets to changing conditions.
- *Mobilize change*: Executive leadership must actively mobilize strategic change.

The process proposed incorporates each of the above principles, but uses a more mundane, project orientated breakdown in terms of scorecard development, scorecard deployment and scorecard operation, as depicted in Figure 6.7. In any event, given the breadth of potential objectives and pitfalls of scorecard projects, the whole initiative should be handled as a formal project with an agreed mandate specifying scope, deliverables and milestones. The latter are especially important as initiatives are commonly stalled by exaggerated analysis in the scorecard development phase and the time implicitly taken until concrete results can appear. Amidst all the intricacies and debate in scorecard rollouts, at a low level, the following basic milestones to demonstrating results should be borne in mind:

[4] Balanced Scorecard Collaborative, Inc., 2002, see `www.bscol.com`.

- First definition of scorecards agreed.
- First data collected and reviewed.
- First targets agreed and linked to appraisal schemes.
- First progress review.

Figure 6.7 presents the overall process for implementing balanced scorecards for IT—the text following goes into detail on the main steps in the process.

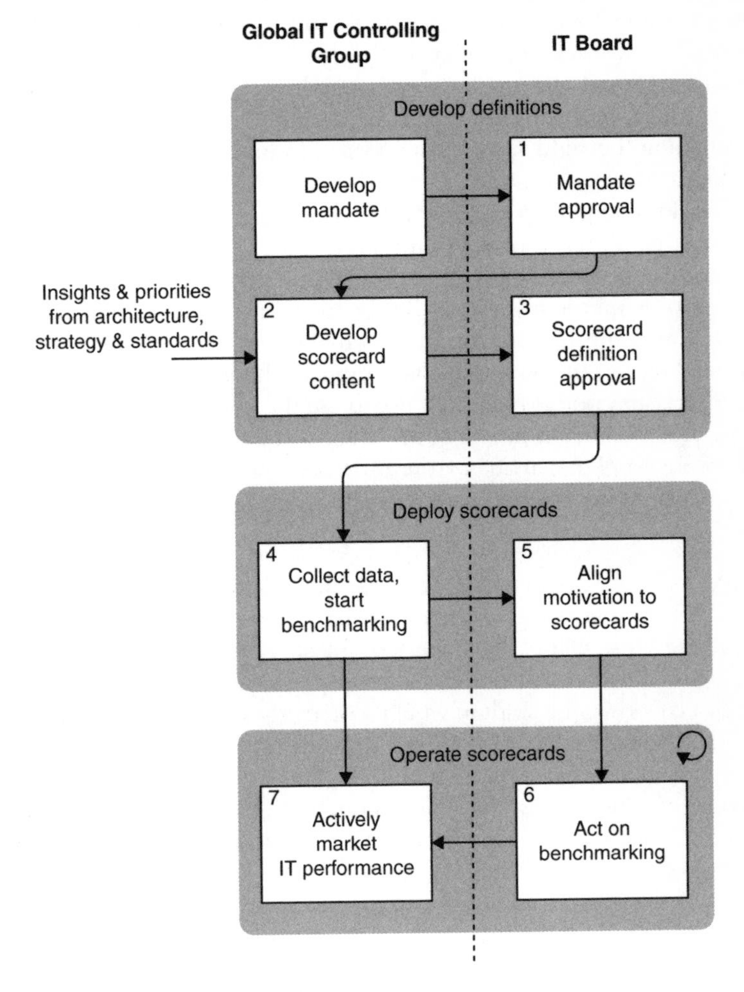

Figure 6.7—Schematic work stream for implementing balanced scorecards for IT

Develop definitions

There are two fundamental ingredients to successfully developing scorecard definitions. The ingredient that traditionally catches much attention is the need to carefully define scorecard content. Despite the compactness of a scorecard, substantial understanding and discipline are required if those few metrics chosen are to focus everyone's efforts meaningfully, while not excluding anything important. The other key ingredient is people and commitment. This is true in all scorecard initiatives, but even for IT scorecards as a simple marketing and diagnostic tool, it can be seen that commitment is crucial. It is not only that affiliate IT departments are burdened with data collection, rather the fact that performance differences across affiliates will be made transparent and widely communicated. Fortunately, scorecards at least provide a balanced form of comparison, but, nevertheless, local IT heads will feel potentially exposed in a similar way to employees when salaries are listed on the department bulletin board. Clearly, as much attention needs to be paid to maintaining the right spirit in the scorecard initiative as to defining perfect scorecard contents.

Key to addressing the people aspect of scorecards is to establish the IT Board as the main governance platform for launching, approving and implementing the scorecard project. While the CIO necessarily plays a strong role, the aim should be preferably for the IT Board to assume overall ownership of scorecards as a mechanism for improvement, with the Global IT Controlling Group leading the process and doing most of the work. The two particularly sensitive decision points for the IT Board are the initial approval of the project mandate and the later approval of the scorecard definition, and the Controlling Group needs to plan activities around consecutive IT Board meeting dates to ensure that both are openly discussed and reach IT Board agreement.

Mandate (Step 1): As in other projects, the mandate is essentially an early formal agreement on the intended work. In the case of IT scorecards, it needs above all to clarify the intended objectives, the team, the timetable for delivering results and, last but not least, implementation policy. The latter can be used to lay down the spirit in which scorecards are introduced, that is, not as further constraints imposed on affiliates by head office, but rather as a genuine method of organizational learning and a point of departure for discussion and improvement. Concerning the team, though Global IT Controlling forms the core, the IT Board should be invited to provide delegates to actively assist in the project, or at least to name people to be consulted in the lead up to scorecard definition. Adequate global representation in the team pools overall expertise and ensures that maximum consensus building takes place early in scorecard definition. Each of these topics needs to be debated and agreed by the IT Board before work on content starts.

Develop Content (Step 2): Two major simplifications to scorecard definition have been made here. The first is that the emphasis on reflecting baseline IT performance means that the scorecard can draw on many established service metrics. The second is that if comparable units are to be meaningfully benchmarked against each other, then the core scorecard definitions need to be the same, so there need only be as many scorecard definitions as there are distinct types of IT organization in the firm. For example, if a firm consists entirely of local IT departments serving respective affiliates, they can all have the same type of scorecard. Should there also be functional IT organizations serving global functions, they can have another scorecard definition. This given, the task consists of developing one or two scorecards. More will be said below on the technical considerations in drafting scorecard content, but in practice and emphasizing the theme of people and commitment, the project team needs to work through the following sequence:

- Collect views on the one or two driving objectives for each respective scorecard quadrant.
- Build consensus on which set of objectives best crystallizes overall IT aspirations and performance.
- Collect information on which metrics can feasibly be used across affiliates to quantify objectives.
- Draft alternative scorecards and document effort required to implement each.
- Collect feedback, refine alternatives and build consensus across the team on recommendations.

Definition Approval (Step 3): When discussing scorecards, it is very easy to become caught up in technical details which should already have been clarified by the core team. In many cases, when presented with a single scorecard for approval, deliberations can take longer than if asked to select a preferred scorecard from three or four alternatives. Whichever approach is taken, agreement should be reached that the chosen scorecard genuinely gives a balanced sense of objectives for IT, and that metrics will give a fair measure of progress. Certainly, the recommendation is not to insist on perfection, but to secure a sensible initial definition and allow explicitly for adaptation later. Following agreement on scorecard content, the project should be promoted to the deployment stage, committing in particular to timelines for starting data collection and presenting collated data for review.

The next few paragraphs return to the technical challenges of developing IT scorecard content, to give some input on possible metrics and the range of considerations that can be taken in constructing a scorecard. Following the scorecard methodology, the first task in developing scorecard definitions is to translate strategy into operational terms, i.e. to express what it is that a business is trying to achieve in an everyday, measurable manner that people can identify with and act on. The standard concept used to do this translation is known as a strategy map and is based on the premise that to achieve, for example, market leadership in profitability, this requires improvement in, say, customer fidelity and brand awareness, and streamlined production processes. This might in turn require a preceding change in the skills and competencies within the workforce. A strategy map traces the dependence of financial success on other enabling improvements back through customer, process and learning domains. With discipline, the result is a coherent and compact set of key objectives from which the final scorecard is derived by identifying relevant metrics for each objective.

In the context of scorecards as a benchmarking tool for IT, strategy maps may not always be the best approach to reaching a set of relevant objectives. As an alternative, the core IT activities of new solutions integration, running applications and running infrastructure can be considered, and the question asked: what needs to happen in each scorecard perspective for service to be improved? For example, perhaps major programmes are in place to develop skills in new technologies such as e-business, but no sooner are they trained than employees leave the company. Under such circumstances, a simple objective could be to develop and retain skilled personnel. It is important that the objectives are coherent and crystallize overall priorities for affiliate IT organizations. If other types of IT organization are present, such as regionalized service centres or functional IT organizations, these in turn will probably need their own sets of objectives according to the organizational type.

Although objectives and interdependencies form the roots for the original derivation of the IT scorecard for an affiliate, the real mid-term focus of attention will shift to the metrics and targets chosen to record progress towards each objective. To help generate ideas, some generic examples of metrics are presented in Table 6.1 and many others can be found in the literature.[5] In each case, the ultimate choice of a metric will be a compromise between the ideal measure of an objective and the data practically available in affiliates, but there are a number of general checks that should be made:

- Does the scorecard contain 16 to 25 metrics equally distributed among scorecard quadrants? Is there a rough balance between measures of recent performance and measures of efforts which will only bear fruit in the future?
- Is each metric clearly and unambiguously defined, meaningful and measurable? Is it within the power of IT to influence values and will values be comparable across different sizes of organization? The latter can be helped by stating values using, for example, per user ratios. Does the frequency of measurement, for example, monthly or annually, suit the business and respective metric?
- Is the distinction made between the core IT activities of integrating new solutions, running applications and running infrastructure? Has a concerted attempt been made to define metrics measuring value to the customer, i.e. business?

The resulting scorecard template can be used directly to manage baseline IT performance in each affiliate IT organization and this will fulfil the original

[5] For example, from Gartner Group, Inc. at `www.gartner.com`.

requirements for benchmarking and marketing across affiliates. There are, however, some straightforward embellishments that can be considered and which can add significant value for head office and affiliates:

- Affiliate scorecards can be consolidated up to a single scorecard reflecting global IT performance. The composition of this global IT scorecard is identical to affiliate scorecards, with each global value calculated as a weighted average of the values in the respective affiliates. The global IT scorecard gives a consolidated view of progress, but also helps individual affiliates position their own operations with respect to the average.
- The generic composition of IT scorecards can dilute the relevance to affiliates. Local general management, for example, may not appear interested in the scorecards, citing absence of local priorities. In such cases, head office can grant affiliates the option of adding their own locally relevant metrics to the mandatory "core" set used for the purposes of benchmarking. Note that for this option to be viable, the number of metrics in the core must be kept as low as possible, and closer to 16 than 25.
- For large affiliate IT organizations, a single scorecard may be at too high a level to be able to serve as an effective tool within the affiliate. Where subordinate IT organizations are large and there is local demand for it, the scorecard can be cascaded down into the organization to give each sub-organization its own scorecard. This is really the second phase in the scorecard methodology to align the entire organization behind an overarching scorecard by giving them their own, adapted scorecards.

Deploy scorecards

Once the initial scorecard definition has been approved by the IT Board, the initiative can be promoted to the deployment phase. In this phase, preliminary data is collected from affiliates, cleaned, stored, analyzed and reviewed for the first time. This will in general itself be a learning process, and while the original concepts behind the scorecard definition may recede, in their place will arise a number of practical obstacles to data collection and unforeseen ambiguities in metrics. It needs to be recognized in advance that this is to be expected and that scorecard definitions will need to be adapted as understanding develops or business conditions evolve. Overall, the mechanics of scorecard data collection need to be learnt, and the process taken further in the following two respects:

Start Benchmarking (Step 4): Unless scorecard definition has been particularly successful, or scorecards extended to include local metrics, experience shows that local IT heads already sense the overall level of performance in their affiliate and interest in their scorecards in isolation may be muted. But interest is much higher when metrics are compared across affiliates. Accompanying a report to the IT Board on overall initiative progress with metric views across affiliates and perhaps neutral highlighting of best and worst performers can galvanize attention. Given that this is still a learning phase, there should be no explicit pressure for action to be taken as a result of findings, but the potential power of the approach will have been demonstrated.

Align Motivation to Scorecards (Step 5): While benchmarking implicitly places some peer pressure on IT organizations to improve, formal scorecard targets should still be agreed for affiliates. In turn, performance towards these targets needs to be linked to personal target setting and incentive schemes to ensure alignment between scorecard and personal objectives. Eighty-five per cent of all successful scorecard projects do this.[6] At the very least, personal objectives should be balanced similarly to the scorecard definition. The exact approach depends both on the management processes within a firm and the business culture, but it remains important that this alignment takes place and that dates for commencing are agreed by the IT Board. Wherever possible, target setting and reviews should be conjoint with established budget setting processes both to avoid repeat work and to contribute to the institutionalization of scorecards. Note that in the absence of historic data on some metrics, IT management will need to be flexible on how binding initial targets are, as in many cases only a best guess can be made on sensible targets.

Operate scorecards

Seen superficially, operating balanced scorecards consists simply of having an organization led by the Global IT Controlling Group to regularly collect, clean and analyze data from affiliates, setting improvement targets to match. As targets are achieved, the scorecard definition itself may also need to be adapted to shift attention to where improvement is required, although the number of changes made annually should be kept down for the sake of mid-term continuity. Yet as it stands, beyond fostering a constructive dialogue between IT managers, the positive impact on the IT organization remains *ad hoc*. The more profound systematic benefits come from long-term commitment to mobilize change and exploit scorecards in two respects:

Act on Benchmarking (Step 6): Within IT management, the scorecard should be made a major component of the dialogue between CIO and local IT heads, and the CIO must be seen to take scorecard improvement seriously. Review of scorecard progress should be a regular slot on the IT Board agenda. Poor performers in particular areas can be invited to personally present action plans for improvement, on which there must be consequential follow-through.

[6] Balanced Scorecard Collaborative, Inc., 2002, see www.bscol.com.

Within the business community, as definitions and data mature, the status of scorecards needs to be promoted and scorecards established as a feature of discussions on baseline IT performance both between CIO and CEO, and local IT heads and their respective general managers.

Actively Market IT Performance (Step 7): Until now in the process, scorecards have only been circulated within the IT management community, but keeping scorecards secret makes execution difficult and misses an excellent opportunity of widely communicating basic performance objectives. Perhaps sensitive financial data that cannot be allowed into competitors' hands can be protected, but, in general, scorecard status should be actively published in all internal media, and in particular the company intranet. Experience shows that the use of "traffic light" red–amber–green highlighting of scorecard values can be particularly effective in helping the general community quickly appreciate the essentials of IT progress. This acknowledgement of weaknesses finds acceptance with the business community, and publication draws public attention to IT successes that are otherwise easily forgotten. The latter can be reinforced, for example, by loudly rewarding best performers with prizes and prominent interviews in internal newspapers.

Overall, balanced scorecards for IT can be a very effective tool for establishing transparent IT performance management that not only focuses on cost. Like a best practice project management methodology, on their own, scorecards remain a ritual. To reap tangible benefits from the significant amount of effort invested, real commitment and organizational momentum must be brought to bear behind scorecards.

Tool support

Tool support is particularly important for balanced scorecards. By nature, scorecards change on a regular basis and are intended for a wide audience, and in this respect, publication of scorecards online makes a lot of sense. Users should have easy, up-to-date access to individual scorecards and be able to navigate swiftly between affiliates and produce summaries of metrics across affiliates or over time. The recommendation is to keep the visualization of scorecard metrics, targets and current values as simple as possible, using red–amber–green highlighting where appropriate, but otherwise avoiding high-tech graphics. Where fields contain sensitive data, access to details can be limited to authorized users.

In parallel to the need to publish scorecards effectively is the back office task of managing data collection, cleaning, storage and analysis. This task includes how data is provided by affiliates, either through automated extraction from existing systems or manual data entry, how data is cleaned and corrected, and how traffic light colours are set. The key requirement is that published data be reliable.

One option for tackling publication and data handling is to use an established scorecard application from the start for both aspects. This has the disadvantage that while wanting to concentrate on scorecard definitions, significant effort is first required to select an application vendor, and the many features that applications offer can be a subsequent distraction. The other option is to delay use of systems to a later stage. Simple publication of scorecards in "MS-Excel" style online can still be effective, while manually managing data collection, though onerous, gives the opportunity of learning more about what requirements really are. The example Web site `www.gitm.biz/perform` shows one possible approach.

Mid-term, as data starts to accumulate and perhaps demand develops for scorecards for further sub-organizations within IT, some type of application will be needed. Many ERP vendors provide scorecard add-ons for their systems and there are also a number of independent vendors specializing in scorecards. A number of these are officially certified by the Balanced Scorecard Collaborative; for more details, see `www.bscol.com`.

Summary

IT control is faced with a challenge. There is significant upward pressure on IT costs for two reasons. Evolving technology has led to increasing business demand for new applications, and expectations and requirements concerning the existing infrastructure are spiralling. The question that businesses ask and Global IT Controlling needs to answer is: "Is it worth it?"

The answer to this question is fundamentally dictated by the balance between added costs and added value brought by IT. The problem is that IT control is traditionally dominated by historical cost control, mainly in the context of IT budgets or individual investment approvals. Controlling IT *value* is relatively new and not yet well established, but building up some form of IT value control is today a necessary complement to cost control, and this chapter has presented three relatively simple instruments for doing so:

- IT accounting through partially allocated cost centres.
- Improved investment approval criteria for IT projects.
- Balanced scorecards in each major IT organization to manage overall IT performance.

The aim throughout is to keep intrusion levels by head office in affiliate operations low. Both the accounting and investment approval changes occur primarily within affiliates without head office intervention. The balanced scorecard is the only direct demand placed on affiliate IT organizations by head office, but even here the scorecards will effectively define a streamlined interface between global and local organizations, and many of the benefits in learning from benchmarking will be realized locally.

7 Value of global IT management – tested

The first chapter of this book posed the question of why a company would want to manage certain aspects of IT on a global basis. This traced the business reasoning back to some combination of business-specific issues such as globalization of customer base and IT-specific issues such as opportunities for improving efficiency. The exact range of IT activities that it makes sense to globalize depends on the business in question, but a reliable initial subset is the planning orientated quartet of architecture, strategy, standards and control. The promise of these global work streams is straightforward:

- *Global IT Architecture*: Understand the support IT provides to the business, and prioritize necessary changes to the underlying IT architecture.
- *Global IT Strategy*: Secure executive business and IT agreement on IT priorities, launch and resource associated initiatives, and cascade priorities and plans down into the organization.
- *Global IT Standards*: Manage complexity and exploit volume synergies through introduction of global standards.
- *Global IT Control*: Provide reliable consolidated performance data and apply benchmarking across sites to learn from best and worst performers.

These are important factors in most businesses and their promise is normally more than sufficient to justify the effort and investment in global IT staff as proposed in Figure 2.7. If you consider this as the initial business case for venturing into global IT management, then the bulk of this book is dedicated to presenting a practical approach to implementing the necessary processes. The question is how to evaluate success, say, 18 months later. At a basic level, you could confirm that the processes are in place and running smoothly. This does, however, miss a subtle point and it is not really the test that counts. Of course, smoothly running processes have substantial merits. The point missed is that as planning-orientated processes, they give direction and context to other IT investments, for example through clearly positioning change projects or ongoing operational costs for some part of the IT infrastructure. So the real test of global IT management is whether the right IT investments are being approved (Figure 7.1).

This brings the focus forward to project and budget approvals as the crunch points where global IT management is ultimately tested. Unless people are

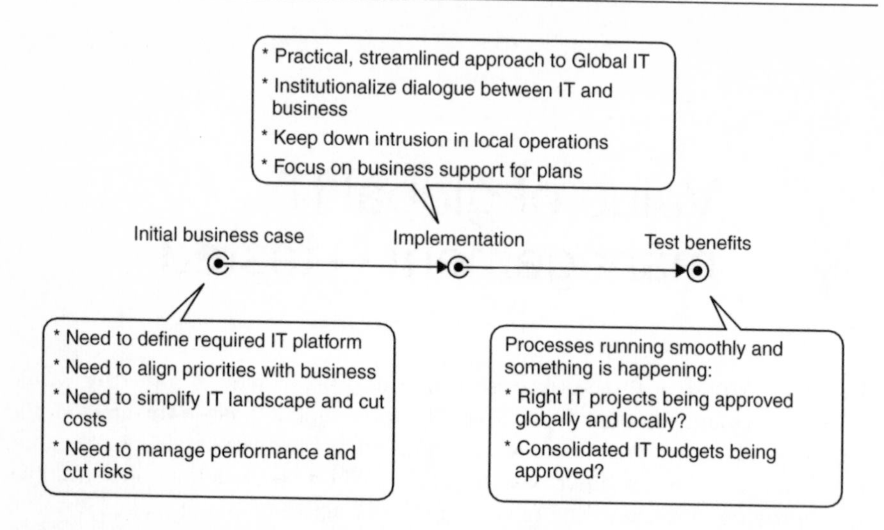

Figure 7.1—The test of global IT management is when important IT investments are approved and changes implemented

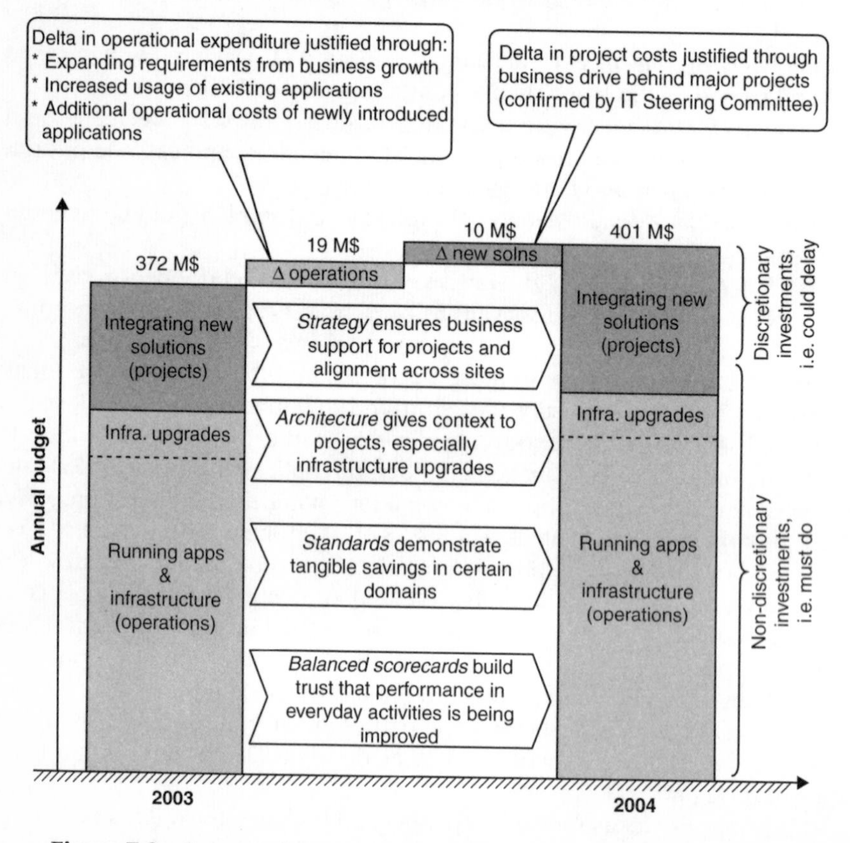

Figure 7.2—Support given to securing IT budgets by global IT processes

persuaded of the wisdom and value of proposed IT investments, projects and budgets will (and should) be rejected. Neglecting to address this relegates global IT management to a paper exercise where nothing happens as a result, and it exposes IT in general to a vicious circle of budget cutting and poor performance. Fortunately, the converse is also true. Good global IT control processes can, for example, show clearly that performance weaknesses are progressively being improved and that, as a whole, operational budgets are at least in line with industry averages. Strategy and architecture can boost the likelihood of project approvals by articulating the alignment with current business strategy. Figure 7.2 highlights the diverse contributions that can be made to achieving budget approvals.

Appreciating the criticality of investment approvals and the contribution that global IT can make casts a new light on global IT management. It promotes global IT from an organization that just takes care of specifically global issues to an organization that is responsible for articulating and managing the value and cost of IT investments as a whole in a firm, even when the majority of value generation may be local.

Appendix: Positioning with established best practices

The basic theme of this book has been to focus on the globalization of processes dealing with IT architecture, strategy, standards and control as a core set of IT activities which it makes sense to globalize. The interaction between these global processes and the many other IT processes has been depicted at a high level throughout the book in a simplified form originally introduced in Figure 2.6, with the main interaction being with detailed local planning processes, the exact form of which has been left intentionally open. This Appendix now returns to the entire set of possible IT processes and places the proposed global processes into the context of established best practices for IT in general. The three main independent players are COBIT, ITIL and PRINCE2 as highlighted in Figure A.1, although there are others that have significant merit. The relation to each of these is described in the next sections.

COBIT®

"Control Objectives for Information and related Technology", or COBIT for short, is an overall framework for reviewing IT organizations that has been developed by the IT audit industry with sponsorship from companies including IBM, PWC and Gartner Group. The framework itself draws on many international standards and is actively used by audit groups throughout the world. The relevance here is to see how the architecture, strategy, standards and control processes presented in this book fit cleanly into the COBIT framework.

COBIT views IT activities as a set of 34 IT processes grouped into the domains of planning and organization, acquisition and implementation, delivery and support, and lastly monitoring.[1] The exact form of any particular IT process is not stipulated, instead the framework concentrates on specifying what a process needs to deliver and how achievement of this goal can be assessed. Specifically, critical success factors, key goal indicators and key performance indicators are documented for each process together with a model for evaluating the maturity of an *in situ* implementation. The ultimate aim of the framework is to be able to objectively compare the maturity of the individual

[1] "COBIT Executive Summary", "COBIT Management Guidelines", July 2000, IT Governance Institute, www.isaca.org.

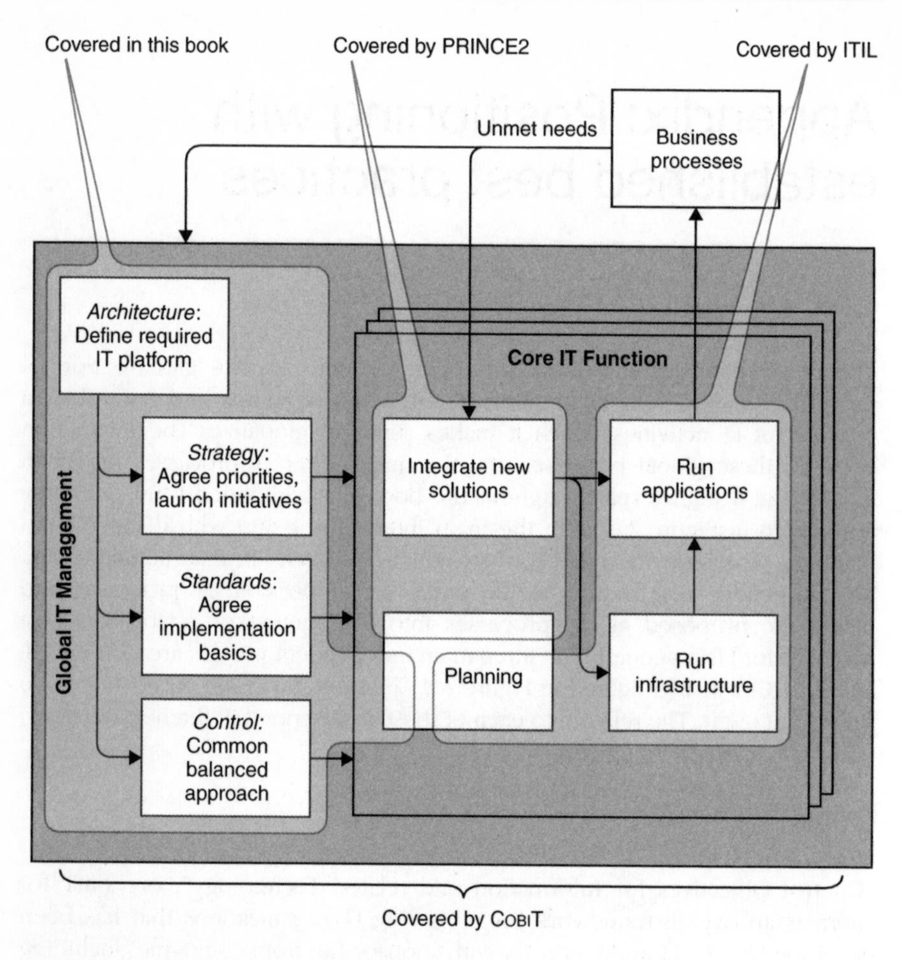

Figure A.1—Positioning of PRINCE2, ITIL and CobiT from the process perspective used in this book

processes that an organization has in place with the degree of business need in each respective domain.

Although there is not a strict one-to-one mapping, the processes presented in this book for architecture, strategy, standards and control can be viewed as viable implementations on a global level for the first six CobiT processes within the planning and organization domain, as shown in Figure A.2. More detail on the correlation between individual processes is summarized in Table A.1. Note how in a global context, a recurrent CobiT demand is that an effective compromise be reached in process implementations between those activities carried out locally and those carried out at corporate level. This compromise features tangibly in the approaches proposed in this book, especially in the cascade mechanism used to translate overall strategic priorities into relevant local form.

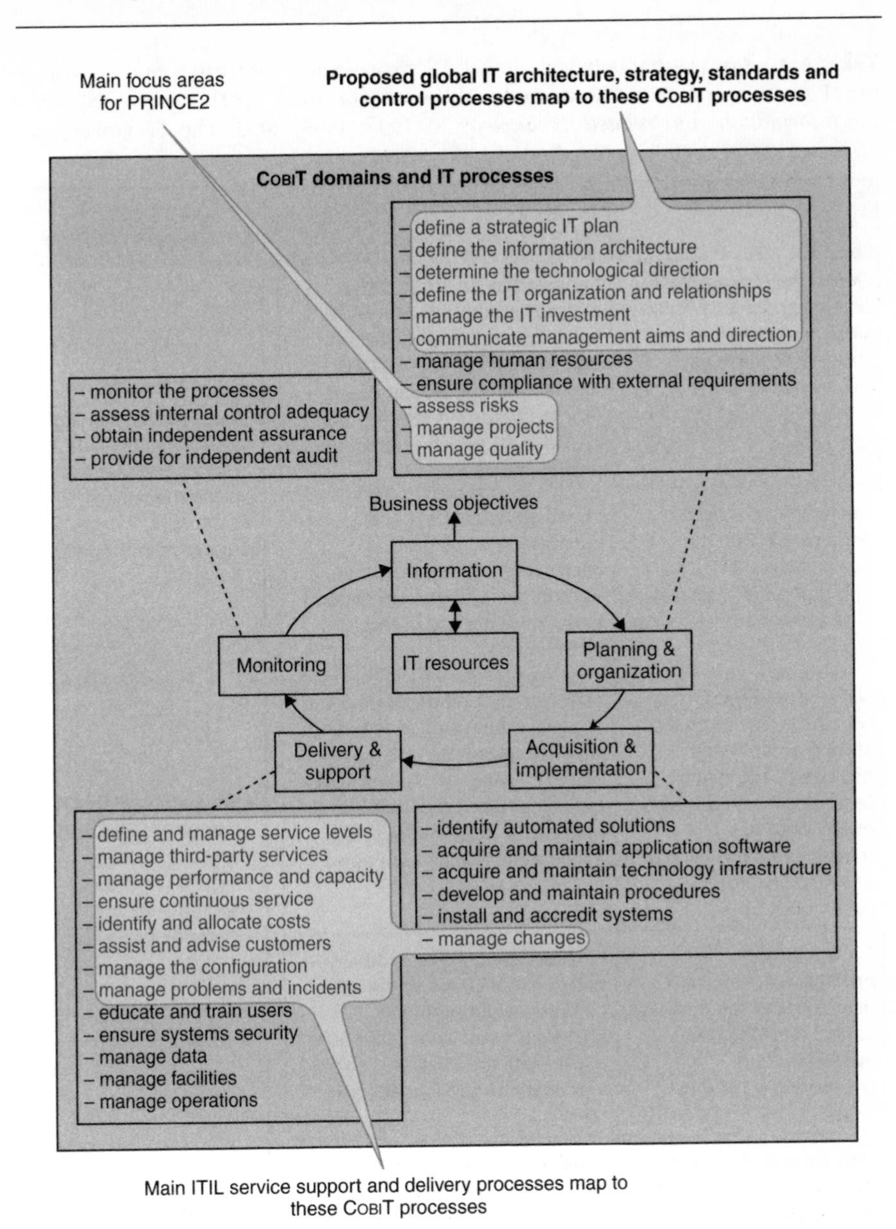

Figure A.2—Positioning of processes presented in this book within the overall CobiT framework. Reprinted with permission from CobiT: Control Objectives for Information and related Technology, Copyright 1996, 1998, 2000, The IT Governance Institute® (ITGI®), Rolling Meadows, IL, USA 60008

Further information on CobiT can be found on the Web site for the Information Systems Audit and Control Association and Foundation under `www.isaca.org`. Certain vendors and consulting firms also maintain their

Table A.1—Correlation between global IT management processes and individual COBIT planning processes. Reprinted with permission from COBIT: *Control Objectives for Information and related Technology* © 1996, 1998, 2000. The IT Governance Institute® (ITGI®), Rolling Meadow, IL, USA 60008

COBIT business goal	Associated COBIT process	Map to global IT management processes
Define the IT organization and relationships with the business goal of delivering the right IT services	"Enabled by an organization suitable in numbers and skills with roles and responsibilities defined and communicated, aligned with the business and that facilitates the strategy and provides for effective direction and adequate control"	Managed on ongoing basis by global IT *architecture* process linking models for business, IT organization, systems
Define the information architecture with the business goal of optimizing the organization of the information systems	"Enabled by creating and maintaining a business information model and ensuring appropriate systems are defined to optimize the use of this information"	
Define a strategic IT plan with the business goal of striking an optimum balance of information technology opportunities and IT business requirements as well as ensuring its further accomplishment	"Enabled by a strategic planning process undertaken at regular intervals giving rise to long-term plans; the long-term plans should periodically be translated into operational plans setting clear and concrete short-term goals"	Managed by global IT *strategy* process and in particular strategy cascade. Standards handled in global IT standards process
Communicate management aims and direction with the business goal of ensuring user awareness and understanding of those aims	"Enabled by policies established and communicated to the user community; furthermore, standards need to be established to translate the strategic options into practical and usable user rules"	
Determine technological direction with the business goal of taking advantage of available and emerging technology to drive and make possible the business strategy	"Enabled by creation and maintenance of a technological infrastructure plan that sets and manages clear and realistic expectations of what technology can offer in terms of products, services and delivery mechanisms"	Managed by global IT *standards* process
Manage the IT investment with the business goal of ensuring funding and controlling disbursement of financial resources	"Enabled by a periodic investment and operational budget established and approved by the business"	Managed by global IT *control* processes, especially balanced scorecard

own comprehensive suites of IT process definitions, one example being IBM's IT Process Model[2] which groups 40 IT processes into eight domains. These models remain in general proprietary and the reader is referred to the respective vendors for further information.

ITIL®

ITIL is the abbreviation for the Information Technology Infrastructure Library, a comprehensive set of best practices for managing IT infrastructure. The best practices were originally compiled by the Central Computer and Telecommunications Agency (CCTA), which has since been integrated into the Office of Government Commerce (OGC) in the UK. The British Standards Institute published its standard "Code of Practice for IT Service Management"[3] based on ITIL.

ITIL is introduced briefly here because, while there is no immediate overlap with the global IT management processes presented in this book, ITIL is becoming a de facto standard in several countries for best practice management of operational IT activities. Referring to the core IT functions of solutions integration, running applications and running infrastructure, ITIL covers the latter two domains as shown in Figure A.1. The more recently developed ITIL components are dedicated to some of the departmental activities shown within the supply view in Figure 2.1 such as operations management or computer installation, but the bulk of ITIL material and its traditional focus is on how to manage the interface between IT activities and the business served. The key underlying concept is *service management.*

In implementing part or all of ITIL, there need not be any radical change in the day-to-day activities of the various IT departments, but what will normally change is a cultural shift towards treating the community of business users as internal customers needing particular services. The provision of these services is seen to be IT's entire *raison d'être*. This cultural shift is reinforced by the service delivery and support processes shown in Figure A.3. These focus explicitly on systematically managing the maintenance of steady state services at the level of the customer and effectively handling service changes in response to evolution in business requirements. The whole aim is to provide tangible value for money and increase customer satisfaction through the focus on the customer as opposed to the operative capabilities that might be in place within an IT organization, but not necessarily needed by the business community.

A move towards implementing a formal service framework should be considered a major project, because of the cultural and organizational changes required for the framework and the task of setting up the individual services

---

[2] "Managing information technology in a new age", IBM whitepaper, IBM Global Services, 2000, www.ibm.com.

[3] "Code of Practice for IT Service Management", 01.01.2003, document PD0005, British Standards Institute.

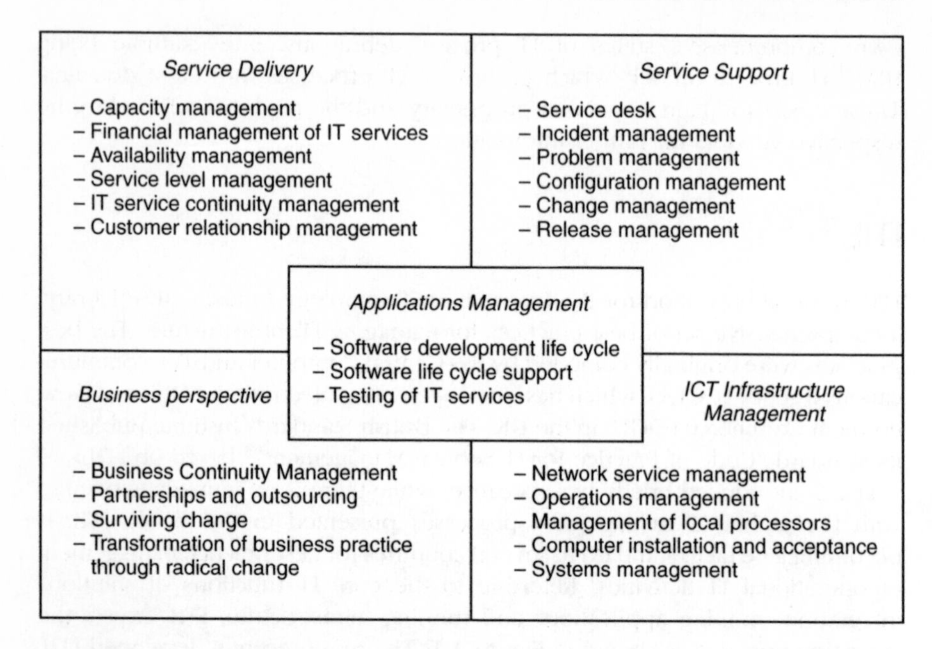

Figure A.3—Composition of ITIL best practice library (note there are overlaps between different domains). Crown copyright material is taken from the Office of Government Commerce's ITIL Service Management publication. © Crown copyright material reproduced with the permission of the Controller of HMSO and Queen's Printer for Scotland

in the chosen service portfolio. For more information on ITIL, the reader is referred to the Office of Government Commerce web site `www.ogc.gov.uk` or the published ITIL manuals.[4] A number of consulting groups and schools also provide ITIL courses and formal ITIL qualification can be obtained through the Examination Institute for Information Science (EXIN) or Information Systems Examinations Board (ISEB) under `www.exin-exams.com` and `www.iseb.org.uk` respectively.

PRINCE2®

Perhaps in response to the notoriously high failure rates for IT projects, there is extensive literature available on IT project management, documenting project experience and a range of methodologies. One particularly popular and successful methodology is PRINCE2 ("PRojects IN Controlled Environments"), which like ITIL was originally developed by the Central Computer and Telecommunications Agency (CCTA). PRINCE2 has become a *de facto*

[4] "Service Support", The Stationery Office, 2000.
"Service Delivery", The Stationery Office, 2001.

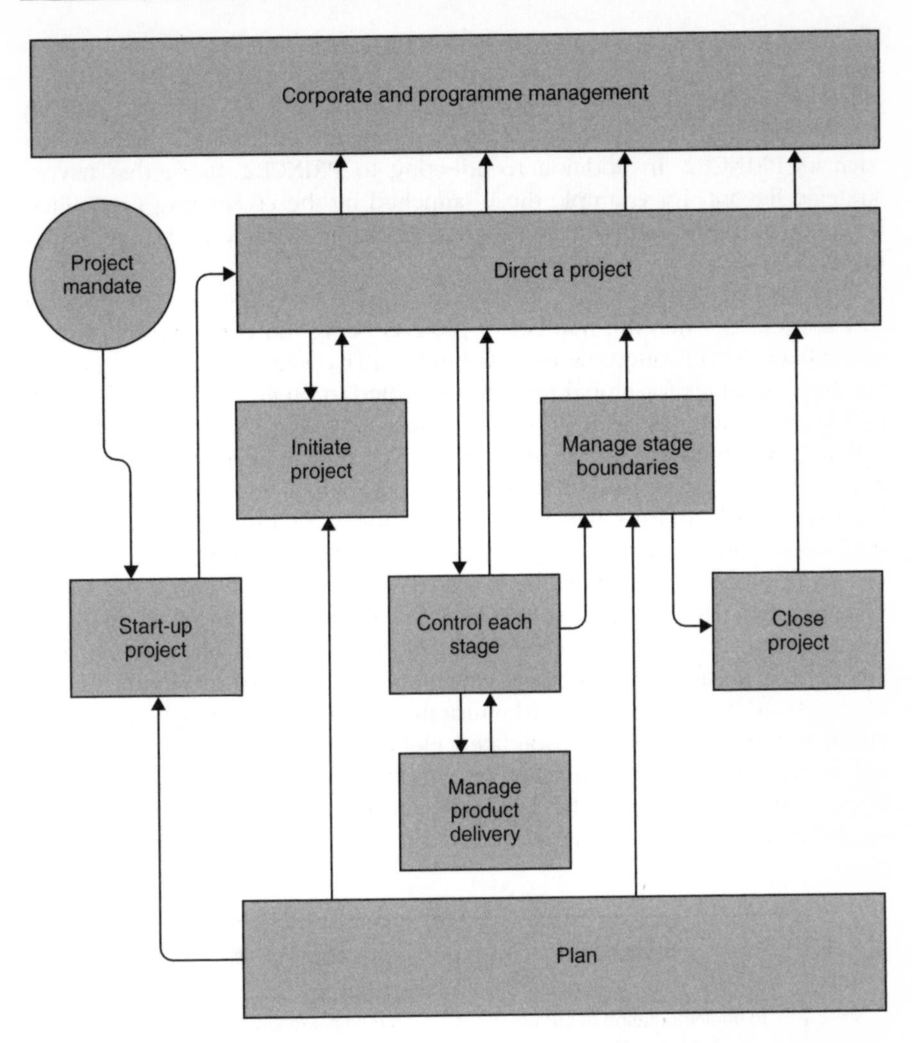

Figure A.4—PRINCE2 process model for project management. Crown copyright material is taken from the Office of Government Commerce's Prince2 process model for project management. © Crown copyright material reproduced with the permission of the Controller of HMSO and Queen's Printer for Scotland

standard in the UK and a number of other countries, and where it has not spread, in its place is usually a comparable alternative.

The overall approach is process based and broken down as shown in Figure A.4. The emphasis is on a systematic approach to leading projects through a series of manageable stages, checking on completion of each stage that the project is still entirely in line with business objectives. Like ITIL, the focus of PRINCE2 is not on the intricacies of implementing complex technology, but on managing the interface between the business and their

IT counterparts with the aim of delivering a solution that meets business needs.

In the context of global IT management, most projects launched globally are of sufficient complexity to warrant using an established methodology such as PRINCE2. In addition to adhering to PRINCE2, those that have a strategic flavour, for example those launched by the IT Steering Committee, will need to follow the guidelines for implementing strategic change presented on p. 75.

One special consideration is how to handle the allocation of priorities across projects when the number of projects being run concurrently starts to accumulate. This is often the case within local IT organizations which need to combine priorities for global projects (inherited through the strategic cascade process in Figure 4.8) with priorities for the many specific local projects and activities which do not feature at a global level, but are nevertheless important locally. Of the many project portfolio or programme management methods available which address this issue, one of the most useful is the approach developed and popularized by J. Ward and P. Griffith which segments the project portfolio according to the business impact of an IT project, as shown in Figure A.5. Note, however, that at least in the early stages of global IT management, the portfolio of expressly global projects is likely to be small and formal portfolio management techniques at a global level run the risk of simply adding unnecessary administrative overhead. Only if local projects are included in one big, consolidated global portfolio is the scale likely to justify explicit portfolio management, although note that such consolidation of planning is contrary to the principles proposed in this book which keep intervention in local planning discrete.

Strategic Applications or systems critical to implementation of current business strategy	*High Potential* Applications or systems that could prove key to future business success
Key Operational Applications or systems on which current business operations depend	*Support* Applications or systems that are valuable, but not critical to business success

Figure A.5—Scheme for IT project portfolio segmentation. Reproduced by permission of John Wiley & Sons Ltd

Further information on PRINCE2 can be found in the various PRINCE2 manuals available or on the Office of Government Commerce (OGC) Web site under `www.ogc.gov.uk`. A list of accredited PRINCE2 consultants and training organizations can be obtained under `www.prince2.org.uk` from the Association for Project Management Group (APMG) which is responsible for PRINCE2 accreditation and certification on behalf of the OGC. Further information on the portfolio management shown in Figure A.5 and the associated management techniques can be found in *Strategic Planning for Information Systems* (J. Ward and P. Griffith, 1996).

Glossary and acronyms

BPR: Business Process Re-engineering, i.e. a method of fundamentally redesigning the flow of activities in a particular business process

BSC: Balanced Scorecard, i.e. mechanism to succinctly direct and manage overall performance

Business application: Program that goes beyond a generic tool such as a spreadsheet to form an integral part of the work flow in a business process

Business case: Fundamental set of reasons demonstrating the value of proceeding with a project, normally in terms of the investment required, the expected return and likely risks

CCTA: Central Computer and Telecommunications Agency, now integrated into the Office of Government Commerce (UK)

CEO, CFO, CIO, COO: Chief Executive Officer, Chief Financial Officer, Chief Information Officer and Chief Operating Officer

Charge-out: Accounting procedure to charge a business function for services offered internally by a department such as information technology. Also referred to as charge-back or cost reallocation

COBIT®: Control Objectives for Information and related Technology, i.e. audit guidelines for accepted best practices for information technology

COGS: Cost Of Goods Sold, i.e. how much it costs to produce goods that are sold

CRM: Customer Relationship Management, i.e. the process of building and exploiting closer contacts with customers

CSF: Critical Success Factors, i.e. those few things that must go right for business success

DW: Data Warehouse, i.e. conglomeration of data from various sources to one massive data collection

EAI: Enterprise Applications Integration, i.e. technology used for simplifying integration and maintenance of interfaces between disparate business applications

e-business:	Term coined by IBM to refer to the extension of a company's business through Internet technologies to customers, suppliers or partners
ERP:	Enterprise Resource Planning, i.e. large-scale, monolithic applications such as SAP® that support multiple business processes
FIM:	Functional Information Manager, i.e. term used in this book for an IT manager dedicated to a specific business function
FTE:	Full Time Equivalent, i.e. one headcount or its equivalent, for example two part-timers
Governance:	Collective term for the institutions and organizational structure that set and maintain high level control of an operation
GM:	General Manager
HR:	Human Resources, i.e. the personnel department
IMAC:	Install, Move, Add, Change, i.e. the standard range of activities provided in desktop service provision
Information silo:	Build-up of information and systems within a business function, but without compatibility with systems used in other business functions
Insourcing:	Bringing operations previously handed over to a third-party service provider back into internal company operations (i.e. the opposite of outsourcing)
ITIL:	Information Technology Infrastructure Library, a set of established best practices focusing especially on service management
KPI:	Key Performance Indicator, i.e. a metric that indicates some crucial measure of business performance
Life cycle:	Concept for better understanding the overall cost structure of a product such as a PC by tracing cost generation from initial purchase right through to disposal
Metric:	Concrete measure for monitoring a particular aspect of performance
NPV:	Net Present Value, i.e. the overall value of a project once cash flows have been discounted to adjust for the time when investments and returns take place
OGC:	Office of Government Commerce (UK), agency behind the development of Information Technology Infrastructure Library
Outsourcing:	Handing operations currently run internally over to a third-party service provider
PRINCE2:	Name of standard project management methodology

RFP: Request For Proposal, i.e. formal tender process for initiating commercial negotiations with multiple suppliers

ROI: Return On Investment, i.e. the level of profit of a project in relation to the investment required

Seven-S, 7-S: Model, originally from McKinsey & Co, for viewing the interdependence of forces that play a role when implementing business change

Sign-off: Explicit signature or approval

Strategy map: Model within the balanced scorecard methodology for tracing the relationships between performance measurements

SWOT: Strengths, Weaknesses, Opportunities and Threats, i.e. simple analysis for considering the current business situation and likely evolution

Value chain: Idea of viewing a business in terms of the sequence of activities that take place, with each activity costing a certain investment and adding a certain value

WAN: Wide Area Network

References

J. Ward and P. Griffith, *Strategic Planning for Information Systems*, John Wiley & Sons, 1996.

L. Applegate, F.W. McFarlan and J. McKenney, *Corporate Information Systems Management: Text and Cases*, Harvard Business School Publishing, 1996.

M. Porter, *Competitive Strategy: Techniques for Analyzing Industries and Competitors*, Free Press, 1980, 1998.

M. Porter, *Competitive Advantage: Creating and Sustaining Superior Performance*, Free Press, 1985, 1998.

J.P. Kotter, Leading change: why transformation efforts fail, *Harvard Business Review*, March–April 1995.

Office of Government Commerce, *Prince2 Process Model for Project Management*, The Stationery Office, October 1999.

Office of Government Commerce ITIL Service Management, *Service Support*, The Stationery Office, 2000.

COBIT, *Control Objectives for Information and related Technology*, The IT Governance Institute®, 1998, 2000.

D. Remenyi, A. Money and M. Sherwood-Smith, *The Effective Measurement and Management of IT Costs and Benefits*, Butterworth-Heinemann, 2000.

M.C. Lacity, L.P. Willcocks and D.F. Feeney, IT outsourcing: maximise flexibility and control, *Harvard Business Review*, May–June 1995.

Bud Porter-Roth, *The Request For Proposal: A Guide to Effective RFP Development*, Addison-Wesley Professional, 2001.

R. Kaplan and D. Norton, *The Balanced Scorecard*, Harvard Business School Publishing, 1996.

TCO Manager for Distributed Computing, Chart of Accounts, Gartner Group Inc., 1999.

Index